Constitutional Stupidities, Constitutional Tragedies

Edited by

WILLIAM N. ESKRIDGE, JR.

and

SANFORD LEVINSON

New York University Press

New York and London

NEW YORK UNIVERSITY PRESS
New York and London

Library of Congress Cataloging-in-Publication Data
Constitutional stupidities, constitutional tragedies / Edited by
William N. Eskridge and Sanford Levinson.
p.   cm.
Includes index.
ISBN 0-8147-5131-8 (cloth : acid-free paper). — ISBN
0-8147-5132-6 (pbk. : acid-free paper)
1. Constitutional law—United States. I. Eskridge, William N.
II. Levinson, Sanford, 1941–
KF4550.A2C668   1998
342.73'02—dc21   97-45470
                    CIP

New York University Press books are printed on acid-free paper,
and their binding materials are chosen for strength and durability.

Manufactured in the United States of America

10 9 8 7 6 5 4 3 2 1

Contents

II   Constitutional Tragedies

Acknowledgments

We are most grateful to Tulane University's Murphy Institute for sponsoring a conference on institutional theory (March 1994), where we developed the original idea of holding a symposium on "constitutional stupidities." We are particularly grateful to John Ferejohn and the other organizers of the conference. Daniel Farber and Suzanna Sherry not only wrote stimulating essays but offered *Constitutional Commentary* as a forum for our initial symposium on this topic. Our colleagues Mike Seidman and Mark Tushnet (Georgetown) and Scot Powe and Jack Balkin (Texas) offered encouragement and suggestions at critical junctures.

The Law and Interpretation Section of the American Association of Law Schools offered us a similar forum for our follow-up symposium on constitutional tragedies; we are especially grateful to Jay Mootz, the chair of the section, for assuring us of this forum and supporting our symposium. The collection of tragedies more than filled a three-hour session. The presenters, whose works are replicated in this volume, were amazing enough, but even more amazing was the ensuing discussion by other scholars at the session. Comments by Jean Love, Larry Kramer, and Mark Tushnet were especially memorable as we developed the tragedy part of the volume. (Our only regret is that Mari Matsuda and Mary Anne Case were not able to turn their excellent presentations into chapters for this collection.)

We are most grateful to Mary Anne DeRosa and Karen Neal of Georgetown, who turned the various draft chapters into usable WordPerfect disks and otherwise facilitated the production of this manuscript. Matthew Michael, a graduate student at Georgetown, helped us with research, editing, and proofreading. Our deans, Judy Areen of Georgetown and Michael Sharlot of Texas, have provided us with moral and financial support for this and other projects. Thank you, deans, and thank you all for your encouragement.

We dedicate this volume to the Americans (and those foreigners who have been the victims of unjust, albeit perfectly constitutional, wars) who have suffered because of the various stupidities and tragedies explored in this volume. Given that the very point of this collection is to ask to what degree these stupidities and tragedies are truly "inevitable"—i.e., forced upon even the most conscientious interpreter of the Constitution—we refrain from specifying any particular victims, lest we implicitly endorse one or another highly controversial theory of constitutional interpretation.

William N. Eskridge, Jr.
Washington, D.C.

Sanford Levinson
Austin, Texas

Introduction

Constitutional Conversations

William N. Eskridge, Jr., and Sanford Levinson

After a day spent at a Tulane University conference on constitutional design, we were walking back to our hotel through New Orleans's Garden District. As we admired the majestic old homes, we also talked about the majestic old Constitution. In a jesting mood, we started speculating about the "stupidest" provision of the Constitution. "Stupidest," in this context, meant the provision that is at the same time most nonsensical and most harmful for today's polity. Thus, a provision sensible in 1789 but not today would qualify, unless its bad consequences were negligible; that is, the mistake was a "harmless error." To continue the stately-mansion metaphor, an ugly gazebo usually would not qualify as a serious flaw, but a structurally unsound roof would. Given that definition, we speculated about what in the Constitution is now the worst provision, and our speculation rapidly involved our colleagues walking with us on that warm, humid day in March 1994.

John Ferejohn, one of the ambulatory colleagues (and, not at all coincidentally, the high priest of the "rational choice" movement that studies the incentive effects of institutional structures) suggested that our joking conversation had a serious point. Academics endlessly debate issues of constitutional *interpretation*, and almost never talk about the flaws inherent in the *document itself*. So, too, the possibility of constitutional stupidities is a feature of the Constitution typically neglected in university, college, and law school courses about the Constitution. Such courses rarely teach the Constitution as a whole; frequently, the approach is nothing more than a series of "great cases," from *Marbury v. Madison* onward. A scholarly conversation about constitutional stupidities would be a useful way to think systematically about the Constitution as a foundational, constitutive document. Also, it could be an important barometer for determining how flawed the Constitution really is, what might be done to address those flaws, and—ultimately—whether it ought to be reexamined in a new Constitutional Convention, like that held in Philadelphia in 1787.

Both inspired and encouraged, we devised an experiment, posing our New Orleans question to several eminent constitutional law scholars.[1] We set one substantive limit, relating to what we consider the Constitution's undoubtedly worst provisions: those clauses of the original document that assumed or assured the existence of slavery.[2] Such provisions epitomize constitutional stupidity—indeed, outright evil—but should not count for our inquiry, because all have been either repealed or rendered irrelevant by the passage of time. Nor should the Eighteenth Amendment, Prohibition, which was repealed by the Twenty-First Amendment, thus replacing a major stupidity with a minor one, as Laurence Tribe argues in this volume (chapter 20). To avoid repetitious essays on slavery and Prohibition, we asked our respondents to nominate constitutional provisions that have survived, and the respondents repaid our request with a surprising range of analyses, set forth in the essays that make up the first half of this volume.

Some of the respondents "resist the question." One of the essays dismisses our project as just a "parlor game" (Philip Bobbitt, chapter 2), but the rest seem to agree that addressing the possibility, the reality, of constitutional stupidity can be intellectually productive as well as practically important. Even postmodernist Lief Carter (chapter 4), who wonders whether we can ever be sure about what is stupid and how bad it is, feels the project opens up constitutional discourse in useful ways. (Indeed, Carter makes a unique as well as valuable suggestion: the Constitution's worst mistakes are the obscure housekeeping provisions that trivialize what should be a grand enterprise.)

Other respondents resist the question's supposed intimation that the Constitution is full of stupidities—which was decidedly not the editors' intent! For example, Daniel Farber (chapter 6) offers the thought that the Constitution is "(almost) perfect." He is virtually alone in that particular conclusion, supportable as it might be (see chapter 22). Everyone else maintains that the Constitution has at least one current and harmful stupidity. Steven Calabresi (chapter 3), one of the document's biggest fans among law teachers, concludes that the constitutional balance of powers no longer operates as well as it originally did and requires massive reform. Like Calabresi, most of the other contributors combine a deep personal respect for the

Constitution, with a critical eye toward its currently harmful "mistakes" (the term Calabresi prefers to "stupidities"). There is nothing about our project that requires any disrespect for the Constitution or its framers; smart people can create rules that over the long term become stupid. For most of our authors, it is their respect and even awe for the Constitution's success that drives their interest in understanding its limitations.

Several respondents resist our question in another productive way: rather than identifying a particular provision that is now stupid, they focus on a pervasive constitutional assumption that no longer holds, to the detriment of our present polity. For Calabresi (chapter 3), the undone assumption is the system of checks and balances among the three branches of the national government. For Robert Nagel (chapter 13), it is the presumed local and decentralized, rather than national and centralized, focus for governance. For Frederick Schauer (chapter 17), it is the assumed passivity of government. All of these assumptions were appropriate ones to make in 1789; all have been undermined by modern trends toward pervasive, centralized government.

The systemic insights developed by Calabresi, Nagel, and Schauer are equally well developed by respondents who identified particular provisions of the Constitution that are today problematic. What unites most of these responses, with the notable exception of Michael Seidman's contribution nominating the criminal procedure provisions of the Bill of Rights (chapter 18), is their emphasis on the Constitution's *structural* provisions rather than its provisions concerning *individual rights*. Nominations for most stupid provision include

- the appointment of the Senate by state (Suzanna Sherry, chapter 19) or the directive that each senator shall have one vote (William Eskridge, chapter 5),
- the Electoral College (Akhil Amar, chapter 1), the mode by which deadlocks in the Electoral College will be resolved in the House of Representatives, and the time lag between a president's election and his taking office (Sanford Levinson, chapter 11),
- the difficult procedures for adopting legislation (Frederick Schauer, chapter 17) and for amending the Constitution (Stephen Griffin, Chapter 8; Mark Tushnet, chapter 21),
- the assumption of decentralized, federalist governance (Robert Nagel, chapter 13) and the assignment of responsibility for voting rules to the states instead of Congress (Jeffrey Rosen, chapter 16),

- the authorization for Congress to adopt laws "necessary and proper" to carry out its assigned powers and the invitation this provided to the Supreme Court to engage in basically disingenuous interpretation of the Constitution (Mark Graber, chapter 7),
- the requirements that the President be a "natural born Citizen" (Randall Kennedy, chapter 9) and be at least thirty-five years old (Matthew Michael, chapter 12),
- the apparent requirement that the vice president must be allowed to preside over his own impeachment trial in the Senate (Michael Stokes Paulsen, chapter 14),
- the assurance of life tenure for federal judges and justices (L. H. LaRue, chapter 10; L. A. Powe, Jr., chapter 15), and
- the housekeeping provisions of the Constitution, which trivialize the document itself (Lief Carter, chapter 4).

In short, the Constitution is chock full of stupid provisions.

Note how the respondents operate under different assumptions about how to determine what is "stupid." For some essays, the metric is legitimacy. Criticizing exclusions from the Presidential Qualifications Clause, Randall Kennedy (chapter 9) and Matthew Michael (chapter 12) make much of symbolic politics: Is it not inconsistent with equal citizenship for the Constitution to exclude the foreign-born and the young adult from aspiring to the presidency? Is that symbolic exclusion not demeaning and without any good justification? Does it not undermine the overall legitimacy of the political enterprise? Jeffrey Rosen (chapter 16) works from legitimacy concerns in criticizing the allocation of voting rules to the states. Particularly striking is Michael Seidman's deployment of legitimacy-based reasoning (chapter 18): he maintains that the role of constitutional conversation is to subject ordinary politics to critique, which enhances the overall legitimacy of the polity. For Seidman, the rights afforded criminal defendants in the Bill of Rights fail this test, because they offer solace rather than critique to the normal politics of criminal punishment.

In contrast, other essays are primarily consequentialist in their assessment of stupidity. Akhil Amar's criticism of the Electoral College (chapter 1) and Sanford Levinson's concern about the time lag between presidential election and office taking (chapter 11) rely mainly on this form of argument: the criticized provision will lead to a disaster someday, and so why not fix it today? Rejecting federal judges' lifetime tenure, L. H. LaRue (chapter 10) and Scot Powe (chapter 15) are also more concerned about bad policy than about legitimacy: Does judicial performance not fall off after ten years? Is a gerontocracy like that of China a good way to grapple with America's legal problems? Most of the other essays share this utilitarian quality: such and such provision is bad because it undermines the polity's ability to make good decisions or has other ill effects.

Yet another, smaller group of essays defines stupidity from a baseline of logic: the Framers chose stupid language whose consequences they did not intend. Michael Stokes Paulsen (chapter 14) catches the Framers in such a mistake. Surely they did not intend the vice president, the presiding officer of the Senate, to preside over his own Senate impeachment trial, but Paulsen argues that there is no escaping the constitutional text on this issue. Likewise, Mark Graber (chapter 7) performs analytical surgery on the Necessary and Proper Clause, whose miswriting was soon corrected by John Marshall's judicial rewriting (see also John Yoo, chapter 38). Unlike Paulsen, we believe a modern-day John Marshall (probably a senator and not a judge) would rescue the nation from the prospect of a tainted vice president presiding over his own impeachment trial, notwithstanding the clarity of the constitutional text.

One final feature of the essays we collected on constitutional stupidity stimulated us to initiate a companion project that forms the second half of the current volume. What joins most of the essays—again, the most notable exception is Seidman's—is their concentration on constitutional provisions whose meaning has not been, for the most part, seriously contested even in these days of hermeneutic uncertainty. No constitutional scholar has seriously maintained that Madeleine Albright or Henry Kissinger, both of them foreign-born, can somehow escape the Natural Born Citizen Clause and be elected President, notwithstanding their superior qualifications (especially their academic prominence!). In John Hart Ely's terms, the respondents shied away from the "open-textured" provisions of the Constitution and, instead, chose provisions that have not been objects of interpretive debate.[3] Indeed, most of the choices were provisions that have not been justiciable, and therefore not subject to judicial construction at all.

One reason the Constitution's stupidities are not emphasized in classes and commentaries is that most academic and judicial attention has focused on the open-textured provisions: not only those of the Bill of Rights (the First through Tenth Amendments) and the Reconstruction Amendments (the Thirteenth through Fifteenth), but also such provisions as those giving Congress jurisdiction to "regulate Commerce" and adopt laws "necessary and proper" for that purpose (Article I, Section 8, Clauses 3 and 18) and vesting the "executive Power" in the president (Article II, Section 1) and the "judicial Power" in the Supreme Court and whatever "inferior Courts" that Congress should establish (Article III, Section 1). Because these provisions are open to much greater interpretive debate, they have been construed in ways that make them unlikely candidates for constitutional stupidities. As Tushnet emphasizes (chapter 21), this is a consequence of human nature: where there is ambiguity, the human mind will avoid constructions that yield stupid results. For this reason, the completion of the stupidities project—and the warm reception it received from many readers, both fellow academics and a more general audience—stimulated us to pose another thought experiment to another collection of constitutional scholars.

For the open-textured provisions of the Constitution—due process, equal protection, free speech—the interpreter needs a theory beyond application of the plain meaning of the constitutional text.[4] Theories of constitutional interpretation fall into roughly two polar categories, with many theories falling between the poles. One theoretical pole is *positivist*, seeking the interpretive answer required or imposed by external sources of law, such as original intent or purpose of the Framers, "neutral principles" found in the Constitution, and constitutional tradition and precedent.[5] The opposite theoretical pole is *normativist*, seeking an interpretive answer that is the most normatively defensible within the constraints of the rule of law.[6] As Ronald Dworkin puts it, the goal should be to construe the Constitution to make it the "best" document it can be, given the constraints of language and our political traditions.[7] Positivist theories tend to be more popular among judges, normativist theories among law professors, who typically claim that positivist judges are "really" following normative approaches when they interpret and apply the Constitution.

A feature of positivist theories of constitutional interpretation is that they pride themselves on reaching results that the interpreter laments, often strongly. (Because positivist theories claim a more "objective" methodology, external to the decision maker, they promise that decision makers with different values will consistently reach the same results.) Among the best examples are those critics of *Roe v. Wade* and its protection of the right to choose abortion who are pro-choice liberals but who nonetheless believe that the Constitution provides few limits on state regulation of that choice,[8] and those supporters of *Johnson v. Texas* and its protection of the right to burn flags who are conservatives personally opposed to flag burning but who believe such unpatriotic conduct can nonetheless be ideologically expressive and therefore protected by the First Amendment.[9]

At the very least, this generates a tension in analysts between their normative visions of a good polity and the demands of the Constitution. It may even generate the possibility of what we call a constitutional "tragedy" if the tension is sufficiently high. After all, the point of many of the "stupidity" essays is that, because of constitutional formalisms, we are stuck with what Fred Schauer calls "suboptimal results,"[10] though, as already noted, no one suggests that the suboptimality reaches the level of genuine tragedy. We therefore asked several prominent academic positivists to identify their greatest constitutional tragedy: What is the worst result they would be required to reach under what they consider the proper methodology for constitutional interpretation? Does this "worst result" constitute a tragedy?[11]

Predictably, our academic positivists argue that the possibility of tragedy gives normative bite to the rule of law. Larry Alexander draws this lesson from Robert Bolt's great play *A Man for All Seasons* (chapter 23): unless law protects the Devil from us, what reason do we have to think the law will protect us from the Devil? Other authors stress classical Greek tragedies (*Oedipus* and *Antigone*) or those written by Shakespeare (*Macbeth*), all of which point to a darker connection between the rule of law and tragedy. Classical tragedy involves the downfall of the hero because of a tragic flaw which the hero cannot escape. Adherence to neutral rules and principles in all cases might be a "tragic flaw" leading to disastrous consequences, even ruin, for the country.

In this spirit, our constitutional positivists nominated some of the most celebrated decisions of American history as tragic: *Marbury v. Madison* (Michael McConnell, chapter 33), *McCulloch v. Maryland* (John Yoo, chapter 38), and *Brown v. Board of Education* (Earl Maltz, chapter 34). *Marbury* is tragic because it is rightly and indeed inevitably decided under a rule-of-law regime, but the power to declare statutes unconstitutional that it vests in the judiciary has been tragic for the country, argues McConnell. *McCulloch*, Chief Justice Marshall's expansive definition of congressional authority under the Necessary and Proper Clause, and *Brown*, Chief Justice Warren's invalidation of segregation as a violation of the Equal Protection Clause, are tragic because they are wrongly decided, according to Yoo and Maltz, respectively. The Supreme Court could not bear to apply neutral principles in those cases, and thereby those great chief justices set a bad example for subsequent judges, generating the judicial hubris (pride and excessive ambition) of which McConnell complains.

The most poignant essay is Gerard Bradley's heartfelt argument (chapter 25) that capital punishment is always immoral and usually—tragically—

constitutional, a conclusion supported by David Strauss's essay from a more liberal, precedent-based constitutional theory (chapter 37), but disputed by Marie Failinger's essay on the death penalty and the right to die (chapter 28). Bradley's essay helpfully addresses the further question: In a capital case, what are the obligations of a judge who is morally or religiously opposed to capital punishment?

At the same time we were asking some of America's leading positivist theorists to name their greatest constitutional tragedy, we posed the same question to leading academic normativists. We were interested in whether normativism always generates constitutional "happy endings." After all, if constitutional interpretation is "justice-seeking," or directed to making the Constitution as morally attractive as possible, then one might well wonder if it would ever be the case that, at the end of the day, *injustice* would be constitutionally mandated or, concomitantly, that even the "best" Constitution would be quite dreadful indeed. To our surprise, most of the normativists are just as tragic as the positivists. Only two essays, by James Fleming (chapter 29) and by Pamela Karlan and Daniel Ortiz (chapter 31), insist that the resolution of an important constitutional issue (the right to die and one person, one vote, respectively) is tragic in the sense that it has horrible consequences but untragic in the sense that it is avoidable through the proper approach. Fleming, in particular, rejects the positivist view that proper constitutional law must have its tragedies. If there is any meaningful ambiguity in the constitutional directive, why not choose the interpretation that ennobles rather than demeans the Constitution? That is a good question for the positivists that dominate the judiciary.

The other normativists agree that tragedies are not only possible but inevitable and plentiful, no matter how excellent the theory. Any theory that vests great discretion in judges is likely to be applied erroneously much of the time, as in the early twentieth century, when the Court deployed the Due Process Clause to invalidate labor-protective legislation (Rebecca Brown, chapter 26). In addition, institutional limits on the judiciary, the "least dangerous branch," render those most directly charged with interpreting the Constitution least able to impose just results on the political process (Christopher Eisgruber and Lawrence Sager, chapter 27). Finally, constitutional cases often demand intrinsically tragic choices between values, as is the case with the death penalty and affirmative action (Marie Failinger, chapter 28; Robert Post, chapter 35).

Other solicited papers further deepened the inquiry about constitutional tragedies. Gary Jacobsohn's essay (chapter 30) is a synthesis of the debate among the positivists and normativists. The problem with a comedic (happy-endings) theory of constitutional law, such as Fleming's and Dworkin's, is that it lacks irony and a sense of limitation. The problem with a tragic (bad-results) theory of constitutional law, such as Maltz's and McConnell's, is its exaggerated sense of law's determinacy. The best approach, according to Jacobsohn, is tragicomedy, which strives for "an accommodation between necessity and manipulation, between the obligation to find the law and the temptation to make it." Consider how such an approach might apply to the tragedies discussed by the various authors.

Theodore Lowi makes the important point that tragedies are generated by history rather than by logic (chapter 32). He nominates strict separation of powers as the greatest constitutional tragedy. The Framers intended for the three branches to operate independently, a design compromised from the beginning of the country's practical history. Circumstances in the latter half of this century, however, have revivified separation of powers under the aegis of "divided government"—a nation faithful to the Founders' vision but ill-suited to modern governance, argues Lowi. (Compare this essay to Calabresi's historical essay [chapter 3], which comes to the opposite conclusion!)

Dorothy Roberts's essay (chapter 36) poses this question: If the Constitution is always tragic for a specified group, does that undermine its legitimacy, either overall or for the members of that group? Roberts asks the question from the perspective of people of color.[12] Jack Balkin (chapter 24) raises similar inquiry from the perspective of people faced with stifling poverty and deploys the question to broaden the conception of constitutional tragedies. Balkin's essay ties together minority perspectives with the classic idea of tragedy, where a hero is undone by the inevitable working-out of consequences from his or her tragic flaw. Under this account, neither people of color nor people in poverty can be tragic heroes, for they do not bring their fate upon themselves. Rather, the tragic hero is We the People. Our tragic flaw is our toleration of slavery, apartheid, the invisible black ghetto, and the devastation wreaked by lack of material resources, coupled with our hope that fate will neither notice nor, more to the point, punish us for our defects. Balkin ominously suggests that this tragic flaw will someday yield a tragic fate—not just injustice for minorities and the poor, but doom for the country.

Although its implications may be complex, the plan of this book is simple. Following this introduction are twenty-one essays proposing various nominations for stupidest provision of the Constitution, arranged alphabetically by author and ending with the editors' reflections on the essays. After the stupidities, of course, are the tragedies, again arranged alphabetically by author and ending with editorial reflections. The last essay in the volume includes the editors' deeper thoughts on the connection between constitutional stupidity and tragedy and between this project and broader debates about constitutionalism. For the reader's convenience, the United States Constitution, as amended, is included as an appendix.

NOTES

1. With the support and encouragement of Daniel Farber and Suzanna Sherry, almost all of the essays in the first half of this volume were originally published in "Constitutional Stupidities: A Symposium," 12 *Constl. Comm.* 139–225 (1995). Ground rules included a limit of one thousand words, which we have relaxed for this volume, and no consultation among the participants. The lack of consultation was meant to ensure, as much as possible, that the answers were not "contaminated" by discovering what other participants were selecting.

2. U.S. Constitution, Art. I, Sec. 2, Cl. 3 (the Apportionment Clause, allotting representatives according to "Numbers," which included "the whole Number of free Persons," but only "three fifths of all other Persons," particularly slaves); Art. I, Sec. 9, Cl. 1 (the Slave Trade Clause, foreclosing Congress from prohibiting the "Migration or Importation of such Persons," namely, slaves, "as any of the States now existing shall think proper to admit," a provision that Article V says cannot be amended out of the Constitution); Art. IV, Sec. 2, Cl. 3 (the Fugitive Slave Clause, prohibiting a state from discharging any "Person held to Service or Labour in one State" who has escaped into another state and requiring the second state to "deliver[] up" to the slave state).

3. John Hart Ely, *Democracy and Distrust* (Cambridge: Harvard University Press, 1981). Mark Tushnet ("The Whole Thing," chapter 21 of this volume), and Pamela S. Karlan and Daniel R. Ortiz ("Constitutional Farce," chapter 31) suggest a reason for this phenomenon: the open-textured provisions, such as the Due Process Clause, cannot fairly be considered "stupid," because what they "mean" is so open to construction.

4. This is not to say that plain meaning has no relevance for these constitutional provisions. There may be certain interpretations that should be disallowed because they are simply inconsistent with the text. Note that the Supreme Court itself sometimes violates this precept. Constitutional liberals embrace concepts of "substantive due process" that seem inconsistent with the plain meaning of the Due Process Clauses of the Fifth and Fourteenth Amendments. E.g., *Roe v. Wade*, 410 U.S. 113 (1973). Constitutional liberals as well as conservatives read the Due Process Clause

of the Fifth Amendment to include an equal protection guarantee against federal regulations (a guarantee explicitly found in the Fourteenth Amendment's limits on state action). E.g., *Adarand Constructors, Inc. v. Pena*, 115 S. Ct. 2097 (1995); *Bolling v. Sharpe*, 347 U.S. 497 (1954). Constitutional conservatives have read the Eleventh Amendment far beyond, and seemingly against, its textual parameters. E.g., *Seminole Tribe v. Florida*, 116 S. Ct. 1114 (1996).

5. E.g., Raoul Berger, *Government by Judiciary* (Cambridge: Harvard University Press, 1977); Robert Bork, *The Tempting of America* (New York: Free Press, 1990); John Hart Ely, *Democracy and Distrust* (Cambridge: Harvard University Press, 1980); Antonin Scalia, *A Matter of Principle* (Princeton: Princeton University Press, 1997); Herbert Wechsler, "Toward Neutral Principles of Constitutional Law," 73 *Harv. L. Rev.* 1 (1959); Henry P. Monaghan, "Our Perfect Constitution," 56 *N.Y.U. L. Rev.* 353 (1981).

6. E.g., Ronald Dworkin, *Freedom's Law: The Moral Reading of the American Constitution* (Cambridge: Harvard University Press, 1996); Rebecca Brown, "Tradition and Insight," 103 *Yale L.J.* 177 (1993); Owen Fiss, "The Supreme Court, 1978 Term: Foreword—The Forms of Justice," 93 *Harv. L. Rev.* 1 (1979); James E. Fleming, "Constructing the Substantive Constitution," 72 *Tex. L. Rev.* 211 (1993); Frank Michelman, "Law's Republic," 97 *Yale L.J.* 1493 (1988); Martha Minow, "The Supreme Court, 1986 Term: Foreword—Justice Engendered," 101 *Harv. L. Rev.* 10 (1987); Lawrence G. Sager, "The Incorrigible Constitution," 60 *N.Y.U. L. Rev.* 893 (1990).

7. Ronald Dworkin, *Law's Empire* (Cambridge: Harvard University Press, 1986).

8. E.g., John Hart Ely, "The Wages of Crying Wolf: A Comment on *Roe v. Wade*," 82 *Yale L.J.* 920 (1973).

9. E.g., Scalia, *A Matter of Principle.*

10. See Frederick Schauer, *Playing by the Rules* (Cambridge: Harvard University Press, 1991).

11. The tragedy essays were presented as part of a panel at the "Law and Interpretation" section of the annual meeting of the American Association of Law Schools (AALS), January 1997. Most of the chapters in the second half of this volume were presented at the AALS meeting.

12. Mari Matsuda also posed the question of constitutional tragedy from a perspective of color and race at the AALS session. Jean Love posed the question from a lesbian and gay perspective during the discussion period. *Bowers v. Hardwick*, she argued, is a constitutional tragedy, because it not only excludes but declares outlaws a productive minority group: lesbians, gay men, and bisexuals.

PART I

Constitutional Stupidities

What is the stupidest provision
of the current Constitution?

CHAPTER 1

A Constitutional Accident Waiting to Happen

Akhil Reed Amar

In the category "Most Mistaken Part of the Current Constitution," I nominate the Electoral College. The ingenious scheme of presidential selection set up by Article II and refined by the Twelfth Amendment was a brilliant eighteenth-century invention that makes no sense today. Our system of selecting presidents is a constitutional accident waiting to happen.

I nominate the Electoral College in part because some constitutional scholars might tend to overlook its flaws. Constitutional Law courses typically stress courts, cases, and clauses that get litigated. Despite the vast constitutional significance of the presidency, it is woefully understudied in law schools today. (It gets far more attention in political science departments—a vestige of the early-twentieth-century world in which academic study of the Constitution was generally nestled in political science—while law schools stressed "private law," like contracts and torts.) Scholars of constitutional law may likewise prefer to focus on clauses that can be "fixed" by creative judicial interpretation. The Electoral College can be fixed only by a formal amendment, and talk of constitutional amendment scares many law professors.

But amendment is exactly what is called for here; the reasons that made the Electoral College sensible in the eighteenth century no longer apply. The Framers emphatically did not want a president dependent on the legislature, so they rejected a parliamentary model in which the legislature would pick its own leader as prime minister and chief executive officer. How, then, to pick the president? The visionary James Wilson proposed direct national popular election, but the scheme was deemed unworkable for three reasons. First, very few candidates would have truly continental reputations among ordinary citizens, so ordinary folk across the vast continent would not have enough good information to choose intelligently among national figures.

Second, a populist presidency was seen as dangerous, inviting demagoguery and possibly dictatorship as one man claimed to embody the "Voice of the American People." Third, national election would upset a careful balance of power among states. Since the South did not let blacks vote, southern voices would count less in a direct national election. Or a state could increase its clout by recklessly extending its franchise. For example, if (heaven forbid!) a state let women vote, it could double its weight in a direct national election. Under the Electoral College system, by contrast, a state could get a fixed number of electoral votes whether its franchise was broad or narrow—indeed, whether or not it let ordinary voters pick electors.

None of these arguments works today. Improvements in communications technology and the rise of political parties make possible direct election and a populist presidency. This is, de facto, our scheme today. Blacks and women are no longer selectively disenfranchised, and states no longer play key roles in defining the electorate or in deciding whether to give the voters a direct voice in choosing electors. Direct national election would encourage states to encourage voters to vote on Election Day, but today this hardly seems a strong reason to *oppose* direct election.

Ingenious, indirect, sophisticated arguments made on behalf of the Electoral College by clever theorists these days are legion, but almost all are makeweight. If the scheme is so good, why does not any U.S. state or any foreign nation copy it? A low-plurality winner in a three- or four-way race is possible even with the Electoral College. Yet such a circumstance could be avoided in a direct national election by single transferable voting (with voters listing their second and third choices on the ballot, in effect combining the "first heat" and "runoff" elections into a single transaction).

The only two real arguments against abolition of the Electoral College are found in federalism and inertia. Only federalism can explain why we should use an electoral college to pick presidents but not governors. But it is hard to see what the federalism argument is *today*. The specter of the national government administering a national election, I confess, does not give me the cold sweats. A razor-thin popular vote margin might occasion a national recount, but states now manage recounts all the time, and new technology will make counting and recounting much easier in the future. (And today, a razor-thin Electoral College margin may require recounts in a number of closely contested states even if there is a clear national popular winner.)

Inertial, Burkean arguments take two forms. First, the argument goes, a change in presidential selection rules would radically change the game in ways hard to foresee. Candidates would not care about winning states, only votes, and campaign strategies might change dramatically and for the worse. But it is hard to see why: given that the Electoral College leader has also historically tended to be the popular vote leader, the strategy for winning should not change dramatically if we switch from one measure to the other. This sets up the second inertial point. The dreaded specter of a clear popular loser becoming the Electoral College winner has not happened in this century: Why worry? But that is what someone might say after three trigger pulls in Russian roulette. One day, we will end up with a clear "loser President"—clear beyond any quibbles about uncertain ballots. And the question is, will this loser/winner be seen as legitimate at home and abroad? If our modern national democratic ethos, when focused on the thing, would balk at a byzantine system that defies the people's choice on election day, true Burkean theory would seem to argue *against* the Electoral College. If We the People would amend the Constitution *after* the loser president materializes—and I predict we would—why are we now just waiting for the inevitable accident to happen?

CHAPTER 2

Parlor Games

Philip Bobbitt

The Constitution is not perfect. Indeed, I do not know what "perfection" is in a constitution, which is an instrument for human hands and thus must bear within its possibilities all the potential for misuse that comes with the user. What I am sure of is that "perfect" does not mean "never needing to be amended," since one important part of the Constitution is its provision for amendment (although I am inclined to believe that few of the amendments to the Constitution were actually necessary).

That said, a competition to find the "stupidest provision of the Constitution" is, to my mind, about the most vapid contest to come along since MTV listeners were asked to suggest names for a litter of puppies owned by a heavy-metal performer. As anyone who has been around dogs knows, their names have to do with their individual natures and the relationships they have with each other and with their masters. Naming them in the abstract is idle, a parlor game.

Designer constitutionalism is a similar pastime. Like political science generally, it is interesting only to the extent that design can be isolated from the many overlapping functions of any political instrument. Political scientists are aware of this, of course. The use of a conceptual strategy, like imagining an alternative constitutional system, for example, is not necessarily marred by the avoidance of the real-world complexity of moral decisions (anymore than is the political philosopher's use of the Kantian veil of ignorance). Rather, these strategies recognize that moral decisions are so very complicated that only by isolating some feature of the political structure in strict laboratory conditions can we arrive at a general thesis. But to the extent that a constitutional question is isolatable, it is a little absurd.

The Constitution functions as an organic whole. All the forms of argument—historical, textual, structural, ethical, prudential, doctrinal—depend entirely on this principle. One cannot begin to construe correctly the "commander-in-chief power" without bearing in mind the Congress's power to appropriate money for the armed forces. Nor can one adequately construe, in any concrete case, the Congress's power to declare war without squaring it with the executive's power to deploy troops where he, and he alone, thinks best. Remove one part of the Constitution and you change another. In a mature democracy, these relationships are sufficiently complicated and well developed that any particular change is likely to have a number of unanticipated consequences, including, often enough, a result conflicting with the campaign by which the change in the Constitution was secured in the first place.

Suppose one of the contributors to this symposium should propose the provision of a senate as the worst provision. The question "Should we have a senate?" was once put to me as a "constitutional question" by my friend Sandy Levinson, one of the editors of this collection of papers. Behind a veil of ignorance, unknowing as to what person one might become or what position in society he or she might have (and therefore unprejudiced to favor any particular group or station), one might well argue that popular majoritarianism is so manifestly an equitable principle that any departure from it is a mistake. Or, similarly, behind this veil one might also argue that the protection of minority points of view can justify such a departure, the likelihood of being a part of some political minority being high in a pluralistic society. Then, I suppose, the focus shifts to empirical evidence, if such is really possible in these matters, to establish whether or not the Senate is in fact protective of the particular minorities with whom the questioner has sympathy.

But in the law we do not live behind such a veil, and to pretend otherwise in order to get clarity and consistency in our principles is to ignore the actual responsibilities we do have. "Should we have a senate?" is a question like then-Governor Reagan's question, "Are you better off now than you were four years ago?", which was used to such powerful effect against President Carter. Of course, this was an irrelevant rhetorical thrust: the question ought to have been "Are you better off now than you would have been if Gerald Ford had been elected?" since neither President Carter nor anyone else can hold time still. Their achievements must be measured against what would otherwise have been but is not, not against what can never be—the suspension of time. The real question for law therefore, because law—unlike political science—does not live without air and the environment of reality, is, Would we or would the Constitution be better off if, for the last two hundred years, we had had no senate? The short answer has to be that "we"—the constitutional We that came into being in 1789—would not be at all better or worse off, since the price of the adoption of the Constitution was the inclusion of the Senate. Indeed, its enshrinement in the Constitution is the only unamendable part of the document.

There are, of course, artlessly drafted provisions—the Twenty-Fifth Amendment, for example, that enabled a discredited President Nixon to name his successor—and there are provisions that, no matter how carefully drafted, have been so construed as to render them useless, such as the Privileges or Immunities Clause of the Fourteenth Amendment. But that does not make them (nor their hopeful ratifiers) stupid, and it certainly does not show that we would have been better off had they not been adopted.

Rather, the reformer must show, not only that it is possible to imagine a world without the egregious provision in which things are better than they are at present, but also that it is possible to actualize such a world in which the system of constitutional interpretation we use remains legitimate. Because that system has made use of the Constitution as a whole, it is not easy to simply begin removing parts that appear inconsequential or offensive without risking the delegitimation of the system of interpretation itself. Some amendments—women's suffrage, for example—fit easily within the whole, because they are consistent with its premises as defined in the Declaration of Independence. For such purposes, Article V exists. Does that mean that a particularly stupid provision was replaced? Or does it mean that the provision for change in the Constitution worked precisely as it should?

When I read that new democracies are being advised by Americans on constitutional questions such as the size of their parliaments, bicameral versus unicameral bodies, presidential versus parliamentary rule, the optimum number of political parties, the criteria for admitting particular parties to participation, the threshold showing by a party to achieve parliamentary participation, the relative strength of the branches, and so forth, I wince. The answers to these allegedly "technical" questions will provide the structure that will guarantee the rights of the people so newly freed. Because these questions do not have any "right" answers in the abstract, they do not have stupid answers either. The correctness of the answers that are chosen will depend upon the adherence on which they are able to rely—which is entirely a matter of the cultural history and idiosyncrasies of the particular country—and on the willingness of citizens to use these structural answers for worthy goals.

The stupidest provisions of a successful constitution like ours are those that, thankfully, have not been adopted—whether their supporters portray the Constitution as an unworkable anachronism or the institutions set up by the Constitution as dysfunctional.

The American constitutional enterprise does not require, I think, constant correction, as if it were a Popperian scheme of ever-improvement, nor profit from the supercilious condescension of those of us who rank its provisions according to escalating stupidity, culminating in the "stupidest." Rather the success of this highly successful enterprise depends upon making only those changes that reinforce its legitimacy in the eyes of our people, which is very seldom a matter, I think, of bringing it in line with the political formulae of theorists. The Constitution needs faith and, if the word is not inappropriate, reverence, as well as modesty before the grave tasks the Constitution sets for us.

CHAPTER 3

An Agenda for Constitutional Reform

Steven G. Calabresi

The U.S. Constitution is, in my judgment, the best constitution human beings have ever devised. Its structural hallmarks of federalism and separated powers work brilliantly to protect liberty from both public and private violence. Government action is hard to obtain (to the dismay of many rent seekers), but where a broad public consensus exists, national law making readily occurs.[1] Individual rights are well secured by the Bill of Rights, the post–Civil War amendments, and an assortment of other clauses, yet most vital public welfare measures usually get upheld. Lastly, the amendment process is tough and hard to navigate, as it should be, but not so much so as to prevent the adoption of such vital alterations of the original design as were accomplished by the Thirteenth, Fourteenth, Fifteenth, Nineteenth, and Twenty-Second Amendments.

In short, the Federalist Constitution has proved to be a brilliant success, which unitary nation states and parliamentary democracies all over the world would do well to copy. I give it most of the credit for the fact that ours is the wealthiest, most technologically advanced, and most socially just society in human history, not to mention the fact that we have with ease become a military superpower that has successfully defended most of the rest of the world from vicious totalitarian despots without in the process being corrupted ourselves. The rest of the world is quite rightly impressed with us, and it is thus no accident that the United States of America has become the biggest single exporter of public law in the history of humankind. Almost wherever one looks, written constitutions, federalism, separation of powers, bills of rights, and judicial review are on the ascendancy all over the world right now—and for a good reason.[2] They work better than any of the alternatives that have been tried.

All of that being said, however, the amended U.S. Constitution is not a perfect document. While I will cheerfully defend it from all enemies foreign and domestic, and while I would even go so far as to form a latter-day Federalist movement to sing its praises, I am confident that the Constitution could still be improved. The overarching "mistake"[3] in the amended document as it has been handed on to us after two hundred years is that the famous Madisonian system of checks and balances does not go far enough. Indeed, I would argue that *each* of the three branches of the federal government has been left insufficiently checked in its exercise of certain core powers. The reason for this is that the Framers wrongly assumed that each of the three branches would devote a great deal of energy to checking abuses by the other two. While this has largely proved to be true, there are some key situations in which each of the three branches is able to act unilaterally in self-interested ways and neither of the other two branches has much incentive to intervene. The point is best illustrated by discussing it in the context of each branch and by suggesting a quick amendment or two that would fix the problem.

Congress

Congressional self-dealing poses the biggest challenge because, contrary to the opinion of many of my colleagues in academia, Congress is by far the most powerful branch of our national government.[4] Congress's power comes from its ability to control the purse strings, pass laws, and conduct oversight hearings and investigations. In the wake of the adoption of the Sixteenth Amendment and of the New Deal revolution in the understanding of the scope of Congress's enumerated powers, senators and representatives have gained unprecedented control over a vast portion of the wealth and income generated by this incredibly wealthy and productive land. They have used this power extravagantly, spending much too much money and passing too many burdensome laws. All too often, the laws and appropriations seem directly designed to further the reelection bids of the sponsors and cosponsors of the ill-designed measures that are being promoted. The net result is that Americans are burdened with an unnecessarily big and wasteful federal government.

This has happened because, sadly, the growth of congressional power over our gross national product has not been met with any growth in the checks on congressional overreaching. To the contrary, constitutional impediments like enumerated powers have been swept away at the same time as important opposing institutions, like the state governments, have been weakened, both through the adoption of the Seventeenth Amendment and, more importantly, by the increase in the number of states from thirteen to fifty.[5] (It is obviously harder for fifty states to organize against national usurpations of power than it would be for thirteen to do so.)

The solution to this problem is to create new checks on our overly big national government by limiting Congress's raw power to overtax, overspend, and overregulate. Various proposals have been introduced or talked about in recent years that would impose precisely these kinds of limits, including proposals for a Balanced Budget Amendment, a Spending Limitation Amendment, an amendment requiring a supermajority of both houses of Congress for approval of any tax increases, a Congressional Term Limits Amendment, and a Presidential Line Item Veto Amendment. Like most other Reagan-Bush Republicans, I endorse *all* of these proposals. In my view, they are a necessary corrective to the excesses of the Progressive/New Deal Era in American public life, which left us saddled with a big, unresponsive, wasteful central government. While this is not the time or place to defend these proposals at length, I see all of them as attempts to achieve a better synthesis of twentieth-century constitutional reforms with the constitutional insights of the founders.

The Executive Branch

The great unwelcome development of the last one hundred years in the executive branch has been the simultaneous collapse of the nondelegation doctrine, the development of presidential-decree law-making powers pursuant to overly broad legislative delegations, and the concomitant growth of democratically unaccountable independent agencies and entities. These developments, the blame for which is directly traceable to the excesses of the Progressive/New Deal Era, need to be vigorously addressed. They have resulted in a bloated, overly powerful, and insufficiently accountable executive bureaucracy.

The solution again is to restore the constitutional system of checks and balances. The nondelegation doctrine should be greatly reinvigorated; if necessary, by constitutional amendment. Proposed statutory reforms that would require congressional approval *before* major rule makings or regulatory changes could take effect should be swiftly enacted. In addition, broad statutory delegations of power to the president should be reviewed by the appropriate congressional committees with an eye toward repealing those delegations that are excessive or that have outlived their usefulness. Most importantly, appropriations for executive-branch programs and staff should be cut sharply and permanently. Finally, the unaccountable bureaucrats in the independent agencies should be put firmly back under the president's control, so the White House can be held accountable for everything they do. No one should hold any policy-making position in the executive branch, except at the pleasure of the president.[6]

The Federal Courts

The imperial federal judiciary is the last institution in need of reform, and the problem here is that the federal courts have improperly misused the post–Civil War amendments to turn themselves into an autocratic engine of domestic social change. Every June, Americans open their morning newspapers and discover without fail that the most important domestic policy questions facing the country are all being resolved, not by their elected representatives in Congress or in the state legislatures, but rather by nine mysterious, black-robed figures who never mix with the voters at a town meeting or stand for election. Somehow, we find ourselves in the ridiculous situation where minor changes in trucking regulation can only be enacted by democratically elected officials subject to the onerous procedural hurdles of bicameralism and presentment, while the most controversial matters of religion and public morality are regularly decided by nine autocrats on a five-to-four vote! This absurd situation would never be tolerated by the nation's governing classes but for the left-wing elitist results it regularly leads to.

The growth of raw, unchecked judicial power has a strange history and largely results, in my opinion, from the unanticipated consequence of combing through the open-ended language of the post–Civil War amendments with the preexisting institution of judicial review.[7] Once that combination was effected, the federal courts gradually discovered that it was politically safer to invalidate state laws rather than federal laws, because the states have no direct "check" on federal judicial overreaching, whereas Congress has several direct "checks" at its disposal, due to its control over the budget for the judiciary and its powers over the confirmation and impeachment of federal judges. By 1937, the federal courts had completely given up their intended role as a "check" on Congress and the president in favor of a new role as a national domestic-policy–making body that could easily reach the states. This transition was no doubt hastened by the Seventeenth Amendment's substitution of direct election of U.S. senators for the prior system of state legislative election.

The solution, today, is to get the federal courts back into the business of enforcing the original Constitution and to get them out of the business of imposing radical social change on the states. This can be done by controlling the appointments process, by reducing appropriations for the judiciary, or by pursuing a few well-chosen constitutional amendments or statutory alterations of federal court jurisdiction. Possible reforms that have been discussed in recent years include (1) a constitutional amendment directing the federal courts to enforce federalism and separation of powers as vigorously as any other part of the Constitution; (2) a statute or a constitutional amendment requiring a three-fourths vote of the Supreme Court or of the en banc session of any federal court of appeal before a *state* law or executive policy could be invalidated; (3) a constitutional amendment requiring that presidential nominations of all Article III judges be sent to the fifty state governors for confirmation instead of going to the Senate, as happens now; (4) a sharp reduction in the appropriation for law clerks, combined with a reduction in the size of the lower federal courts; (5) a statute relimiting the injunctive powers of the federal courts, perhaps by designating the U.S. Court of Appeals for the District of Columbia Circuit to be the *only* federal court with equity jurisdiction anywhere in the country; (6) a statute eliminating facial challenges to statutes in federal courts, which, if successful, wipe out the entire statute, in contrast to more modest, "as applied" challenges; (7) incorporating recent salutary developments with respect to the justiciability doctrines into the core federal jurisdictional statutes; and, lastly, (8) a statute forbidding the use of head-swelling aristocratic forms in federal court, like the wearing of black robes, the title "Your Honor," and the designation "The Honorable."

I currently have no opinion as to how many of the above reforms would need to be enacted to get the federal judiciary to stop misbehaving. Perhaps the needed "check" can be accomplished just through the appointments process, coupled with the threat of reform, or maybe something more drastic will be needed. I favor doing as little as possible, *so long as the federal courts stop misbehaving.* If they continue on the path they are on, then sterner measures will be required and will be forthcoming.

In conclusion, the key "mistake" in the Constitution is that the system of checks and balances has been diluted too much by the unanticipated effects of constitutional amendments and changes over the last two hundred years.

All three branches of the federal government need to be reined in through a general restoration of the system of checks and balances.[8]

NOTES

1. For a normative defense of American constitutional federalism, see Steven G. Calabresi, "'A Government of Limited and Enumerated Powers': In Defense of *United States v. Lopez*," 94 *Mich. L. Rev.* 752 (1995). For a normative defense of the American constitutional system of separation of powers, see Steven G. Calabresi, "Some Normative Arguments for the Unitary Executive," 48 *Ark. L. Rev.* 23 (1995).

2. See sources cited in note 2. See also Steven G. Calabresi, "Thayer's Clear Mistake," 88 *Nw. U. L. Rev.* 269 (1993).

3. I prefer the term "mistake" to the more emphatic term "stupidity," because many of the flaws I identify could probably not have been foreseen to be flaws when they were incorporated into the Constitution. Indeed, most of the flaws I mention are the unanticipated results of the synthesizing of new constitutional amendments with the provisions of the original document.

4. But see Michael Stokes Paulsen, "The Most Dangerous Branch: Executive Power to Say What the Law Is," 83 *Geo. L.J.* 217 (1994) (wrongly describing the executive branch of the government as being the most dangerous); Martin S. Flaherty, "The Most Dangerous Branch," 105 *Yale L.J.* 1725 (1996) (same).

5. Both the adoption of the Seventeenth Amendment and the increase in the number of states were necessary, and in many ways salutary, developments. My regret is that *other* mechanisms were not established over the years to rein in the power of our overly big national government.

6. See Calabresi, "Unitary Executive"; Steven G. Calabresi, "Some Structural Consequences of the Increased Use of Ethics Probes as Political Weapons," 11 *J. L. & Pol.* 621 (1995).

7. I use the word "unanticipated" in text because, although I am certain that the framers of the post–Civil War amendments hoped those amendments would be judicially enforced, I am equally certain that the generation of Americans who died and sacrificed to overturn the substantive due process decision in *Dred Scott* did not mainly intend to empower the federal judiciary by enacting their amendments. They thought and hoped that *Congress* would mainly enforce the amendments, and they certainly were not friends of judicial activism.

8. I am grateful for the helpful suggestions of Gary Lawson, Thomas W. Merrill, and Christopher Rohrbacher.

CHAPTER 4

"Clause and Effect"

An Imagined Conversation with Sanford Levinson

Lief H. Carter

Foreword

This essay reprints, unmodified, the essay that originally appeared in *Constitutional Commentary*. I then add some remarks appropriate to this expanded volume.

I could not rewrite my original essay and stay faithful to its argument. That argument, in a nutshell, claims that truth abides in context, not text. Context—both the pragmatic elements of specific problems and the moods and expectations which surround them—powers all discourse, including constitutional discourse. We use constitutional texts more like steering wheels than engines, to move discourse in directions we desire. And since each of us desires to move in our own direction, we will never fully agree on textual meaning.

The same principle governs this collection. The context for the initial collection of thousand-word essays on constitutional stupidities so thoroughly drove my original contribution that I might reach an entirely different conclusion now that we write for an edited book with a much longer word limit. Freely expanding and thus changing my essay would thus have me commit, as they say in the postmodern trade, a "performative disjuncture."

The Original Essay

LC: Good to hear from you. I'm honored to join such good company as Farber and Sherry. Please send the details.

SL: There is no written description. The basic idea is to select your least favorite clause of the current U.S. constitution and in one thousand words, explain why you would love to see it expunged. It should be something you think has significance for current governance; you get no points by condemning the Fugitive Slave Clause.[1]

LC: That assignment, for a pragmatic postmodernist like me is harder than you think. You remember that part in my Pergamon book where I show how significant clauses in the Constitution have been interpreted, in both short runs and long, in quite contradictory ways.[2] "Clause and effect" views of constitutional law fail to make sense of two hundred years of constitutional history. Reality is so completely socially constructed that any one clause out of context is just a string of words. Any suspect clause that "has significance for our current governance" could go anywhere and hence shouldn't be expunged.

SL: When will you postmodernists learn to stop hiding behind that social-construction line? Of course we construct. Please get on with doing a little social construction for us.

LC: I'm not hiding, and I am constructing. I believe that legal language, like all language, has no intrinsic meaning out of context. Even if I could defend the proposition that a certain clause has done the most damage "so far," I could never show that such a clause could not support a different and highly desirable construction in the future. Legal language is just a discipline we impose to define the nature of our disagreements in trustworthy enough ways that we don't go out and kill each other.

SL: You take the Stanley Fish position?

LC: Yes, but just the hook, not the line and sinker. The hook of course is that legal rules in their very ambiguity play a role in forming a kind of wisdom that transcends the rules. (Remember Fish's exasperated basketball coach in "Fish vs. Fiss"?) But unlike Fish, I think current antifoundationalist thought only marks our transition from one foundationalist paradigm to another. Fish says we will continue to pretend we achieve foundationalist determinacy. My line (and sinker, though I don't particularly like the metaphor) is that liberalism has struggled for three centuries to construct a foundational, natural-law–like belief in the natural reality of substantive indeterminacy, and hence a political commitment to the desirability of skepticism, mystery, and tolerance.

SL: Yes, I know the pragmatic line and sinker: If it works, it's "true." You're about to tell me that you can therefore take any constitutional clause and argue coherently both for and against expunging it. So try expunging the Due Process Clause (or for that matter the Equal Protection Clause) of the Fourteenth Amendment.

LC: Pieces of expunge cake! Without such clauses, would the late-nineteenth-century courts have been able to confine Fourteenth Amendment privileges and immunities to the right to travel, especially in light of Article IV privileges and immunities? We might have incorporated basic rights far earlier than we did and confronted the evils of Reconstruction and its aftermath much sooner. And the Equal Protection Clause is pure legal gobbledygook, since all laws backed by sanctions inescapably discriminate and create inequalities: laws against murder treat those who murder differently from those who don't, and so on.

SL: Would you care to justify the Fugitive Slave Clause?

LC: Sure, but remember I'm mainly trying to argue against clause and effect. As a tool for defining differences—for focusing moral thought and for prodding us down that bloody road toward our aspirations (to focus our "constitutional faith," as someone put it)—it may well have been necessary to enshrine the devil of slavery in our Constitution in order to have something to drive out of the temple.

SL: Well, I agree it would not make sense to expunge, say, the Cain and Abel story from the Bible because we're offended by it.

LC: Right. Such biblical and constitutional clauses "work," or rather we find all sorts of ways of using such tools to produce work that we value. And the "we" in this sentence matters. Social construction of reality means that the only point in my saying what I would expunge would be to construct something useful for you and our audience.

SL: So you're writing this article like a Socratic dialogue to dramatize that truth is not "there" apart from social life. So let me play along and guess: You will expunge that which is least susceptible of doing work, right?

LC: Yes, but not necessarily by expunging that which is inherently confusing. As I said, the Equal Protection Clause is inherently confusing. And the truistic Tenth Amendment has done work, at least for Bill Rehnquist and George Will and more than a century of police-power fans. I can only argue for expunging (because they do no work) some part of the Constitution which we constitutional students and scholars find useless, i.e., have the hardest time remembering.

SL: You mean the least litigated clauses?

LC: Nope. We'll never know if we might have had a president under thirty-five. And the story, which I heard first from Mark Tushnet, about the eighteen-year-old guru-televangelist-cum-presidential-candidate who claims that according to his religion, which is protected by the First Amendment (which amends the Thirty-Five-Year-Old President Clause), he is reincarnated and really a wise seventy-year-old, still works for me in class. I propose instead that our readers take the following short closed-book test and submit their results to Suzanna Sherry. Whichever question gets the most wrong answers becomes our socially constructed expunge winner. Here's the test:

1. After a putatively disabled president declares in writing that he is not disabled, what is the minimum possible number of days he must wait before resuming the powers of his office without confronting constitutionally approved congressional opposition?
2. Who counts the votes of the Electoral College, and who supervises the counting?
3. Define the constitutional meaning of "Corruption of Blood." In what context, if any, is corruption of blood permissible?
4. True or false: The president may convene both houses of Congress together but cannot convene only one house.
5. What is the maximum permissible geographical size of the District of Columbia?
6. True or false: A vote of one fifth or more of the total members of either house is sufficient to . . . Well, you get the idea.

SL: But the rule here is to expunge what you think has the most negative significance for modern government. How can you argue that the least known and most trivial clauses are the most damaging clauses?

LC: I'd like to argue that these clauses trivialize and "demoralize" the Constitution, but I don't really believe that. I have to fall back on the performance problem you've created for me. You've given me a thousand-word limit, and you have not permitted me to add anything, only expunge. Social construction being as indeterminate as it is, I wouldn't dare just take out, say, the references that support the death penalty without adding a prohibition. Take the word "life" out of the Due Process Clause? It you want to pin me down, I'd delete separate election of the president and have him or her serve at the pleasure of the Congress, parliamentary style, but I can't begin to defend that coherently in a thousand words, or do it without adding new clauses.

SL: Aha! So rules do have effects.

LC: Then how come I'm already way over my thousand-word limit?

Afterword

I trust readers now see why fidelity to my original argument, not mere laziness or overwork, obligated me to leave my text "as was." It will not, however, contradict its message to apply it in this afterword to other arguments, as they have been revised for publication in book form, to further my point. More specifically, I shall state briefly for each of the first seven alphabetically arrayed articles (in the original symposium organized by Eskridge and Levinson) what I take to be a strong counterargument. The point is not that I am right and they are wrong. (My alphabetical scheme requires me to counter my own argument in due course.) Rather, the mere presence of credible and serious counterarguments suggests that "stupid" clauses can, if we shift perspectives and contexts, do nonstupid constitutional work.

• Akhil Reed Amar (chapter 1). The argument against the Electoral College concedes that federalism may well have justified the initial textual arrangement. The stupidity, if any, thus lies in our not amending the Constitution to provide direct presidential election now. Thus the textual stupidity resides in the roadblocks to amending created in Article V. But Amar objects to the Electoral College now because he fears that one day we will have a minority president. Well, we have had one in Bill Clinton, at least in his first term. Is there a huge political difference between the authority of a president (Clinton) who has received less votes than the combined votes of his two opponents (Bush and Perot), and the authority of a president who has received less votes than one opponent? Grant that we could document such a real difference in public support and legitimacy, we must also acknowledge that federalism as a political value seems on the upswing these days. On what basis does our supposed "real difference" so outweigh current enthusiasms for federalism as to make retaining the Electoral College, and the autonomy it may give to state politics, stupid?

• Philip Bobbitt (chapter 2). Sorry, sir, but this collection does not rival MTV essay contests to name the puppies of rock stars. (For starters, it is not a contest.) A poll of what notable members of our little academic community think about constitutional issues, issues that do not receive much public or academic attention in our ordinary conversations, helps me and, I trust, others to think interesting new thoughts. There is nothing unfaithful about seeking improvement. Even the pope does it. Besides, these essays are a great liberal-arts teaching device. In the teaching context, it emboldens us to ask our students, "What would *you* say is the silliest thing in our constitutional order?" Alert readers will note that I heartily endorse Professor Bobbitt's main thrust. But asking the "stupid" question is entirely useful in the context of liberally educating our young on matters constitutional. Without such an education, Bobbitt's much-desired constitutional reverence will be hollow and most illiberal.

• Myself. Sorry, Lief. Your quiz at the end and your proposal to rank the things we cannot remember and have so far had no utility does not quite prove your point. These clauses do fill in structural holes without which we would have some really stupid textual silences. Of course you try to cover that by saying these clauses really serve the purpose of by-laws and undercut the moral pull of the document we actually study. But in practice these trivial clauses do not demoralize. Constitutional contests over the "big issues"—abortion and gun control, for example—may demoralize some as they energize others. If, as you claim, the context of political debate about the Constitution is what matters, then these clauses are not stupid, just immaterial to the larger constitutional debates of our time.

• William N. Eskridge, Jr. (chapter 5). The criticisms of Akhil Amar's position largely apply here. The objections to "one senator, one vote" make some not-obvious assumptions about the organization of state political systems in the present, not just in the past. Would Wyoming or Alaska continue to function effectively in their internal operation as polities if they were effectively stripped of voice and power at the national level? The post hoc argument that sagebrush states produce unhappy policy results (and I happen to share Eskridge's policy views on these issues) does not go far to prove that the textual arrangement is itself stupid, at least not until we assess the consequences of a different Senate on state political autonomy.

• Daniel A. Farber (chapter 6). About all that can be said critically of Farber's piece is that he, like Bobbitt, refuses to play by the rules. Even in his pseudo-Panglossian world, he could have picked his least favorite clause. If constitutional things necessarily work out tolerably well, do we constitutional commentators have justifiable job security?

• Mark Graber (chapter 7). The Necessary and Proper Clause stupid? What scholastic world is he living in? I thought the world in which "good" texts spoke for themselves died with, say, Galileo. (Does Graber condemn reading the Equal Protection Clause into the Bill of Rights?) The Necessary and Proper Clause is a perfect example of a clause that has, in some contexts, done useful work. The fact that the same work might well have been done without it (e.g., by playing with the Commerce Clause more directly) does not make this clause stupid. As Graber documents, the clause focused important Federalist/anti-Federalist debates and conversations about the nature of the union we created. Its imprecision itself strikes me as a desirable endorsement of a nonliteralistic approach to constitutional meaning. If we say it is stupid because of the uses to which John Marshall put it, do we have any choice but to replay the old Federalist version of "I like chocolate . . ." once again?

• Stephen M. Griffin (chapter 8). And here we come to the crux, which I take to be Amar's main point: the provisions for formal constitutional change by amendment are too difficult. We therefore resort to undemocratic judicial subterfuge to bring about needed change. Well! I now live in a sagebrush state, Colorado. This state managed a few years ago to amend, by the majority of those casting ballots, its state constitution so that any person suffering discrimination based on the belief (including, presumably, a false belief) that the person was gay, lesbian, or bisexual (in orientation, not necessarily behavior!) had no judicial or other remedy for this discrimination. Under its terms, suppose my hypothetical employer, a homophobic zealot, fires me in breach of our mutual contract of employment because he believes (the truth does not matter) that I am gay. Colorado's now mercifully dead Amendment 2—thanks to an unbroken string of judicial decisions from Colorado's trial courts to the U.S. Supreme Court—would, read literally, strip the Colorado courts of their power to issue me a remedy for breach of contract. Call limited democracy and the judicial power to check and balance the temporary whims of some voters stupid? That is highly debatable.

I do not (and cannot, from my perspective) claim to have refuted the seven arguments I have challenged. In fact, they are for the most part elegant and stimulating and useful and therefore fun. I mean only to support my own position: stupidity, like truth, abides in context, not text. Stupidity and truth are, perhaps sadly, easily contested. Acts of political will, not intellectual analysis, normally determine what we shall, for a time, call stupid. Its better to settle things than to settle them right. None of us branded the Supremacy Clause, and the judicial power it is used to justify, stupid.

NOTES

1. Professor Levinson's first statement is his e-mailed response to my request for details. All other "SLs" are purely my own invention. I could never hope to replicate Sandy's fine blend of articulate probing and gentle civility.

2. See Lief H. Carter, *Contemporary Constitutional Lawmaking: The Supreme Court and the Art of Politics* 22-23 (New York: Pergamon Press, 1985).

CHAPTER 5

The One Senator, One Vote Clauses

William N. Eskridge, Jr.

Article I, Section 3, Clause 1 of the Constitution provides that the Senate "shall be composed of two Senators from each State, . . . and each Senator shall have one Vote." Amending the original Constitution's method for selecting senators, the Seventeenth Amendment, Section 1 repeats this language precisely. The requirement that each state have two senators was part of the "Great Compromise" reached in Philadelphia and may still be defensible today; it assures that the Senate will be a deliberative body with relatively few members and, plausibly, that the interests of the states qua states might be better represented. The requirement that each senator shall have one vote was also part of the Great Compromise but is much harder to defend today. In my opinion, the One Senator, One Vote Clauses are the most problematic ones remaining in the Constitution. Indeed, they are hard-wired into the Constitution, as the proviso to Article V states that "no State, without its Consent, shall be deprived of its equal Suffrage in the Senate."

The One Senator, One Vote Clauses flout the constitutional principle of "one person, one vote." If Citizen A's legislator represents one hundred thousand people, while Citizen B's legislator in the same chamber represents ten thousand, Citizen A is being treated unequally under the assumptions of our political culture. To prevent this kind of vote dilution, the Supreme Court has required equality in district size for other kinds of elections. Indeed, in *Reynolds v. Sims*,[1] the Court held that state senates apportioned like the national Senate violate the Equal Protection Clause of the Fourteenth Amendment. The Court rejected the argument that equal protection was satisfied so long as one of the two legislative chambers followed the one person, one vote principle:

> The right of a citizen to equal representation and to have [his or her] vote weighted equally with those of all other citizens in the election of members of one house of a bicameral state legislature would amount to little if States could effectively submerge the equal-population principle in the apportionment of seats in the other house. . . . Deadlock between the two bodies might result in compromise and concession on some issues. But in all too many cases the more probable result would be frustration of the majority will through minority veto in the house not apportioned on a population basis[.]

The same problem inheres in the One Senator, One Vote Clauses: they sacrifice the "right of a citizen to equal representation and to have [his or her] vote weighted equally with those of all other citizens." If the constitutional baseline in a representative democracy is one person, one vote, then the One Senator, One Vote Clauses are presumptively problematic.

How problematic? Does the sacrifice of majority-rule values undermine the dynamic operation of energetic government? Does the sacrifice subserve a larger goal? I hypothesize that the One Senator, One Vote Clauses have negative but not disastrous effects on energetic government, but neither do they have a single tangible benefit. Their primary effect in today's polity is to distribute political benefits from the rest of the country to the fourteen "sagebrush states" of the West and Great Plains (Alaska, Arizona, Colorado, Idaho, Kansas, Montana, Nebraska, Nevada, New Mexico, North Dakota, Oklahoma, South Dakota, Utah, and Wyoming).

The sagebrush states have almost one-third of the votes in the Senate, but less than one-tenth of the people in the country. Although the sagebrush senators are not completely homogeneous, they do exhibit bloc-voting characteristics and predictably affect closely divided chamber votes. Three recent examples: if Senate votes were weighted according to their states' representation in the House (each senator receiving half of the state's House allotment), the Senate would have voted 295–140 to override President Bush's veto of the 1990 civil rights bill, would have rejected the nomination of Judge Clarence Thomas for the Supreme Court in 1991 (albeit in a close vote, 224–211), and would have overwhelmingly (238–165) voted to remove the ban on entry into the United States of people who are infected with the HIV virus (a move that was defeated by 52–46 when proposed in 1993). Consider each example in more detail.

The first example reveals the limitations of my objection. Even if the Senate had overridden President Bush's veto in 1990, it is not clear that the House would have done so. What is clear is that a civil rights bill was enacted in 1991. At most, then, the net effect of the One Senator, One Vote Clauses was not to defeat the legislation but to delay it and, more importantly, to skew the content of the political compromise ultimately adopted. The 1991 civil rights statute was a diluted version of the 1990 bill; it provided fewer statutory rights to people claiming unlawful job discrimination.[2] Sagebrush senators provided the margin for sustaining the president's veto and, hence, for relocating the legislative bargain at a point less favorable to victims of job discrimination, especially African Americans. This was precisely the reason (quoted above) that the Supreme Court in *Reynolds* rejected state senates that diluted one person, one vote principles.

That the one senator, one vote rule is strongly antimajoritarian is cause for concern, but that concern might be ameliorated if the rule served a substantive value. For example, the Framers required bicameral approval and presentment to the president so as to assure that hasty majorities would not override individual liberties or unsettle the rule of law.[3] The obvious benefit of the One Senator, One Vote Clauses would be to protect individual liberties by slowing down or defeating at least some kinds of legislation. An immediate problem with such an argument, today, is that legislation in the modern administrative state is often deregulatory (tending toward less government). Slowing down or defeating deregulatory proposals is not libertarian, as that term is commonly understood. Another problem is that the Framers also hoped for energetic government that solved important public problems. The ultimate normative question is this: Does the sagebrush bloc contribute to a useful balance between liberty and energetic regulation?

I doubt it. Sagebrush values are often billed as libertarian or law and order, but the sagebrush senators' voting records are not distinctively libertarian or sensitive to rule of law values. As a group, these senators are libertarian when it comes to private rights to government land in the West and to taxing the government for environmental regulations. They are not libertarian when it comes to farm subsidies, defense spending, and the Alaska Pipeline. (The sagebrush senators were decisive in the Senate's insistence that pipeline decisions affecting the environment be unreviewable.) Moreover, these senators are relatively unsympathetic to the liberty of racial, ethnic, or sexual-orientation minorities. For instance, they consistently vote for gratuitously antihomosexual measures having no defensible policy rationale.[4] Their overwhelming vote against admitting HIV-positive immigrants, for example, was antilibertarian and without any defensible medical justification.

The Thomas confirmation vote,[5] which was western- more than southern-driven, reflects the far-reaching importance of sagebrush overrepresentation for issues of governance generally. Unlike the House, the Senate's consent is needed not only for the enactment of legislation but also for the confirmation of federal judges, agency heads, and department officials, as well as for ratification of treaties (by a two-thirds supermajority). As a result, the sagebrush group not only has influence in Congress beyond any democratic or other normative justification but also has similarly indefensible influence on foreign policy, the composition of the judiciary, and public administration.

The overrepresentation of small-population states (especially the sagebrush states) in the Senate does not affect every issue that comes before Congress; in fact, it probably has no decisive effect on a majority of issues. When it does have a decisive effect, the phenomenon is antimajoritarian but perhaps defensible according to some other normative criterion. I am open to such justification, but the most obvious one (rugged individualism) is not supported by the actual behavior of sagebrush senators, either recently or historically.[6] Worse, the public costs of sagebrush overrepresentation ought to increase rather than diminish over time. If the most critical domestic issues facing the United States as the millennium approaches are those associated with urban areas—ghetto segregation, drug and health epidemics, violent crime, the collapse of public education, a widening chasm between rich and poor, racial strife—the underrepresentation of urban interests not only deprives the Senate of its presumptive role as the more farsighted chamber of Congress but also undermines the country's ability to deal with its most festering problems.

NOTES

1. 377 U.S. 533 (1964).

2. For a key example, the 1990 bill explicitly overrode several Supreme Court decisions retroactively. The 1991 statute was silent on the issue, and the Supreme Court predictably construed the statute not to have retroactive effect. See *Landgraf v. USI Film Products*, 114 S. Ct. 1483 (1994).

3. See *INS v. Chadha*, 462 U.S. 919 (1983).

4. Or, conversely, sagebrush senators vote strongly against elementary liberties for gay people. The proposed Employment Non-Discrimination Act of 1996 (ENDA), which would have protected against sexual-orientation job discrimination, was defeated by a slender 50–49 vote in the Senate on September 10, 1996. The sagebrush senators voted nineteen to nine against ENDA. The bill would have passed the Senate had voting been by population rather than one senator, one vote.

5. Nineteen sagebrush senators (sixteen Republicans, three Democrats) voted for Judge Thomas, and only nine (all Democrats) voted against him. The overall Senate vote was 52–48 in favor of Judge Thomas. The only other region to support Judge Thomas was his home region, the South, including border states (nineteen senators for, fifteen senators against). The Midwest, East, and Pacific Coast senators opposed Judge Thomas's confirmation (fourteen senators for, twenty-four senators against).

6. The sagebrush senators have been a distinctive voting bloc throughout the post–New Deal era. They have decisively influenced national policy through their strong support of McCarthyism in the 1940s and 1950s, their alliance with southern senators to sink strong civil rights laws in the 1950s, their Court baiting and uncritical support for the nation's Indochina policy in the 1960s and 1970s, and their opposition to environmental, health, and safety regulation in the 1970s and 1980s.

CHAPTER 6

Our (Almost) Perfect Constitution

Daniel A. Farber

I doubt that we would write the Constitution in quite the same way if we were to undertake the task afresh. Would anyone today actually propose giving the Providence metropolitan area the same representation in one branch of the legislature as half the West Coast? Nor do I doubt that there are details of the Constitution in need of improvement. (Like the editors of this volume, I regard slavery as too obvious a failing to require discussion here.) The interesting question is not whether the Constitution might not have been improved here or there. As with any human document, the answer is undoubtedly "yes."[1] But the more significant question is whether changes in the text would produce large practical benefits—or to put it another way, whether any parts of the Constitution (again putting aside slavery) have produced major social harms. On this score, I am quite skeptical.

The individual-rights side of the Constitution is probably the easiest with which to deal. No doubt each of us can think of individual rights that should ideally be protected in the Constitution but are not mentioned there. Still, it is hard to identify any individual rights that are truly precluded from recognition by the constitutional text. What prevents the judicial recognition of additional individual rights is usually not the text. Instead, it is the same thing that prevents their explicit incorporation into the Constitution: the lack of any strong national consensus in their favor. Liberals must be aware, for example, that the chances of getting the Supreme Court to recognize a constitutional right to welfare are just as small as getting Congress to pass such an amendment, and for roughly the same reason: most people in this country think the idea is nuts. On the other hand, if our society were really prepared to recognize such a right, room could be found in the existing text, as Professors Michelman and Tribe pointed out some years ago. Thus, if there is an objection regarding the treatment of individual rights, it is not really to anything written in the Constitution, but rather to our constitutional culture.

Much the same can be said about federalism. The extensive transformation of federal-state relations over our history shows just how much leeway the current Constitution allows in this regard. The fundamental decision to encourage some forms of local autonomy seems sound, and so is the equally fundamental decision to establish a unified nation. In the past two centuries, the balance between the two has shifted as our constitutional culture has changed, but most of the important changes have been extratextual.[2]

This brings us to the separation of powers, the area where the text is in many ways the most explicit. The fundamental decision here was to eschew a parliamentary form of government. At least since Woodrow Wilson, this decision has been roundly criticized in some quarters. It seems less than obvious to me, however, that England or the continental European countries have been better governed on average than has the United States.

What about the details of the structure of government? The institution of party government has transformed the Framers' original expectations about how the system would work; here, political culture has turned out to mean more than original intent. Hence, it is especially important in this setting to consider how the system has actually worked, rather than merely the words in the document.

The Senate seems most vulnerable to criticism, since it violates the general principle of "one person, one vote," which we otherwise endorse. It is true that in theory a small proportion of the population in strategic geographic locations could gain vastly disproportionate power through the Senate. Yet this seems to have happened rarely if ever in our history; I cannot offhand recall any instance of popular outcry against the "malapportionment" of the Senate.

In practice, senators have not responded solely to the interests of their own states. Presidential elections have played an important role in ameliorating the problem: senators have an interest in assisting their party to win in those contests, and historically many senators have themselves been aspiring presidential candidates. Hence, senators have tended to have a somewhat national, rather than purely local, outlook. Also, the longer terms served by senators have probably encouraged them to take a Burkean view of their function, just as the Framers hoped. On balance, then, the Senate seems to have worked tolerably well. Indeed, if it had not, it quite likely would have suffered the fate of the House of Lords by now.

In short, the imperfections of the original text matter much less than what we have made of the Constitution over two centuries. This conclusion could be considered an extension of the Coase Theorem. Constitutions do matter, because they raise the transaction costs of enacting various legal measures. But in the long run, the rules cannot prevent the ultimate political balance of a society from working itself out—through amendments, judicial interpretation, or new institutions, such as political parties. In the end, society gets its way; if we dislike the results, we must put most of the blame on our contemporaries rather than the Framers.

NOTES

1. To take a perhaps minor example, the Natural Born Citizen Clause of Article II, which prevents immigrants from aspiring to the presidency, has always struck me as an unfortunate expression of nativism. See Randall Kennedy, "A Natural Aristocracy," chapter 9 of this volume.

2. The Reconstruction Amendments are the exception that proves the rule. Even there, the critical shift of power to the national government during the Civil War and Reconstruction took place in the political (and ideological) arena.

CHAPTER 7

Unnecessary and Unintelligible

Mark Graber

No constitution produced after much deliberation by reasonably intelligent persons is likely to contain passages that are "foolish; dull in intellect; nonsensical."[1] Many constitutional provisions quickly outlived their original purpose (the Electoral College) and others are venal (the not-so-oblique protections of slavery). Nevertheless, contemporary claims that some constitutional provision is plainly stupid probably overlook the intelligent reasons why that particular clause was inserted into the Constitution or the sound reasons the Framers had for choosing that particular language. Constitutional language that seems foolish from some perspectives probably remains in the text because the provision in question serves the interests of a minority large enough to block a contrary amendment, and not because Americans lack the intelligence to perceive or the energy to repeal nonsensical constitutional clauses.

The problem of identifying stupid constitutional provisions would be different if "stupid" meant "mistaken . . . deleterious, or . . . least favorite."[2] This assignment would have provoked an extended meditation on what constitutional provision is most responsible for my least favorite aspect of American constitutionalism, "the depressing past [and present] that characterizes American welfare."[3] The Fourteenth Amendment may be at fault. Alas, the Reconstruction Congress used such vague phrases as "due process" and "equal protection" instead of explicitly stating that "all citizens have a right to be provided by government with certain basic necessities." Several distinguished commentators do believe the former phrases, in conjunction with the Ninth Amendment, provide sufficient foundations for various constitutional rights to livelihood.[4] Still, even if Frank Michelman and others are correct about what the Constitution means, more explicit constitutional protection might have overcome the constitutional scruples of those justices and political actors who have hitherto been unwilling to recognize unenumerated constitutional welfare rights.[5]

An alternative approach would have examined the extent to which specific constitutional institutions are responsible for the unwarranted degree of economic inequality in the United States. If, for example, our constitutional commitment to federalism helps explain American failures to guarantee all persons a decent standard of living,[6] then every constitutional clause that limits national capacity to combat poverty should be considered a leading candidate for the stupidest provision in the text. At this point, however, my colleague Ric Uslaner will be quick to insist that no change in constitutional language or institutions will likely be effective in the absence of a sympathetic political culture.[7] In this light, progressive reformers should note that Mary Ann Glendon's study of constitutional approaches to welfare in Western nations found no correlation between explicit constitutional protection for welfare rights and the level of actual welfare benefits provided to poor people.[8]

The problem with all meditations of this sort, however, is that "stupid" does not mean "mistaken . . . deleterious, or . . . least favorite." Opponents of an expanded Great Society may be terribly mistaken. Some may even be guilty of class or race prejudice. Still, "stupid" is hardly the right word to describe the several Nobel Prize winners in economics who have devoted careers to criticizing the welfare state. Moreover, even if the title *Constitutional Stupidities* is a rhetorical flourish, the term "stupidities" conceals important problems of constitutional politics. As the history of civil rights in the United States and my previous discussion of comparative welfare policies suggest,[9] a constitutional clause recognizing rights to certain necessities is likely to be a mere scrap of paper in the absence of a social commitment to achieving greater economic equality and opportunity in the United States.[10]

In fairness to Professors Levinson and Eskridge, I should acknowledge that the above reflections on "stupidity" were primarily intended to cover my misreading or, more likely, forgetting the question this essay was supposed to answer. Given nearly two hundred years of Constitution-worship in the United States, the editors of this volume have done their country an enormous service by forcing both contributors and readers to contemplate possible constitutional imperfections. Still, if the other papers in this section take "stupid" to mean "mistaken," one essay that takes "stupid" to mean "foolish" may provide a useful comparison. Explanations of constitutional foolishness are likely to be different from explanations of constitutional mistakes, and each form of constitutional error may have different consequences.

If any provision in the Constitution merits the appellation "stupid," the Necessary and Proper Clause seems the best candidate for this honor.[11] Article I, Section 8's concluding declaration that "the Congress shall have the Power . . . To make all Laws which shall be necessary and proper for carrying into Execution the foregoing Powers" is nonsensical on its face. Understood literally, the clause prevents the national legislature from exercising vital constitutional powers. More significantly, the Necessary and Proper Clause satisfies several crucial historical tests for foolishness. The Framers did not seriously consider the meaning of "necessary and proper," and prominent defenders of the Constitution subsequently confessed that the provision was unnecessary and improper.

The Necessary and Proper Clause apparently establishes a constitutional standard that legislation rarely meets. No necessary means exist in many cases for realizing certain purposes. For example, in a room with two doors, it is not "necessary" to use either particular door in exiting (though one may well be more "convenient"). Although many policies help further such government goals as reducing poverty, promoting peace, or preventing crime, no single legislative strategy seems the necessary means for achieving those ends. The phrase "necessary and proper" also obliterates the distinction between constitutionality and wisdom, a distinction central to the Framers' goal of eliminating basic regime questions from normal political discourse.[12] A measure that is unwise cannot be a necessary means for achieving some important constitutional purpose. Hence, a literal reading of the Necessary and Proper Clause suggests imprudent measures must be unconstitutional. A justice sympathetic to progressive welfare policies, for example, would seem constitutionally obligated to void the Personal Responsibility and Work Opportunity Reconciliation Act of 1996,[13] because no social democrat would consider Clinton-Gingrich welfare policies the necessary means for reducing poverty (or achieving any other legitimate social end). Of course, judicial proponents of laissez-faire who take "necessary and proper" seriously would be as constitutionally obligated to strike down virtually every Great Society measure as unnecessary or improper means for realizing greater social equality.

The Framers could have avoided these constitutional thickets had they followed Massachusetts and authorized the national legislature to enact "wholesome and reasonable orders, laws, statutes, and ordinances."[14] No one outside of John Marshall and Alexander Hamilton, however, seriously contends that "necessary . . . means no more than needful, requisite, incidental, useful or conducive to."[15] "Necessary means" may not be "those means without which the grant of power would be nugatory," as Jefferson suggested.[16] Unfortunately, no one, including the constitutional Framers, seems to know the precise point of the phrase "necessary and proper."

The records of the Constitutional Convention do not provide an intelligent justification for the Necessary and Proper Clause or indicate that the words "necessary and proper" were the product of a conscious compromise between proponents and opponents of broad national power. The Committee on Detail neither explained its decision to incorporate into Article I Charles Pinckney's suggestion that Congress be explicitly authorized "to make all laws for carrying the foregoing powers into execution"[17] nor its insertion of the phrase "which shall be necessary and proper" into Pinckney's proposal.[18] The convention as a whole apparently perceived these alterations as stylistic and accepted without debate the Committee on Detail's handiwork.[19] Thus, not only do we have no understanding of how the Framers interpreted "necessary and proper," but the paucity of deliberation also suggests that the delegates were unaware that the phrase had the potential to wreak havoc both among proponents and opponents of the Constitution.

This history helps explain how language as foolish as "necessary and proper" slipped into the Constitution. The Necessary and Proper Clause did not reflect any value choice that later generations might regard as mistaken. Rather, the available evidence suggests that no one regarded that provision as being of any particular significance. The delegates seemed to perceive the phrase "necessary and proper" as a mere rhetorical flourish, not worth debating. They had far more important constitutional issues with which to deal. Besides, everyone wanted to go home.

Delegates who nevertheless thought the phrase "necessary and proper" would clearly demonstrate that Congress did not have an unlimited right to pass laws were quickly disabused of that foolish notion by anti-Federalist commentators. Leading opponents of the Constitution immediately pointed out that as long as Congress retained the power to determine what laws were "necessary and proper," the Necessary and Proper Clause would not in practice limit congressional discretion in any way.[20] "Necessary and proper" was a stunningly poor candidate for guiding legislative judgment, Brutus pointed out, because it is "utterly impossible fully to define this power."[21] Thus, not only did the infelicitous phrase "necessary and proper" undermine the Framers' effort to create a constitution of limited and enumerated powers, the ambiguity of the Necessary and Proper Clause belies the founding generation's belief that written constitutions would require "no sophistry; no construction; no false glosses, but simple inferences from the obvious operation of things."[22] No provision more clearly demonstrated that the American Constitution would not interpret itself.

Constitutional defenders proved unable to respond to these anti-Federalist criticisms. When Hamilton claimed that "the national government" would be the "judge of the necessity and propriety of the laws to be passed for executing the powers of the Union,"[23] he was repeating rather than responding to anti-Federalist attacks. More generally, the authors of *The Federalist Papers* attempted to defuse controversy over "necessary and proper" by claiming that the clause was an "unfortunate and calumniated provision"—or superfluous.[24] Hamilton "affirmed with perfect confidence that the constitutional operation of the intended government would be precisely the same if these clauses were entirely obliterated."[25] "Had the Constitution been silent on this head," James Madison wrote, "there can be no doubt that all the particular powers requisite as means of executing the general powers would have resulted to the government by unavoidable implication."[26] In short, Publius admitted that the phrase "necessary and proper" was pointless, perhaps even stupid.

Consensually stupid constitutional provisions do not survive long as actual constitutional guides or limitations. Thus, the Supreme Court in *McCulloch v. Maryland*[27] apparently neutered the Framers' misfeasance by reading the Necessary and Proper Clause out of the Constitution, substituting by verbal subterfuge a "Wholesome and Reasonable" Clause such as that found in the Massachusetts Constitution. The phrase "necessary and proper," however, still haunts constitutional theory from its perch in interpretive limbo. *McCulloch* is typically the first or second major case of constitutional interpretation that law students read. In constitutional English, they learn, "necessary" does not mean necessary. This lesson prepares students to accept without question that in constitutional English "no law" does not have to mean no law, that "interstate commerce" may simply mean commerce, that "due process" may somehow encompass a right to an abortion, and, for that matter, that "stupid" can mean "mistaken . . . deleterious, or . . . least favorite." One consequence of this linguistic practice is that constitutional commentators often speak in a dialect that citizens uninitiated in the mysteries of constitutional law find arcane.[28] Judicial decisions that speak in a similar tongue, Joseph Goldstein correctly notes, have "forced [the general public] to turn more and more to specialists, to experts in constitutional law, in order to gain some understanding of the structure of government and of our fundamental rights as individuals and as members of a group."[29]

Moreover, by accepting these interpretive sleights of hand from the very beginning, law students and professors routinely overlook what should be the central question of constitutional theory: Why should one interpret a constitution that may contain stupid, outdated, or venal provisions? The answer may be that constitutions are compromises between people with very different notions of what is stupid, outdated, or venal.[30] The constitution of any heterogenous society, therefore, is likely to contain provisions that seem mistaken and provisions that seem foolish from any given perspective. For this reason, methods of constitutional interpretation that permit commentators and justices to ignore the plain English meaning of constitutional language may simply result in provisions that seem mistaken or stupid from one perspective being replaced by interpretations that seem mistaken or stupid from another.

NOTES

1. This is a definition of "stupid" in *Webster's Scholastic Dictionary* 355 (Airmount Publishing, 1966).

2. Sanford Levinson and William N. Eskridge, Jr., "Constitutional Stupidities: A Symposium," 12 *Const. Comm.* 139, 140 (1995). If "stupidest provision" is shorthand for the "clause of the current Constitution [I] would . . . least recommend to someone currently engaged in the project of constitution drafting, as in Eastern Europe" (*id.*), the obvious choice would be the first seven words of the Preamble, "We the People of the United States."

3. Michael B. Katz, *In the Shadow of the Poorhouse: A Social History of Welfare in America* xii (New York: Basic Books, 1986).

4. See Charles L. Black, Jr., "Further Reflections on the Constitutional Justice of Livelihood," 86 *Colum. L. Rev.* 1103 (1986); Frank I. Michelman, "Foreword: On Protecting the Poor through the Fourteenth Amendment," 83 *Harv. L. Rev.* 7 (1969); Peter B. Edelman, "The Next Century of Our Constitution: Rethinking Our Duty to the Poor," 39 *Hastings L.J.* 1 (1987).

5. Of course, by providing explicit constitutional recognition of welfare rights, the persons responsible for the Fourteenth Amendment might have weakened the rhetorical case for finding other unenumerated constitutional rights.

6. See Katz, *Shadow of the Poorhouse* x.

7. See Eric M. Uslaner, *The Decline of Comity in Congress* 165–67 (Ann Arbor: University of Michigan Press, 1993) (noting that changing congressional rules or

procedures will not change outcomes unless there has been a previous change in congressional ends).

8. Mary Ann Glendon, "Rights in Twentieth-Century Constitutions," 59 *U. Chi. L. Rev.* 519, 531 (1992).

9. See note 8, above, and the relevant text.

10. For a longer discussion of the problems with "constitutional stupidities," see Mark A. Graber, "Conscience, Constitutionalism and Consensus: A Comment on Constitutional Stupidities and Evils," in Ian Shapiro, ed., *NOMOS XXXIX: Integrity and Conscience* (New York: New York University Press, 1997).

11. Honorable mention should go to the presidential election system, which was based on the Framers' stubborn refusal to admit that political parties would probably develop in the United States just as they were developing in every other protorepublic.

12. See Jeffrey K. Tulis, *The Rhetorical Presidency* 30–32 (Princeton: Princeton University Press, 1987).

13. 110 Stat. 2105 (1996).

14. "Constitution of Massachusetts—1780," in William F. Swindler, ed., *Sources and Documents of U.S. Constitutions*, vol. 5, at 97 (Dobbs Ferry, N.Y.: Oceana Publications, 1975). That no other eighteenth century constitution had a necessary and proper clause provides another historical indicium for stupidity. Presumably, the more intelligent the clause, the more likely its equivalent would be found in other constitutions.

15. See Alexander Hamilton, "Opinion on the Constitutionality of the Bank, February 23, 1791," in Jacob E. Cooke, ed., *The Reports of Alexander Hamilton* 88 (New York: Harper & Row, 1964); *McCulloch v. Maryland*, 17 U.S. (4 Wheat.) 316, 413 (1819) (Marshall, C.J.). See also William Winslow Crosskey, *Politics and the Constitution in the History of the United States*, vol. 1, at 392–93 (Chicago: University of Chicago Press, 1953) (suggesting that the Necessary and Proper Clause recognized that the federal government had broad power to legislate for the general welfare).

16. Thomas Jefferson, "Opinion on the Constitutionality of a National Bank," in Merrill D. Peterson, ed., *The Portable Thomas Jefferson* 205 (New York: Viking Press, 1975).

17. Max Farrand, ed., *The Records of the Federal Convention of 1787*, vol. 3, at 598 (New Haven: Yale University Press, rev. ed., 1966).

18. *Id.*, vol. 2, at 168, 344–45.

19. The convention did quickly vote down as "unnecessary" Madison's proposal to insert "and establish all offices" between "laws" and "necessary." *Id.* at 345. No one, however, considered whether the phrase "necessary and proper" or the entire clause was also unnecessary.

20. See "Letters of Centinel," in Herbert Storing, ed., *The Complete Anti-Federalist*, vol. 2, at 177 (Chicago: University of Chicago Press, 1981); "Essays of Brutus,"

in *id.* at 365, 389–91, 421; "An Old Whig," in *id.*, vol. 3, at 24; "Address by Sydney," in *id.*, vol. 6, at 113; "A Countryman," in *id.* at 86.

21. "Essays of Brutus" 390. See also *id.* at 421; "An Old Whig," 24; "Letters from The Federal Farmer," in *The Complete Anti-Federalist* 247.

22. Jonathan Elliott, ed., *The Debates in the Several States on the Adoption of the Federal Constitution* 285 (Philadelphia: J. B. Lippincott Company, 1836) (quoting John Jay). See H. Jefferson Powell, "The Original Understanding of Original Intent," 98 *Harv. L. Rev.* 885, 902–13 (1985).

23. *Federalist* No. 33 (Hamilton), at 203, ed. Clinton Rossiter (New York: New American Library, 1961).

24. *Id.* at 202.

25. *Id.*

26. *Federalist* No. 44 (Madison), at 285.

27. 17 U.S. 316 (1819).

28. Robert Nagel, for example, points out that in constitutional English, "unreasonable" does not really mean without reason. Robert F. Nagel, *Judicial Power and American Character: Censoring Ourselves in an Anxious Age* 129–32 (New York: Oxford University Press, 1994).

29. Joseph Goldstein, *The Intelligible Constitution: The Supreme Court's Obligation to Maintain the Constitution as Something We the People Can Understand* 17 (New York: Oxford University Press, 1992).

30. See Mark A. Graber, "Why Interpret? Political Justification and American Constitutionalism," 56 *Rev. Pol.* 415, 434–37 (1994); *Lochner v. New York*, 198 U.S. 45, 76 (1905) (Holmes, J., dissenting).

CHAPTER 8

The Nominee Is . . . Article V

Stephen M. Griffin

In any list of least favorite constitutional provisions, we should not ignore the provisions protecting slavery, such as Article I, Section 9, Clause 1 (providing that the slave trade could not be prohibited prior to 1808) and Article IV, Section 2, Clause 3 (the Fugitive Slave Clause). These provisions may have been superseded, but they have not been expunged from the text and should not be forgotten.

That said, there are a number of constitutional provisions that have always struck me as questionable. Article I, Section 4 leaves the procedures for holding federal elections in the hands of the states. This has meant that there has never been a uniform law of voter registration (contributing to election fraud and lower turnout in the twentieth century than in the nineteenth) or a uniform federal ballot (leading to voter confusion in some states).[1] The method of presidential election specified in Article II, Section 1 was an unstable compromise, resulting in the need for the Twelfth Amendment only fourteen years after the Constitution was ratified. It would also have been better had the Framers tried to define at least a minimal conception of the "judicial Power" in Article III, Section 1 (or, for that matter, the "executive Power" in Article II, Section 1).

My nominee, however, is Article V, which has historically operated to make the Constitution very difficult to amend.[2] It is true that the question of how to provide for change poses difficult choices for those who create a constitution. If a constitution makes change too easy, there is a risk that it will not structure politics but be hostage to it. But making change too difficult may cause political instability or force change to occur through a nonconstitutional process. The procedure for change that the Framers provided in Article V appears to reflect a judgment that making change too easy is the greater danger.

The Framers were successful in making formal constitutional change exceedingly difficult. Since 1791, the Constitution has been amended only sixteen times (or seventeen, depending on your view of the validity of the Twenty-Seventh Amendment). The provisions of Article V have undoubtedly played a role in causing this low rate of amendment. The second round of approval by a supermajority of state legislatures or conventions seems especially daunting. By requiring the concurrence of both national and state legislatures, Article V comes close to requiring unanimity to approve any amendment as a practical matter.

An important study by Donald Lutz confirms what many commentators have long suspected, that the U.S. Constitution is one of the most difficult constitutions in the world to change.[3] This creates a serious problem for American constitutionalism. Since the Framers chose to err on the side of making amendment difficult, they ran the risk that Article V might make the Constitution irrelevant as circumstances changed. Most commentators would concede that the Constitution has changed a great deal through means other than those stipulated in Article V, primarily judicial interpretation. It must also be stressed, however, that the Constitution has changed through ordinary political means, that is, without formal amendment or a Supreme Court decision. The development of political parties in the nineteenth century and the establishment of independent regulatory agencies and a different conception of the presidency in the twentieth century are familiar examples of this kind of change.

By making it difficult to change the Constitution, the Framers forced a significant amount of constitutional change off the books and thus limited the ability of the Constitution to structure political outcomes. To the extent that we believe that constitutionalism should play this role, we should favor making change through Article V easier. It is not clear that there is a real need, for example, for the supermajority requirement for approval by state legislatures or conventions. If the concurrence of only a majority of states were required, then some of the amendments approved by Congress but never ratified by the required supermajority would have become part of the Constitution. It appears that this includes the 1789 Reapportionment Amendment, the 1810 Titles of Nobility Amendment, the 1924 Child Labor Amendment, and the 1972 Equal Rights Amendment.[4] I am sure that different scholars would have different opinions as to whether these amendments were desirable. I confine myself to two observations: that approval of the Child Labor Amendment might have given additional constitutional legitimacy to the New Deal and that we would be better off with the ERA.

The crucial point, however, is that making amendment easier would have the effect of encouraging additional amendments to keep the Constitution up to date. Perhaps a supermajority of Congress should be sufficient to approve any amendment. While the contrary view, that amending the Constitution must be done with caution, is understandable, this view is in some tension with the goals of American constitutionalism. Making amendment difficult does not avoid constitutional change; it simply encourages change to occur through other means. If we value deliberative change, we should favor making constitutional amendment less difficult.

A final questionable aspect of Article V is the provision "that no State, without its consent, shall be deprived of its equal suffrage in the Senate." For practical purposes, this makes it impossible to change representation in the Senate to a population basis. The power the present system of representation gives to states with small populations increasingly appears to be an anachronism.

NOTES

1. See Jeffrey Rosen, "Divided Suffrage," chapter 16 of this volume.

2. On matters of amendment and much more, see Sanford Levinson, ed., *Responding to Imperfection: The Theory and Practice of Constitutional Amendment* (Princeton: Princeton University Press, 1995).

3. See Donald S. Lutz, "Toward a Theory of Constitutional Amendment," 88 *Am. Pol. Sci. Rev.* 355, 362 (1994), reprinted in Levinson, *Responding to Imperfection* 237–74.

4. Here I rely on the very useful study by Richard Bernstein. See Richard B. Bernstein, with Jerome Agel, *Amending America: If We Love the Constitution So Much, Why Do We Keep Trying to Change It?* 45–46, 140–43, 177–81, 301–3 (New York: Times Books, 1993).

CHAPTER 9

A Natural Aristocracy?

Randall Kennedy

> No Person except a natural born Citizen, or a Citizen of the United States, at the time of the Adoption of this Constitution, shall be eligible to the Office of President; neither shall any Person be eligible to that Office who shall not have attained to the Age of thirty five Years, and been Fourteen Years a Resident within the United States.
> —UNITED STATES CONSTITUTION, ARTICLE II, SECTION 1, CLAUSE 5

One concrete way of measuring the extent to which people affiliated with different social groups are full and equal members of this nation is to ask whether a person associated with that group could plausibly be elevated to the highest office in the land. The added difficulties, solely on the basis of race or gender, that an African-American or female presidential candidate faces, regardless of that person's talents, are a testament to the extent to which this society is still marked by racism and sexism. One might take some minimal comfort, though, in recognizing that their difficulties are the consequence of social biases rather than formal legal barriers, for the very point of the passage quoted above from Article II of the Constitution is to declare in effect that *any* native-born American over thirty five years of age who has resided in the United States for fourteen years is eligible to serve as President.[1] It thus exemplifies—by being inclusive—what is among the best aspects of the American political tradition.

Yet the Presidential Qualifications Clause also illustrates one of the least admirable parts of that tradition.[2] The reason, therefore, that I choose this provision as my least favorite part of the Constitution is that, with one now-meaningless exception—persons who were citizens of the United States at the time the Constitution was adopted—it wholly *excludes* from eligibility for the presidency all persons who are not native born.

Formally barred from the presidency, then, are people who may have invested their all, even risked their lives, on behalf of the nation—some of them even before becoming citizens, many others afterward.[3] This idolatry of mere place of birth seems to me an instance of rank superstition. Place of birth indicates nothing about a person's willed attachment to a country, a polity, a way of life. It only describes an accident of fate. It is a truly "immutable" aspect of one's biography, in today's world more so even than ethnicity or gender.

All citizens of the United States should have an equal legal right to vie for the nation's highest office. More precisely, any inequalities in that right should require full defense, as perhaps can be given in regard to the disqualification of impeached presidents or those who have already served two terms. But Article II imposes a totally *unjustified* inequality. There are many reasons that Henry Kissinger should not have become president, but his having been born in Germany is certainly not one of them. The natural-born citizen requirement embodies the presumption that some citizens of the United States are a bit more authentic, a bit more trustworthy, a bit more American than other citizens of the United States, namely, those who are naturalized. It establishes the most literal kind of "natural aristocracy," wholly different from Jefferson's own invocation of that notion, in regard to eligibility to become head of state.[4]

It may be that the clause is of more symbolic than "practical" importance. Yet Justice Holmes pointed out many years ago that we "live by symbols" and even clichés. It is important that a formal proposition of American life is that *every* native-born American child can conceivably grow up to become president, and we can legitimately criticize American politics to the extent that any such aspirations are frustrated by the unwillingness of people to judge candidates only on the basis of achievement rather than ascription. Such aspirations ought not be denied to naturalized citizens of the United States, regardless of the fortuity of place of birth.

NOTES

1. There are, of course, two caveats to the statement in the text. Article 1, Section 3, Clause 7 allows Congress, upon impeaching federal officials, to disqualify them from "hold[ing] and enjoy[ing] any Office of honor, Trust or Profit under the United States," and the Twenty-Second Amendment disqualifies anyone who has al-

ready served two terms as president. Neither presents the kinds of problems generated by the clause under discussion.

2. See the important article by Rogers Smith, "Beyond Tocqueville, Myrdal, and Hartz: The Multiple Traditions in America," 87 *Am. Pol. Sci. Rev.* 549 (1993).

3. One would be curious, for example, to see how many Medal of Honor winners have been ineligible for the presidency, to mention only the most obvious category of individuals who have proved their devotion to the United States quite literally above and beyond any normal call of duty.

4. I wrote this piece as a contribution to the Eskridge and Levinson symposium on "constitutional stupidities." Because the "rules" of the symposium included a Rawls-like "veil of ignorance" in regard to choices made by other participants, I did not learn until later that Robert Post had also chosen this clause. See Robert Post, "What Is the Constitution's Worst Provision?" 12 *Const. Comm.* 191 (1995). I am delighted to incorporate by reference his eloquent denunciation of its implications.

[Eds.: For purposes of this book, Professor Post submitted a piece on constitutional tragedy, which we publish in place of his piece on constitutional stupidity. Both are worth reading, but another "rule" of this collection is that no author got to write on both stupidity and tragedy.]

CHAPTER 10

"Neither Force nor Will"

L. H. LaRue

If we are to choose which provision of the Constitution has turned out to be the stupidest, we must be allowed to use hindsight. The Constitution includes some provisions that made good sense in their day but on which time has been hard. With the use of hindsight, I choose the second sentence of Section 1 of Article III: "The Judges, both of the supreme and inferior Courts, shall hold their Offices during good Behaviour. . . ."

Perhaps there are others who, like me, find the phrase "during good Behaviour" to be highly ambiguous. And some of these may even join me in finding the standard interpretation of that phrase rather strange. But I waive all such matters, and I am willing to go forward on the assumption that a community consensus has settled the meaning of the phrase, which is that our judges shall serve for life, unless they choose to resign or are impeached. Having accepted that "good Behaviour" means "life tenure," I will say that this provision is stupid.

However, I admit that this judgment does draw heavily upon the use of hindsight, and I do not wish to impugn the judgment of the drafters. When they wrote, the project of constitution making was new, and the relevant experience was lacking. Having an independent judiciary was more theory than reality for them, and they had not experienced a regime in which judges declared governmental acts to be unconstitutional. Of course, judicial review was not foreign to them; they were familiar with the precedents and approved of the concept. Even so, it was not a lived reality. In setting up this new and powerful institution, they had to proceed upon assumptions, and it is not strange that some of these assumptions should turn out to be false.

Consider, for example, Hamilton's famous discussion of the judiciary in *Federalist* No. 78. Recall that the context for this discussion is whether the judiciary would have the capacity to upset the political balance of power.

> Whoever attentively considers the different departments of power must perceive that, in a government in which they are separated from each other, the judiciary, from the nature of its functions, will always be the least dangerous to the political rights of the Constitution; because it will be least in a capacity to annoy or injure them. The executive not only dispenses the honors but holds the sword of the community. The legislature not only commands the purse but prescribes the rules by which the duties and rights of every citizen are to be regulated. The judiciary, on the contrary, has no influence over either the sword or the purse; no direction either of the strength or the wealth of the society, and can take no active resolution whatever. It may truly be said to have neither FORCE nor WILL but merely judgment; and must ultimately depend upon the aid of the executive arm even for the efficacy of its judgments.[1]

When I read this passage, I am always charmed by the elegance of such classic eighteenth-century prose, and it always takes me a little while to cast off its spell and descend to the ugly task of analysis. When I do, my first reaction is, "How quaint!" And, indeed, analysis seems almost beside the point. To be charmed by the antique quality of this paragraph is perhaps the only appropriate response; Hamilton's world seems so far removed from ours that it is otiose to assess his description of the judiciary as though it were a description of our judiciary. Consider, by way of a parallel, his description of the president as dispensing honors and holding the sword and his description of Congress as commanding the purse and prescribing rules. There is an antique charm to this description, but it would be both churlish and irrelevant to dissect it, to test its accuracy as political science. (Today, I suppose, if one wished to talk about "the political rights of the Constitution," one would start with the role of money and the mass media in politics, and go forward from that starting point.) We should not be surprised, of course, that we differ from Hamilton in our most fundamental assumptions about government and law, but perhaps it may be worthwhile to emphasize that we do indeed differ from him in how we understand judging. For example, I do not think that many (any?) scholars would say today that judging does not involve "force or will." Hamilton was confident that he could draw a line between political will and judicial judgment; I think that most of us are not quick to assume that this can be done.

Perhaps one way to highlight the difference between Hamilton's assumptions and our own is to look at his description of the "job qualifications" for a judge, which appears somewhat later in *Federalist* No. 78:

> There is yet a further and weighty reason for the permanency of the judicial offices which is deducible from the nature of the qualifications they require.

It has frequently been remarked with great propriety that a voluminous code of laws is one of the inconveniences necessarily connected with the advantages of a free government. To avoid an arbitrary discretion in the courts, it is indispensable that they should be bound down by strict rules and precedents which serve to define and point out their duty in every particular case that comes before them; and it will be readily conceived from the variety of controversies which grow out of the folly and wickedness of mankind that the records of those precedents must unavoidably swell to a very considerable bulk and must demand long and laborious study to acquire a competent knowledge of them. Hence it is that there can be but few men in the society who will have sufficient skill in the laws to qualify them for the stations of judges. And making the proper deductions for the ordinary depravity of human nature, the number must be still smaller of those who unite the requisite integrity with the requisite knowledge.[2]

We have, in recent years, witnessed some rather interesting controversies over judicial appointments, and I trust it takes no citation to remind everyone that the participants in the debates differed sharply about "qualifications." Your memory may differ from mine, but I do not recall anyone arguing that a deep, scholarly knowledge of the precedents was the fundamental prerequisite for the job. Why not? Because none of us believes that our judges are "bound down by strict rules and precedents which serve to define and point out their duty in every particular case that comes before them." None of us believes that Hamilton has correctly described the type of judiciary, the type of judges, that we live with today. Of course, it would be foolish to criticize Hamilton for failing to be a prophet on this point. But I do feel free to criticize those among us who refuse to wake up and see that our reality is different.

Let us proceed then from assumptions that match our day:

1. we have a strong and independent judiciary;
2. our judges have the power to change the law, both common law and constitutional law;
3. our judges will exercise their power to change the law based upon their judgments about justice and utility;
4. this power to change the law is not unlimited, since there are political, institutional, and moral restraints that all judges feel;
5. this power has been used in the past sometimes for the good, sometimes for the bad;
6. we ought to accept and preserve this power, but we should also limit it.

If you grant these assumptions, then the question arises, Should we give these judges, especially those who sit on the Supreme Court, life tenure? No.

I would limit their tenure. For example, one might guarantee life tenure as a judge, but limit the period for which a judge might serve on any one court. Perhaps a Supreme Court justice should serve on that court for only ten or fifteen years, and then move down to a lower court. I pick a term of about that length because I think that most Supreme Court justices do their best work during the period of their fifth to tenth years. As a rough generalization, I would say that it is uphill to that plateau, and then downhill afterwards. By downhill, I do not mean that they tend to become senile; they just run out of new ideas. After their tenth year, almost all judges start defending what they did in their early career; consequently, it would be good for them to move on. Any argument over details of my proposal, however, would be idle unless there is agreement on fundamental principle.

Is there agreement on fundamental principle? At this point, I should be launching into a review of the possible arguments, pro and con. And were I really clever, I could use this dialectic of pro and con to generate the requisite fundamental principles by which we could assess whether changing the Good Behaviour Clause in Article III, Section 1, Sentence 2, would be a good idea. But my imagination fails me. I simply cannot imagine why anyone would argue that a judge should have life tenure on the Supreme Court. My imagination is not that good.

NOTES

1. *Federalist* No. 78, (Hamilton), at 465, ed. Clinton Rossiter (New York: New American Library, 1965).

2. *Id.* at 471.

CHAPTER 11

Presidential Elections and Constitutional Stupidities

Sanford Levinson

Amendment XII: The person having the greatest number of votes for President, shall be the President, if such number be a majority of the whole number of Electors appointed; and if no person have such majority, then from the persons having the highest numbers not exceeding three on the list of those voted for as President, the House of Representatives shall choose immediately, by ballot, the President. But in choosing the President, the votes shall be taken by states, the representation from each state having one vote. . . . ; and a majority of all the states shall be necessary to a choice. . . . The person having the greatest number of votes as Vice-President, shall be the Vice-President, if such number be a majority of the whole number of Electors appointed, and if no person have a majority, then from the two highest numbers on the list, the Senate shall choose the Vice-President. . . .

Amendment XX: The terms of the President and Vice-President shall end at noon on the 20th day of January. . . .

On November 4, 1980, Ronald Reagan decisively defeated Jimmy Carter, the incumbent president (who had himself defeated an incumbent president four years before). Perhaps more to the point, in the 1980 election the electorate "repudiated" much of the legacy of the Democratic Party and declared its preference for leadership in a significantly different direction.[1] Ronald Reagan did not, however, take office until January 20, 1981. On November 8, 1992, the incumbent, President George Bush, garnered less than 40 percent of the popular vote; Bill Clinton was elected with 43 percent of the popular vote, while Ross Perot got 19 percent. Again, a desire for "change" was widely viewed as one of the meanings of the election. Clinton, of course, did not take office until January 20, 1993.

Although the 1996 election turned out to be far more sedate than might have been expected, it is surely not beyond possibility that a serious third party will challenge the hegemony of the Democrats and Republicans as the millennium approaches. It is not easy, for example, to see how the Republican Party can long maintain its uneasy alliance of buccaneer free-market libertarians and social conservatives committed to a strongly regulative state, nor is it a sure thing that the Democratic Party will not fracture over the extent to which the welfare state should be cut back. Indeed, had Ross Perot not basically discredited himself by his antics in 1992 and thereafter, it is possible that his Reform Party would have played a serious role even in the 1996 election. If Perot can bring himself to take a backseat, the Reform Party might well become a serious force in American politics.

In any event, as I write these words in February 1997, the assumption is that the Democratic candidate will be the current vice president, Al Gore, who for my purposes can be imagined as the next best thing to an incumbent president running for reelection. Gore will surely run on the record of the Clinton-Gore administration, promising, with due modification, "more of the same." Assume two possible alternative scenarios, though, in addition to an electoral victory by Gore. The first is simply that he is defeated by a candidate, most likely a Republican, who promises a radical departure from "the failed policies of the Clinton-Gore administration." The second is that the presence of a strong third (or even fourth) party results in no candidate's gaining a majority of the electoral votes, so that the election is thrown into the House of Representatives.

Consider first the easier (and far more common) case: the defeat of an incumbent, followed by a ten-week hiatus in which the repudiated administration continues to possess the full legal powers of the modern American presidency. George Bush, the most recent such repudiated president, illustrated the range of these powers by sending troops abroad (to Somalia) and by pardoning criminals (Elliot Abrams) and possible collaborators in arguably illegal conduct (Caspar Weinberger).

Although I believe that this hiatus is in fact extremely stupid, it may not be an example of a "constitutional stupidity" insofar as it is not in fact constitutionally required, though it is certainly influenced by constitutional considerations. We vote for presidential electors on the first Tuesday after the first Monday in November not by constitutional command but rather because of Congress's exercise of its authority, given by Article II, Section 1,

Clause 4, to set a nationally uniform election day.[2] So, as a technical matter, my concerns about the gap between election and inauguration do *not* require changing our Constitution at all; Congress need only set the election on, say, the first Sunday following the New Year in January, with the electors to meet the following Wednesday[3] and Congress in turn to receive the electoral-vote count on the next Monday. Inauguration could then occur unproblematically on January 20, unless, of course, no candidate had received a majority of electoral votes (to which I shall return presently).

What is wrong with the present way of doing things? First, there is something profoundly troubling, to a democrat, in allowing repudiated presidents to continue to exercise the prerogatives of what is usually called the "most powerful political office in the world."[4] But theoretical troublesomeness is scarcely the worst consequence. Perhaps the Civil War was inevitable, but it seems clear that its outbreak was not at all hindered by the maintenance in office of the monumentally ineffectual President James Buchanan, coupled with the extraordinary coyness of his successor, Abraham Lincoln, who was not authorized to take power until March 4, 1861, Inauguration Day prior to the Twentieth Amendment. Similarly, the response to the Great Depression was scarcely helped by the open discord between Herbert Hoover and Franklin Roosevelt between November 1932 and March 1933. Indeed, one motive for the Twentieth Amendment was precisely to overcome this four-month hiatus and its perceived disadvantages. Those who framed the Twentieth Amendment were onto something important; they simply did not go far enough. The best test of this proposition is a simple question: Would anyone reading this essay seriously recommend to any foreign country that it adopt an election-inauguration structure like our own?[5]

The consequences go beyond the mischief that can be done by a tired, perhaps bitter, repudiated incumbent. Our current structure directly contributes to the pernicious practice of candidates feeling no need whatsoever to identify anyone who would occupy high positions in their administrations. Were there only, say, ten days between election and inauguration, a candidate would *have* to identify such occupants, and voters would therefore have a far greater sense of what sort of administration they were actually likely to get. My colleague Scot Powe chides me elsewhere in this volume for believing that voters care about the future secretary of Housing and Urban Development. Fair enough, but do *no* voters care about the likely identity of the secretaries of state and defense and the attorney general (for starters)? What if, for example, Colin Powell had publicly agreed to accept a position as Bob Dole's secretary of state? Probably nothing could have saved

Dole's bid for the presidency (except earlier disclosure of the extraordinary financing procedures engaged in by the Clinton campaign), but it is hard to believe that such an announcement would not have shifted at least some votes to the Republican column. Why do we persist in reposing blind faith in elected quasi-kings (or, in the future, queens) to choose "the best and the brightest" to exercise power over our national destiny and personal security?

But maybe we need the extra time so that Congress can choose the president and vice president when no candidate gets a majority of the electoral votes. This consideration would amply explain the gap in time between the popular vote and the ultimate inauguration of the new president, given the necessity for an intervening election (in this case by Congress) to choose who will actually lead the executive branch. Still, would any sane person choose, in 1997, the system bequeathed us by the Framers and the drafters of the Twelfth Amendment, in which the House of Representatives votes by state instead of by member? Even if one rejects Suzanna Sherry's and Bill Eskridge's denunciations of the Senate's malapportionment, it seems inexplicable that anyone would accept, let alone glory in, the possibility that a majority of state delegations in the House of Representatives, representing far less than a majority of the national population, would inflict their choice upon the rest of the country. And even if one can explain why the Senate gets to choose the vice president, why restrict the list to two, unless we simply want to assure that there *will* be a vice president, who can thereupon assume the office of the presidency should the House continue to be deadlocked among the three candidates from whom it picks?

The scheme established by the Constitution is a constitutional crisis waiting to happen. Consider the following possibility:[6] Candidate A wins a majority of the popular vote, but only a plurality of the electoral vote. (She is, for example, enormously popular in the Northeast but loses, extremely narrowly, in California, Texas, and Florida.) The remainder of the electoral votes are split between the other "major party" candidate, B, and a third-party insurgent, C. (Recall that George Wallace won forty-six electoral votes in 1968.) Because no one has a majority, the election goes to the House for resolution.

Assume now that Party A has narrow control of the House, in part because of a sweep of California and Texas. This means, obviously enough, that a majority of the members of the House would support the candidate of their party for election to the presidency. One might also imagine that Candidate C calls on the House to elect A, not only because she did in fact get more popular and electoral votes than the other candidates, but also because C in fact believes that she would make the better president. This can be termed the "no-crisis" solution.

But now assume that a majority of the states are in fact controlled by members of Party B, which did unusually well in those states with only one to three representatives (e.g., Idaho, Wyoming, North Dakota, Montana, Vermont, New Mexico). These members, of course, believe that Candidate B would make a splendid president (or perhaps it is enough to know that they believe that Candidate A is "unfit" to be president). Emphasizing the wisdom of the Framers, they blithely cast their votes for B, who thereupon becomes the president. Is this a tolerable result? Would there be any reason for adherents of A not to march in the streets, at the very least, and to condemn the new administration as illegitimate? Perhaps the adherents of B will patriotically forego their constitutional advantage and vote contrary to their actual preferences—something they need not do in a one-member, one-vote procedure. This seems to be a thin reed on which to place the American government.

It should be clear by now that only the most blind, almost literally mindless, ancestor worship can generate any affection at all for our present scheme of electing and then installing in office our chief executive. The election-inauguration gap, fortunately, does not require full-scale constitutional reform. But the procedure for resolving gridlock in the Electoral College most certainly does. Some, like Akhil Amar, would abolish it outright and move to straightforward popular vote. Perhaps that is the best solution, but we need not decide that now, so long as the potential for mischief generated by the Twelfth Amendment is in fact eliminated. The Constitution in this respect is like a suspension bridge with a cable that is on the verge of tearing apart, with an untold capacity for damage to the innocent drivers below. If we are serious about building a sound bridge to the next millennium, then we should take care of this fundamental threat to the stability of our political system. The Constitution in this respect is irredeemably stupid; our continued failure to recognize this and to do something about it *now*, before the full damage is done, is far worse.

NOTES

1. I borrow the term "repudiation" from Steven Skowronek's important book *The Politics Presidents Make: Leadership from John Adams to George Bush* 37 (Cambridge, Mass.: Belknap Press, 1993).

2. 3 U.S.C.A. § 1 (1985)(codifying 62 Stat. 672, June 25, 1948).

3. It should be clear that I am not discussing the merits of the Electoral College as such.

4. The same might be said, incidentally, in regard to "lame-duck" or, even worse, out-and-out defeated members of Congress. Any true democrat should, at the very least, be troubled by the ratification of GATT by the lame-duck Congress in December 1994 instead of the newly elected Republican Congress that, for better or worse, represented an even sharper repudiation of the prior Democratic majority than Clinton's election did of the Bush Administration. Indeed, John Copeland Nagle has written a superb essay, "A Twentieth Amendment Parable," suggesting that the deep meaning of that amendment "was to abolish lame duck sessions of Congress," save perhaps for emergencies (such as outbreak of war) in which decisions simply *had* to be made rather than wait for the new, far more democratically legitimate, Congress. (See John Copeland Nagle, "A Twentieth Amendment Parable," 72 N.Y.U. L. Rev. 470 [1997].) Once again, though, this problem could be solved without constitutional amendment if we simply changed Election Day to mid-December. It is, in any case, not clear to me why the country benefits from the eight-week gap between legislative elections and installation in office, but that is the subject for another essay.

5. This question assumes that the country has in fact chosen to have a strong president elected separately from its legislature. As Mark Tushnet notes, in "The Whole Thing," chapter 21 of this volume, almost no other countries have in fact opted for our distinctive political structure, and several of the contributors to this volume suggest that it might be we, rather than they, who have made the fundamental mistake.

6. The scenario that follows was suggested by Mark Tushnet.

CHAPTER 12

The Presidential Age Requirement and Public Policy Agenda Setting

Matthew D. Michael

As this volume illustrates, several provisions in the Constitution have outlived their usefulness and now can be viewed as mere "stupidities." These stupidities become much more worrisome, however, when they transcend the realm of mere obsolescence to engender significant practical problems for the American polity. One area in which these types of troubling provisions seem concentrated is in the Constitution's requirements for the selection of the president. Indeed, the Electoral College endures perennial assault because of the prospect that a candidate with a majority of popular votes might lose the presidency, while the nativist requirement for presidential candidates strikes some observers as promoting an aristocracy.[1] While both of these provisions certainly challenge important normative underpinnings of democracy, it is the age requirement for attaining the presidency that potentially poses the greatest practical problem for current issues of American public policy. With the growing importance and conflictual nature of intergenerational issues such as Social Security, the United States should level the presidential playing field by opening the possibility of presidential election to citizens under the age of thirty-five.

Article II bluntly states that "neither shall any person be eligible to that Office [President] who shall not have attained to the Age of thirty five Years." Yet there seems little substantive support for such a provision. Were a new Constitution to be drafted today, it seems exceedingly dubious that such an age restriction would be included. There seems nothing "magical" about the thirty-fifth birthday: one can legally become a congressman, senator, or Supreme Court justice by the age of thirty. Perhaps the most logical clue to the rationale for the presidential age restriction is suggested by Hamilton's exegesis in *Federalist* 68: the presidency was to be sought only by citizens with "the requisite qualifications ... [,] pre-eminent for ability and virtue."[2] Such an age restriction seems normatively akin to the nativist requirement that Randall Kennedy attacks in chapter 9 of this volume.

Beyond important symbolism, however, the age requirement projects a large shadow onto the practical realm of United States public policy. Indeed, a new character is gaining saliency in an increasing number of policy debates. Other eras could be said to have been divided largely by type of livelihood (e.g., agrarian versus manufacturing), economic status (e.g., rich versus poor), or race lines (e.g., black versus white). The coming era, though, seems likely to promise a new cleavage, pitting the so-called "Generation Xers" against the "Baby Boomers." Such a battle is most easily discerned in resolving how to manage the intergenerational transfer programs that will generate trillions of dollars of unsustainable future liabilities.

While policy makers today are acutely aware of the need for action, intergenerational issues seem oddly absent from the policy agenda. Perhaps one key reason is the logical clinging of the elderly to the status quo: one recent study found that only 4 percent of senior citizens had an unfavorable view of Social Security.[3] Thus, recent reforms to Medicare provided only a superficial remedy to postpone that program's demise by a scant few years, while presidential candidates have campaigned on mere generalities about "reform," "commissions," and the like where Social Security is concerned. The policy process for meaningful reform—restructuring, privatization, or some combination of the two—remains quagmired in the status quo.

I would maintain that one contributory reason for this inertia is the lack of visibility for intergenerational issues that the absence of Generation X presidential candidates has caused. Because of the Constitution's Article II restrictions, Generation Xers have been precluded from seeking that office, clearly the most important in the nation. Granted, few, if any, legitimate presidential candidates have emerged in American history between the ages of thirty-five and forty. Yet, with the growing import of intergenerational issues, this option should be available for a certainly affected group. How can a government be representative when one of its most burdened minorities—studies indicate that a 30–40 percent payroll tax will be needed to sustain the current system of intergenerational transfers—is excluded from the most visible branch?

A Generation X candidate (say, age thirty) would likely not stand much of a chance at winning the presidency. Indeed, Madison's prediction would apply in such a circumstance: "The influence of factious leaders may kindle a flame . . . but will be unable to spread a general conflagration."[4] Still, such a candidate could produce several important benefits for public policy.

First, a younger candidate could inspire increased electoral participation in what has historically been the least participatory age cohort. Indeed, the 1992 "outsider" candidacy of Ross Perot drastically increased participation among otherwise disaffected and nonparticipatory citizens. In a democracy, candidacies that are able to energize segments of the population to vote may themselves be intrinsically salutary.

From a public policy perspective, the most important practical benefit that a Generation X candidate could confer is to thrust the issue of entitlement reform squarely onto the policy agenda. Even though Perot stood no realistic shot at victory in 1992 (especially after his summer antics), his candidacy was perhaps the driving force behind the subsequent obsession with budget balancing. Similarly, the virtually single-issue campaign of Steve Forbes greatly boosted the prospect of a flat tax—and, more generally, of tax relief—appearing on the policy agenda. Indeed, there are numerous precedents for single-issue presidential candidates affecting future policy agendas. The age requirement of Article II, however, has prevented Generation X candidates from galvanizing interest in issues peculiarly affecting the youngest generation of eligible voters.

Generation Xers might instead be encouraged to mobilize their efforts to elect congressmen and senators who will give emphasis to addressing intergenerational issues. Simply stated, this option is second best, for the president is clearly the chief agenda setter. Clinton Rossiter expounded on the many "hats" of the president: he is, in effect, the national spokesman.[5] John Kingdon corroborated this assertion empirically: 91 percent of the officials he surveyed responded that the president is the most important actor in the policy process in setting the agenda.[6] While alternative specification is usually left to Congress, it is clear that the most effectual agenda-setting institution is that of the presidency. For that reason, access to the presidency—of which candidacy is surely an important component—is a key means of access to the policy agenda.

Overall, one must realize that removing the age requirement for seeking the presidency is not merely a means to address an isolated issue. Although Social Security reform is extremely important, it represents only one example of how the future of public policy seems likely to pit generations against one another, be it over entitlements (Social Security/Medicare), education (Stafford loans, AmeriCorps), or even foreign policy (future wars, drafts). Such intergenerational conflicts have never so clearly cleaved the nation in its past as they appear to be doing with the coming of the twenty-first century. With the demographics clearly giving the Baby Boomers a plurality of votes in these intergeneration electoral battles, the least that the United States could do is to give Generation Xers an effective platform from which to speak and influence the agenda.

NOTES

1. See Akhil Reed Amar, "A Constitutional Accident Waiting to Happen," chapter 1 of this volume; Randall Kennedy, "A Natural Aristocracy?" chapter 9 of this volume.

2. *Federalist* No. 68 (Hamilton), at 414, ed. Clinton Rossiter (New York: New American Library, 1961).

3. Michael Tanner, "Public Opinion and Social Security Privatization," *Social Security Privatization*, Aug. 6, 1996, at 4.

4. *Federalist* 10 (Madison), at 84.

5. Clinton Rossiter, *The American Presidency* (Baltimore: Johns Hopkins University Press, 1960).

6. John H. Kingdon, *Agendas, Alternatives, and Public Policies* (New York: HarperCollins College Publishers, 2d ed., 1995).

CHAPTER 13

The Last Centrifugal Force

Robert F. Nagel

The Constitution of 1787 was debated against a backdrop of rebellion, defiance, and factionalism. Disintegration seemed almost a law of nature. As Hamilton put it, "[I]n every political association which is formed upon the principle of uniting in a common interest a number of lesser sovereignties, there will be found a kind of eccentric tendency in the subordinate . . . orbs by the operation of which there will be a perpetual effort in each to fly off from the common center."[1] Proponents of the Constitution appealed to this centrifugal principle, not only in explaining the need for a stronger national government, but also in minimizing the risks of centralization.

Thus the authors of *The Federalist* argued that there was a greater likelihood that the states would encroach on national authority than that the central government would usurp state authority. Again invoking the laws of physics, they repeatedly urged that human affection is "weak in proportion to the distance or diffusiveness of the object."[2] While "the strong propensities of the human heart would find powerful auxiliaries in the objects of State regulation,"[3] the operations of the national government would be less tangible and therefore "less likely to inspire an habitual sense of obligation."[4] Supported by the loyalty of their citizens, states would be "at all times a complete counterpoise, and, not infrequently, dangerous rivals to the power of the Union."[5]

Not only would the natural affinities of the people provide pressure against nationalistic excesses, but state governments themselves would stand ready "to mark the innovation, to sound the alarm to the people."[6] Indeed, once alerted, the people would be able—through their state governments—to create "[p]lans of resistance,"[7] which ultimately would be backed by "trial of force."[8] To modern ears, of course, this reference to armed resistance sounds "off the wall" (at least to those in the mainstream of American politics), but the argument is pursued doggedly. *The Federalist* contains projections of the likely maximum number of soldiers in a national army (not more than "twenty-five or thirty thousand men")[9] and envisions an encounter between that army and state militias "amounting to near half a million of citizens with arms in their hands."[10]

All this ferocious talk of conflict is easily ignored today; we are more inclined to notice the legal and institutional assurances than the arguments based on the psychology of loyalty and the methods of popular resistance. The more primitive bases for decentralization, however, must have seemed plausible to a people who had fought a war for independence and then lived through a period of political chaos.

In any event, the authors of *The Federalist* turned out to be right, at least for much of our history. The centrifugal tendency was dramatically manifested in the great armed struggle over slavery and in the violent resistance to school desegregation. Less dramatically (and more appealingly), it can be seen in the continuing vitality of state and local governments.

Nevertheless, it is now obvious that the Federalists vastly underestimated the forces that favor centralization. Their claim that the operations of the national government would involve relatively abstract matters unlikely to generate "affection, esteem, and reverence towards the government"[11] ignores two of the most visible and potent powers of government: the power to make war and the power to spend public funds. Moreover, it is absurd to insist, as *The Federalist* does, that the tangible concerns of local government are a source of popular allegiance *and* that these concerns will hold only "slender allurements"[12] for the ambitions of national leaders. Even putting aside the obvious political incentives for invading areas of state regulation, there remains the great driving force of idealism. If the twentieth century holds no other lessons, it has emphatically taught that the rationalistic passion for engineered progress demands uniformity. Finally, when the Constitution was being debated, the logistics of the proposed national government were in doubt. The authors of *The Federalist* conceded indeterminacy as to how the government would actually operate in the near term, and they certainly had no vision of how it would operate over a longer span of time. It goes without saying that many of the centrifugal forces that existed in their world simply do not exist in a country linked by airplane, television, and computer.

It is not surprising, then, that it has been impossible to confine a strong national government to specific enumerated powers. Control over all that "variety of more minute interests"[13] that the Federalists assumed would remain local is now shared between the states and nation. So complete is the nationalization of our political culture that most modern scholars, confronted by this claim that the basic theory of power allocation in the Constitution has been proven wrong, can be expected to ask only why anyone would care. Our present circumstance is this: In a time when thousands of citizens routinely communicate their various opinions to their representatives by fax or telephone or postcard, a large segment of the population does not feel sufficiently connected with government to vote, let alone to participate in more sophisticated and costly ways. In a time when a presidential candidate thinks it appropriate to answer questions about his underwear, government is seen as distant. In a time when an endless supply of official standards, rules, and exceptions is routinely issued, government is seen as unresponsive. In a time when decision-making authority has been shifted from the shadowy doorways of local legislatures to the elevated sanctums of Washington, the influence of special interests is believed to be pervasive and inexorable.

The Federalists told us this would not happen. Under their theory, national representatives were to be deliberative, while state governments kept policies aligned with local circumstances. The Constitution was to combine public spiritedness with responsiveness. But that theory assumed that the natural operation of centrifugal political forces would ensure that the objectives of national policy remained defined and limited. Now that the welfare of ordinary life is a concern of Washington, D.C., faction is combined with distance. Government can be both personal and remote, solicitous but unsatisfying. Given the powerful forces that have produced centralization, it is doubtful that tinkering with constitutional text could significantly change our present circumstance. Adding the word "expressly" to the Tenth Amendment or narrowly defining "commerce among the states" would not alter any of the underlying realities. Institutional checks, such as the recurrent proposal to give state legislatures a veto over certain classes of federal legislation, hold more promise. But the Federalists were right that the people in the states will act as a counterpoise to federal power only if the popular will exists to utilize mechanisms of resistance. By invoking the centrifugal principle, the proponents of the Constitution largely presumed such a culture, but as a fallback they also argued that local resolve might be fortified if national policies were ineffective. This suggests the depressing conclusion that today even a modest movement toward a constitutional redistribution of powers depends upon sustained ineptitude at the top.

NOTES

1. *Federalist* No. 15 (Madison), at 34, ed. Clinton Rossiter (New York: New American Library, 1961).

2. *Federalist* No. 17 (Hamilton), at 199.

3. *Id.*

4. *Id.* at 120.

5. *Id.*

6. *Federalist* No. 44 (Madison), at 286.

7. *Federalist* No. 46 (Madison), at 298.

8. *Id.*

9. *Id.* at 299.

10. *Id.* at 299.

11. *Federalist* No. 17 (Hamilton), at 120.

12. *Id.* at 118.

13. *Federalist* No. 17 (Hamilton), at 119.

CHAPTER 14

Someone Should Have Told Spiro Agnew

Michael Stokes Paulsen

Let us assume that I am elected vice president and am an evil, diabolical man. I behave badly, even criminally in office. The House of Representatives impeaches me. I solemnly march into the Senate chamber for my trial. My team of lawyers takes its place in the designated spot on the floor. And I pick up the gavel and assume my post as the presiding officer at my own impeachment trial.

Under Article I, Section 3, Clause 4 of the Constitution, the vice president of the United States is "President of the Senate." Clause 6 of the same section of Article I specifies that the Senate "shall have the sole Power to try all Impeachments." Thus, the vice president of the United States is the presiding officer at his own impeachment trial. Q.E.D.

There is no way around this one. Nowhere does the Constitution say that the vice president is stripped of his power as presiding officer of the Senate just because the business at hand is his own impeachment trial. Article I, Section 3, Clause 5 specifies that the Senate's chosen "President pro tempore" serves "in the *Absence* of the vice president, or when he shall exercise the Office of President of the United States" (emphasis mine). The vice president is not "absent" when he is before the Senate for his impeachment trial, and he certainly is not exercising the office of president of the United States.

The power of each house of Congress to make its own rules of proceedings pursuant to Article I, Section 5, Clause 2 cannot be used to strip the vice president of his specific constitutional prerogative—one of the few he has—as president of the Senate, or to accomplish the same thing by deeming the vice president "absent" if he is impeached. Unlike the House, which has unrestricted power to choose its speaker and other officers (and thus can strip the speaker of his powers if they like), the Senate is stuck with the vice president. Its rules-of-proceedings power is bounded by the fact that the vice president of the United States must remain the presiding officer of the Senate.

It follows that the Senate may not, consistent with the President of the Senate Clause, effectively deprive its president of the power to preside by making his rulings impotent or by vesting a superior power to preside in some other officer, or in a committee, or in the body as a whole. Otherwise, given an inch, what would prevent the Senate from taking a full mile and using its rules power to deprive the vice president of his right to preside in a wide range of other circumstances? What would prevent the Senate from rendering "president of the Senate" an empty title by adopting a rule making all of the vice president's rulings subject to the veto of some other officer, or of a committee, or of the Senate as a whole?

The President of the Senate Clause clearly forbids any action by the Senate that would deprive the vice president of the power to preside over the Senate—in *any* circumstances. Nothing in the text of the Constitution suggests that the power of the vice president to preside over the Senate is any different just because he happens to be the object of an impeachment trial. That, alas, is the whole problem.

Indeed, the omission of any such exception can scarcely have been accidental, for the Impeachment Clause specifically provides that the chief justice, not the vice president, presides when the president of the United States is impeached. Applying the principle of *expressio unius est exclusio alterius* (the inclusion of one thing implies the exclusion of all others), it is clear that if the Framers had meant to disqualify the vice president in the case of his own impeachment, they would have said so.

But they did not. Now *that* is stupid.

CHAPTER 15

Old People and
Good Behavior

L. A. Powe, Jr.

Just what was wrong with the Nine Old Men? Their votes? Not taken as a whole, for the "Old" included Brandeis.[1] That their judicial philosophies were without redeeming social value? Again, it cannot be, for their philosophies ran the gamut from the liberal Brandeis to the moderate Hughes to the conservative Sutherland to the almost limitlessly reactionary McReynolds. No, what was wrong with them is that they were old, that they had not left the Court, and that they intended to outlast the new political order. Butler, the youngest of the group over seventy, had been born the year after Appomattox. Their understanding of government and economic collapse stemmed from their experiences as adults with the depression of 1893.[2]

If the Court was aged in 1936, it was more so in 1984, with five justices having been born during the Roosevelt Administration—*Theodore* Roosevelt's administration. Brennan, Burger, Powell, Marshall, and Blackmun knew radio via the crystal set[3] and reached adulthood during either the Coolidge or Hoover Administrations. As the oldest quintet in Supreme Court history, their votes could have (had they not split) determined the constitutional rules and aspirations for late-twentieth-century America. What allegedly rational system could place individuals of that age in positions of influence and authority? The answer, straight from the text, is a Constitution that allows judges to continue until they are ready for their graves.

Life tenure (or "during good Behaviour" as Article III, Section 1 words it) creates the real possibility of imitating a society like China, where power is wielded by the oldest among it. Even if their minds are every bit as good as they were when they were appointed,[4] there is no good reason in a democracy to vest so much power in people whose formative experiences are from an age decidedly different from that of most of the current populace.

We cannot hold the Framers entirely to blame. Life tenure was the way they defined an independent judiciary (which is the correct objective). For their generation, life expectancy was shorter, and people who viewed public service as a duty[5] rather than an opportunity internalized their own term limits by willingly retiring from public life. Even for the initial generations, however, the Supreme Court seemed to generate an unwillingness gracefully to leave the center stage. Of the first sixteen appointees to the Court (this includes Jefferson's), fully ten stayed on the bench until death. Excluding the flukes of Goldberg and Fortas, the two shortest tenures since the Kennedy presidency were those of Burger and Powell, each of whom stayed until he was almost eighty.

No wonder. Today justices enjoy a job that has good pay, high prestige, manageable hours, great vacation opportunities, and no heavy lifting,[6] so they last longer and longer. And as they age, their formative experiences grow ever more distant from those of the 250,000,000 people whose Constitution they interpret and whose lives they periodically affect. Their age and the imposition of their almost systematically out-of-date views (even if on occasion they get it right)[7] are costs that we the people ought not and need not bear in order to maintain an independent judiciary. Life tenure is the Framers' greatest (lasting) mistake.[8]

There are at least three interrelated problems with life tenure. First, in Sandy Levinson's words, justices "have stayed too long at the fair."[9] Their formative adult experiences took place forty years earlier in a society often unrecognizable in the present. It is one thing to elect such individuals to govern; it is another to have them govern because elected individuals approved of them twenty or thirty years earlier. Second, the political order that created their ascendancy (and for which they may have some fond feelings) may also be receding into history. Yet, like the Four Horsemen or, alas, Brennan and Marshall, they try to live and serve until that old political order can somehow restore itself (and therefore replace them with younger lawyers of similar ideology). Third, as shown by the Reagan and Bush Administrations, there are incentives for a current governing coalition to appoint youthful justices so that those appointees will have at least thirty probable years of service on the Court. This virtually guarantees that the first and second problems will crop up at some point.

All of the above is likely. None of it is necessary.

If life tenure is the problem and an independent judiciary the goal, then any number of solutions are possible, but the one that immediately suggests itself is a nonrenewable eighteen-year term (salary continuing on retirement), with vacancies occurring every two years.[10] The turnover would remain roughly the previous average (2.2 years) but would be less random. A two-term president would get four appointments, and the Court could not be packed[11] with appointees of a single party unless that party were able to win three consecutive presidencies.

Eighteen years is long enough to learn the job and then do it well and to guarantee independence from the elected branches, while short enough to avoid the unseemly problems that life tenure creates.

NOTES

1. One might (though I would not) condemn Brandeis for his vote in *A.L.A. Schecter Poultry Corp. v. United States*, 295 U.S. 495 (1935), which invalidated the National Industrial Recovery Act of 1933.

2. See Felix Frankfurter, "Twenty Years of Mr. Justice Holmes' Constitutional Opinions," 36 *Harv. L. Rev.* 909 (1923), reprinted in Philip B. Kurland, ed., *Felix Frankfurter on the Supreme Court, Extrajudicial Essays on the Court and the Constitution* 119–20 (Cambridge, Mass.: Belknap Press, 1970) ("[T]he 'Constitution' which the [justices] 'interpret' is to a large measure the interpretation of *their own experience*" [emphasis in original]).

3. So, too, did White, who was born during World War I.

4. A highly unlikely (although possible) occurrence. Word processors and law clerks, both in ample supply, can better maintain consistency for justices than in earlier days, when they had to do their own work.

5. They would have referred to it as "a sacrifice."

6. Nor circuit riding.

7. Sandy Levinson, who has articulated similar views, observed that Brennan and Marshall held on too long. See Sanford Levinson, "Contempt of Court: The Most Important 'Contemporary Challenge to Judging,'" 49 *Wash. & Lee L. Rev.* 339, 341 (1992). In making that claim, which I believe more strongly than he does, Levinson acknowledged that the two were among his heroes. That, I think, is part of the problem. When judicial liberalism can only be defined by octogenarians, something forward-looking has been lost. One would think that someone under seventy might be able to articulate successfully what a judicial liberal should do. And if no one under seventy can, then maybe the breed *should* be extinct.

8. It is, of course, not their only one. Guns, grand jury indictments, and civil juries (the explanations why Justice Black's incorporation theory could not get five

votes) are mistakes anyone can find in the Bill of Rights. And even more egregious is giving people living in areas smaller than a respectable Texas ranch two United States senators. See "The Big Country," *Texas Monthly*, Feb. 1985, at 103: "When a Texas ranch is respectably large, it is invariably likened to Rhode Island. A ranch of 671,360 acres has exactly as much land as Rhode Island; therefore its area should be expressed as 1 RI." The XIT Ranch came to 4.78 RIs. All the postage-stamp–sized states should be combined into a single real state that could then elect two senators or, alternatively, if they wish to remain small, they should be limited to a single senator.

9. Levinson, "Contempt of Court" 341.

10. Sandy Levinson offered this solution earlier, though he noted that he had borrowed the eighteen-year notion, and its rationale, from an essay that appeared in the *Wall Street Journal*. He might have offered further reflections on lifetime tenure in this collection of essays had he not believed it an even greater failing that the electorate does not know who the secretary of Housing and Urban Development (and his or her cohorts) will be prior to casting a ballot for presidential electors. Is it unfair to wonder why, if the vice president does not matter to voting behavior, the identity of the cabinet will?

11. I admit that I am assuming no deaths and few unexpected retirements. It is arguable that some justices might view eighteen-year terms the way John Jay, John Rutledge, and Thomas Johnson viewed their "life" appointments in the 1790s and thus be more willing to exit what might become a less prestigious Court. It goes without saying that I would run this risk.

CHAPTER 16

Divided Suffrage

Jeffrey Rosen

The biggest constitutional mistake? As the recent wave of constitution making in Eastern Europe suggests, future Solons and Lycurguses are not likely to be very interested in quibbling over the details of a Bill of Rights. Instead, the critical question is how to structure democratic elections. And on this point, the most misguided provision in the Constitution is not the Electoral College, which remains theoretically mystifying but has not bothered anyone for more than a century. Far worse are Sections 2 and 4 of Article I and (if I am allowed more than one villain) Section 2 of the Fourteenth Amendment, which divide responsibility for defining the nature and scope of suffrage between Congress and the states. This unfortunate compromise, more than any other, is responsible for all the most traumatic electoral crises since Reconstruction.

"To have reduced the different qualifications in the different States to one uniform rule would probably have been as dissatisfactory to some of the States as it would have been difficult to the convention," Madison explained apologetically in *Federalist* 52.[1] Allowing the states to restrict the suffrage in different ways was the only politically feasible compromise, because "it cannot be feared that the people of the States will alter this part of their constitutions in such a manner as to abridge the rights secured to them by the federal Constitution."[2]

But of course, abridging federal constitutional rights is precisely what the states proceeded to do in their decisions restricting the suffrage in the nineteenth century and manipulating electoral districts in the twentieth. Maybe there was some logic for allowing states to exclude broad classes of voters in 1789, when only propertied, educated citizens were thought capable of casting informed votes. But in an age when uniform as well as universal suffrage has been embraced as a national ideal, it makes little sense to tolerate a patchwork of inconsistent and parochial state restrictions.

More fundamentally, the constitutional tragedy of the post-Reconstruction era—the subversion of African-American suffrage by the states—could have been avoided if the Reconstruction Republicans had granted Congress plenary control over the franchise, as Senator Jacob Howard and Congressman George Boutwell proposed. Imagine how the racial politics of the next century might have been transformed if the Committee on Reconstruction had endorsed Boutwell's draft of the Fourteenth Amendment ("Congress shall have the power to abolish any distinction in the exercise of the elective franchise in any State, which by law, regulation or usage may exist therein"), or Howard's draft ("Congress shall have power to make all laws necessary and proper to secure to all citizens of the United States in each State the same political and elective rights and privileges").[3] Instead, by refusing to displace the states' control over the franchise, and by compounding the error with Section 2 of the Fourteenth Amendment, the Reconstruction Congress paved the way for the nullification of the Fifteenth Amendment in the 1890s, as defiant states restricted black suffrage with literacy tests, grandfather clauses, dual registration requirements, and so forth.

Similarly, the great redistricting crises of the twentieth century—malapportionment, partisan gerrymandering, and the confusion over race-conscious districting—might have been avoided or moderated if states had been stripped of their powers to draw congressional districts. The pressures on redistricting were not apparent until the rapid population growth after 1850, when the contrast between city and country became increasingly dramatic. But gross malapportionment might have been less likely to persist for more than a century if landed interests had not been free to lobby self-interested state legislators, with the results that Hamilton predicted in *Federalist* 60.[4] And the implementation of the Voting Rights Act might have been less tortured if self-interested state legislators had not been free to balance the irreconcilable goals of incumbency protection and proportionate racial representation with the inflexible requirements of population-based districting.

The solution for future constitution makers? Giving Congress exclusive control over the franchise would not entirely solve the problem, since the siren calls of self-dealing and incumbency protection would still be hard to resist. What is needed is to tie Ulysses to the mast with some kind of precommitment strategy. Perhaps the solution would be to delegate power over suffrage and districting to an administrative body that is less vulnerable to partisan interests. One model is the independent commission responsible for making recommendations to Congress about military base closings, whose recommendations had to be accepted or rejected as a package. Another is the Federal Reapportionment Act of 1929, which charged the president with reporting to Congress both the state-by-state results of the decennial census and a strictly numerical apportionment of representatives, and delegated responsibility for certifying the apportionment to the clerk of the House of Representatives.[5]

Should the national election laws be constitutionalized? "It will not be alleged that an election law could have been framed and inserted in the Constitution which would have been applicable to every probable change in the situation of the country," Hamilton said in *Federalist* 59.[6] But why not? Today, many countries have inserted election laws into their constitutions, including Australia, Belgium, Canada, Greece, India, Ireland, Italy, Mexico, the Netherlands, Portugal, Sweden, and Switzerland.[7] The best argument against constitutionalizing the national election laws is that the national legislature should be free to experiment with proportional and mixed representation systems; experimentation is more difficult once the rules are constitutionally entrenched. So perhaps the institutional arrangements for adopting and amending election laws, but not the laws themselves, should be specified in the Constitution. Blue Ribbon commissions, fast-track legislation—there are plenty of possibilities. Just make sure to exclude the states as ruthlessly as possible.

NOTES

1. *Federalist* No. 52 (Madison), at 326, ed. Clinton Rossiter (New York: New American Library, 1961).

2. *Id.*

3. Benjamin B. Kendrick, *The Journal of the Joint Committee of Fifteen on Reconstruction* 54–55 (New York: Columbia University Press, 1914).

4. *Federalist* No. 60 (Hamilton) at 366-73.

5. See, e.g., Samuel Issacharoff, "Judging Politics: The Elusive Quest for Judicial Review of Political Fairness," 71 *Tex. L. Rev.* 1643, 1665 (1993).

6. *Federalist* No. 59 (Hamilton) at 362.

7. Andrzej Rapaczyrnski, "Constitutional Politics in Poland: A Report on the Constitutional Committee of the Polish Parliament," 58 *U. Chi. L. Rev.* 595, 622 and n. 51 (1991).

CHAPTER 17

The Constitution of Fear

Frederick Schauer

At various places along the Massachusetts Turnpike, a limited-access toll road with a speed limit of sixty-five miles per hour in most places, there are signs cautioning drivers not to back up on the turnpike if they have missed their desired exit. These signs tell us much about Massachusetts drivers, since in most other states we could not imagine the need for such signs, precisely because we could scarcely imagine the possibility of drivers even contemplating the behavior that Massachusetts sees a need to warn against.

The phenomenon on the Massachusetts Turnpike is hardly unique, for with some frequency we learn about the proclivities of a population by learning about the behavior that it is necessary explicitly to prohibit. There are numerous "No Spitting" signs in Hong Kong, but few in Switzerland; and when I saw a sign on a supermarket cash register in Woodstock, Vermont, announcing that discount coupons would not be accepted unless the customer purchased the item for which the coupon was designated, my initial reaction was surprise, for just like the out-of-state driver on the Massachusetts Turnpike, it had never occurred to me that anyone would engage in the behavior that the supermarket was prohibiting. Just as an assertion presupposes the plausibility of its negation[1]—"You are sober" is not a compliment—so too does a prescription presuppose the empirical likelihood of its violation.

As they tell us much about Massachusetts drivers, the signs on the turnpike also instruct us in constitutional jurisprudence. Like the signs on the turnpike and the warnings in the supermarket, constitutional provisions tend to presuppose the likelihood of the behavior they prohibit. Just as there are no signs on the turnpike prohibiting throwing Molotov cocktails at other vehicles, and no signs on the Hong Kong ferries prohibiting fare avoidance, so too do we rarely see constitutional provisions addressed to theoretically or logically possible occurrences that are in practice unlikely to occur within the relevant domain. Just as the signs on roads and ferries prohibit what the sign posters believe is actually likely to happen, so too do the drafters of constitutions go out of their way to address what they see as genuine threats. Given, for example, South Africa's recent history of abuse of power by the police and prosecutors, it is not surprising that the new South African Constitution is extraordinarily detailed in its regulation of police and prosecutorial practices.[2] Similarly, it is only to be expected that discrimination on the basis of language is prohibited in the constitution of multilingual Canada but not in the constitution of monolingual Mexico.

Yet what is a genuine threat or possibility at one time may be less so at another. Few students of American history fail to understand the perceived need, in 1791, for the Third Amendment, prohibiting the quartering of troops in private houses, yet for the same reason it is unlikely that the Third Amendment would find its way into a constitution newly written in 1997. That the Fourteenth Amendment makes no mention of discrimination on the basis of gender or sexual orientation is historically unsurprising, just as it is historically unsurprising that gender discrimination is explicitly prohibited in virtually every one of the new constitutions now emerging throughout the world, and that discrimination on the basis of sexual orientation is prohibited by some, such as the aforementioned Constitution of the Republic of South Africa.

From this perspective, the imperfections of the Constitution of the United States, in 1997, are likely to be imperfections of two types (paralleling the statistician's distinction between Type I and Type II errors): guarding against problems that no longer exist (Type I error, the false positive) and not guarding against problems that exist now but did not exist, or were not then perceived as existing, at earlier times (Type II error, the false negative). As examples of the former, we have not only the Third Amendment, whose prohibition of a nonproblem is relatively costless,[3] but also the more costly efforts to guard against dangers now perceived as less dangerous than they were in other times, such as the Seventh Amendment right to trial by jury in civil cases and the Second Amendment right to keep and bear arms. The cost of the Seventh Amendment comes not only from the expense and delay of a civil jury trial but also from the possibility of more suboptimal verdicts from juries than from judges. The cost of the Second Amendment comes from the way it has legitimated a certain rhetoric and politics that probably makes gun control more difficult or more limited than would otherwise be the case. If this is so, and if guns are dangerous, then the costs of the Second Amendment are apparent. In both the Second and Seventh

Amendment examples, therefore, it is at least arguable that the problem toward which the provision was originally directed is now less pressing and that the costs of the provision itself are not insignificant. Such provisions, in 1997, may by the excess imposition of constraint (the false positive) entail costs no longer justifiable by even the long-term benefits. (Not all parts of the Constitution can or should be evaluated by even a nonquantified cost-benefit analysis, but some parts can be, and a careful look at constitutional imperfection would try to examine whether the costs of some constitutional provisions (or nonprovisions) greatly outweigh their benefits.)

The converse problem exists with respect to the false negative, the erroneous nonimposition of constraint. As examples here, we might think of the lack of (textual) protection for the right to privacy or the right to be free of discrimination on account of gender or sexual orientation. And many people believe (although I am not one of them) that the lack of term limits and the lack of a constitutional requirement of a balanced budget are perfect examples of the eighteenth-century Constitution's failure to anticipate all of the problems of the twenty-first-century United States.

Yet although it is evident that there are existing constitutional provisions that produce false positives, and nonexisting constitutional provisions whose nonexistence produces false negatives, the difficulties created by guarding against what are now nonproblems and not guarding against what are now problems are not restricted to particular constitutional provisions. Rather, the eighteenth-century Constitution, in the large, adopts a certain attitude about the state itself, an attitude not unlike the one that Massachusetts appears to adopt with respect to people who are armed with automobiles. This attitude is best characterized as one of risk aversion, for with respect to exercises of governmental power, the overwhelming perspective of the eighteenth-century Constitution, not surprisingly, is that risk aversion is preferable to risk preference or even risk neutrality in thinking about the inevitably uncertain consequences of any form of governmental behavior.

When we think of the Constitution as risk-averse, we associate it in some ways with skepticism about human motivation. This is not inconsistent with a Lockean and rights-based understanding of the Constitution's inspirations, but it is also not inconsistent with a Hobbesean perspective on officials, for the risk-averse Constitution—"If men were angels . . ."—has as dim a view about concentrations of state power as Hobbes had about human nature in general. Whether it be the rejection of a parliamentary system in favor of strong (and therefore cumbersome and frequently gridlock-creating) interbranch checks and balances, or the existence of numerous requirements for supermajorities (as, for example, with the trial of impeachments, the amending of the Constitution, and the ratification of treaties), and the various side constraints[4] or trumps[5] of the Bill of Rights, an underlying theme of the Constitution is and has always been that the dangers of mistaken governmental action (again, the Type I error, or the false positive) are more to be feared than the dangers of mistaken governmental inaction (the Type II error, or the false negative).[6] To adapt Blackstone's maxim about the criminal law, the philosophy of the Constitution appears to be that, in a world of uncertainty about the consequences of any governmental action, it is better that ten good things go undone than that one bad thing be permitted.

Perhaps such a libertarian, risk-averse, and government-distrusting view of the state is still appropriate. Although we hear much talk of governmental "gridlock" these days, perhaps that talk is misguided, and perhaps now, just as in the eighteenth century, the expected danger of governmental overreaching (as with any expected value calculation, would be the probability of governmental error multiplied by the consequences of such an error) may be far greater than the expected danger of governmental impotence. Indeed, it is not implausible to suspect that modern technological developments—consider how much easier modern technology has made it to invade someone's privacy—have increased rather than decreased the expected danger of governmental error, and thus increased rather than decreased the appropriate degree of risk aversion toward governmental action with uncertain consequences and uncertain application.

But perhaps not. Perhaps the greatest dangers come from governmental inaction, dangers that we see when we look, for example, at governmental inaction with respect to health care and many other issues of social policy. If we were in 1997 to redraft the Constitution, knowing what we know today about the world and the history of this country, would we be as concerned as our forebears were in 1787 about guarding against the excesses of another George III, or would we be, comparatively, less concerned about that problem and more concerned about the problem of governmental inaction?

Thus, no amount of attention, however appropriate it might be, to individual clauses and individual constitutional doctrines can transcend the fact that the degree of distrust of government in the United States appears to exceed that of most other countries in the world, including many in which the citizens have far more reason to distrust their government than we have to distrust ours.[7] And it is not implausible to hypothesize that this degree of distrust is not only reflected in the Constitution and in particular constitutional decisions but is also, in part, a product of the Constitution and a particular form of risk-averse and government-distrusting constitutional culture. If we are attempting to identify constitutional imperfection, therefore, we might be well advised not to focus on various clauses or doctrines that might be made better (or whose elimination might make the Constitution better), but instead to consider whether the constitutional structure and culture we now have has imperfectly calibrated, in light of the problems we now face, the trade-offs between the dangers of erroneous government empowerment and the dangers of erroneous government disempowerment.

The overarching theme of the Constitution of the United States, and the "who's to say/where do you draw the line/parade of horribles/foot in the door/thin edge of the wedge/camel's nose in the tent/slippery slope" rhetoric it has engendered, is one of fear, a fear which in 1787 or in 1791 was quite properly aimed at the state. Yet just as the signs on the Massachusetts Turnpike would be misguided were Massachusetts drivers to become more sensible, so too would the target of the eighteenth-century Constitution—governmental tyranny—be misguided if the target had shifted. Whether the target has so shifted is a question that is both political and empirical. But the measure of the imperfection of the Constitution is the extent to which the *entire* Constitution, as written, as interpreted, and as understood, is aimed at a danger that occupies a different position on the spectrum of all dangers than it did more than two centuries ago. If that is the case, then the imperfections of American constitutionalism should not be trivialized by identifying the occasional flaws in this or that clause, or this or that interpreting case. To pick out a clause or two, or a case or two, as imperfect is implicitly to endorse the remainder. But whether the remainder, in the large and not in the small, is worthy of endorsement is an issue, in an era of constitutional transformation throughout the world, that cannot safely be ignored.

NOTES

1. See John Searle, *Speech Acts* (Cambridge: Cambridge University Press, 1969).
2. "Every person arrested for the alleged commission of an offence shall . . . have the right as soon as it is reasonably possible, but not later than 48 hours after the arrest or, if the said period of 48 hours expires outside ordinary court hours or on a day which is not a court day, the first day after such expiry, to be brought before an ordinary court and to be charged or to be informed of the reason for his or her further detention, failing which he or she shall be entitled to be released." Republic of

South Africa [Interim] Constitution, Act No. 200 of 1993 (Government Gazette, vol. 343, no. 15466), Chapter 3, § 25(2)(b).

3. That there has never been a Supreme Court case enforcing the Third Amendment is good evidence of the fact that it imposes few constraints on governmental action, although on occasion even nonenforced constitutional provisions (such as the Second Amendment) may influence public and political discourse in a government-constraining way. For the one case in which a direct Third Amendment right was upheld, at least partially, see *Engblom v. Carey*, 677 F.2d 957 (2d Cir. 1982).

4. See Robert Nozick, *Anarchy, State, and Utopia* (New York: Basic Books, 1974).

5. See Ronald Dworkin, *Taking Rights Seriously* (Cambridge: Harvard University Press, 1977).

6. For a more extended analysis, see Frederick Schauer, "The Calculus of Distrust," 77 *Va. L. Rev.* 653–68 (1990). See also Einer R. Elhauge, "Does Interest Group Theory Justify More Intrusive Judicial Review?" 101 *Yale L.J.* 31–110 (1991).

7. See Peter Taylor-Gooby, "The Role of the State," in Roger Jowell, Sharon Witherspoon, and Lindsay Brooks, eds., *British Social Attitudes: Special International Report* 35–58 (Aldershot, England: Gower Publishing, 1989); Peter Taylor-Gooby, "What Citizens Want from the State," in Roger Jowell, Lindsay Brooks, and Lizanne Dowds, *International Social Attitudes* 81–102 (Aldershot, England: Gower Publishing, 1993). According to the 1991 World Values Survey, citizens of the United States, not surprisingly, trusted government more than did the citizens of Nigeria (41.5 percent compared to 26.1 percent), but, suprisingly, citizens of the United States trusted government less than did the citizens of (then) Czechoslovakia (43.6 percent), Chile (59.4 percent), Latvia (57.8 percent), Lithuania (58.7 percent), and Estonia (64.7 percent). I am grateful to my colleague Pippa Norris for drawing my attention to these figures.

CHAPTER 18

Criminal Procedure as the Servant of Politics

Louis Michael Seidman

Any assessment of what the Constitution is bad at must be grounded in a theory of what it is good for. So let me begin with a brief statement of such a theory: the Constitution is mostly good for providing a platform, external from our ordinary politics, from which current arrangements can be criticized.

This theory does not entail the view that all that matters is criticism. Any sensible political system requires legitimation as well as destabilization. The theory merely asserts that our ordinary political processes already provide very powerful legitimation. We do not need *constitutional law* to endorse results that our existing political system has already endorsed.

Nor does the theory entail the view that constitutional law necessarily privileges change. Political systems need to change, but they also need to maintain continuity. Although the Constitution can promote change, it can also appropriately entrench the status quo by providing a platform to criticize proposals for change.

The theory *does* entail the view that a constitutional provision that does no more than make us more satisfied with outcomes that already satisfy us is not accomplishing anything worthwhile. Constitutional law should serve as a corrective to ordinary politics and is corrupted when it becomes the servant of politics.

If one shares my view of what the Constitution is good for, it follows, I think, that it is quite bad at dealing with problems of criminal procedure. If the Constitution were doing its job, it would obstruct and destabilize our political impulses concerning crime control. Yet today, the Fourth, Fifth, and Sixth Amendments function mostly to make us satisfied with a state of affairs that should trouble us deeply.

Here are two facts about American criminal law. The United States has the most elaborate and detailed constitutional protections for criminal defendants of any country in the world. The United States also has the second highest incarceration rate of any country in the world.[1]

The relationship between these two facts (if, indeed, there is one at all) is controversial. Some critics of the Fourth, Fifth, and Sixth Amendments argue that they stymie effective law enforcement, thereby encouraging crime and requiring a high incarceration rate. Although this connection is theoretically possible, it is quite implausible. The best data available suggest that criminal procedure protections are doing very little to obstruct successful prosecutions. For example, only a tiny percentage of criminal cases are lost or "no papered" because of Fourth Amendment problems.[2] Virtually every empirical study of the impact of *Miranda* suggests that it has not reduced the rate at which suspects confess.[3] The poor quality of criminal defense work has led some distinguished commentators to conclude that counsel now serves primarily as a barrier to the defendant's participation in his own trial.[4]

In contrast, some defenders of the Constitution's criminal procedure provisions argue that incarceration rates would be even higher were these protections unavailable. This claim is similarly implausible. By now, the Fourth Amendment is so riddled with exceptions and limitations that it rarely prevents the police from pursuing any reasonable crime control tactic.[5] Although the Supreme Court continues to insist on the ritualistic reading of *Miranda* warnings, judges have virtually gone out of the business of actually policing the voluntariness of confessions and regularly sanction the sort of coercive tactics that would have led to the suppression of evidence a half-century ago.[6] The courts have been satisfied with formal rules requiring the presence of counsel in the courtroom, while tolerating actual courtroom performances that make a mockery of the formal protections.[7] And even when a defendant can demonstrate that the prosecution has violated minimal Fourth, Fifth, and Sixth Amendment protections, the recent evisceration of habeas corpus means that there may be no court available to entertain his or her claim.[8]

It seems unlikely, then, that the criminal procedure amendments have either exacerbated our crime problem or provided an effective bulwark against police and prosecutorial overreaching. A third possibility is more plausible: constitutional protections intended to make prosecution more difficult instead serve to make the prosecutor's job easier.

This reversal of the historic mission of the criminal procedure amendments functions on both the individual and the global level. In individual cases, criminal procedure protections make the punishment we inflict on criminal defendants seem more acceptable. Although the amendments do little to make the prosecutor's job harder, people commonly believe that they obstruct the prosecution of dangerous criminals. Some doubt and ambivalence that might otherwise accompany the use of violent and coercive sanctions is thereby dissipated.

On the global level, criminal procedure protections serve to redirect and exacerbate the popular anger about crime. While crime rates have remained static and even declined slightly in recent years,[9] the rate of incarceration has skyrocketed.[10] There is no easy way to demonstrate that the crime rate would not be higher if we had incarcerated fewer people, but, at a minimum, these statistics demonstrate that the increased rate of incarceration is not caused by an increase in crime. Instead, it seems to be fed by the public *perception* that crime is out of control and that still more draconian punishments are necessary to deal with it.

Popular misconceptions about criminal procedure protections feed this perception. Because people believe that "legal technicalities" set large numbers of guilty and dangerous criminals free, they think that too many miscreants are escaping punishment. Because they believe that the problem could be brought under control if only the "legal technicalities" were changed, they fail to focus on the bankruptcy of mass incarceration as a crime-fighting strategy.

In the United States today, over one million people are imprisoned, the largest number in our history and the second largest in the world (in terms of percentage of population).[11] One out of every 193 adult Americans is behind bars, and the total inmate population is roughly equivalent to that of the city of Phoenix.[12] Despite the absence of any evidence that these extreme measures have helped to control crime, political pressures grow for still more prisons, longer sentences, and more executions.

The criminal procedure amendments have done nothing to slow this decline into barbarism. Instead, they have contributed to an atmosphere that promotes acceptance of a situation that ought to shock us.

NOTES

1. As of June 1994, there were 1,012,851 men and women incarcerated in state and federal prisons. See *State and Federal Prison Population Tops One Million*, De-

partment of Justice Press Release, Oct. 27, 1994. The United States is now behind only Russia in incarceration rates. It has an incarceration rate more than four times that of Canada, more than five times that of England and Wales, and fourteen times that of Japan. See Steven A. Holmes, "Ranks of Inmates Reach One Million in a 2-Decade Rise," *N.Y. Times*, Oct. 28, 1994, at 1.

2. In the course of an opinion arguing that the exclusionary rule imposes unacceptable costs, Justice White was forced to concede that "[m]any . . . researchers have concluded that the impact of the exclusionary rule is insubstantial." *United States v. Leon*, 468 U.S. 897, 908 n.6 (1984). A General Accounting Office study showed that in federal criminal prosecutions, 0.4 percent of cases were not prosecuted because of illegal search problems. Evidence was excluded in 1.3 percent of cases studied, and only 0.7 percent of those resulted in acquittals or dismissals. Report of the Comptroller General of the United States, *Impact of the Exclusionary Rule on Federal Criminal Prosecutions* 8–14 (Washington, D.C.: Government Printing Office, 1979). Studies of state prosecutions yield similar data. See National Institute of Justice, *Criminal Justice Research Report—The Effects of the Exclusionary Rule: A Study in California* 1 (1983); Thomas Y. Davies, "A Hard Look at What We Know (and Still Need to Learn) about the 'Costs' of the Exclusionary Rule: The NIJ Study and Other Studies of 'Lost' Arrests," 1983 *Am. B. Found. Res. J.* 611.

3. For a good summary of the empirical evidence, see Stephen J. Schulhofer, "Reconsidering *Miranda*," 54 *U. Chi. L. Rev.* 435, 455–61 (1987).

4. See Lloyd Weinreb, *Denial of Justice: Criminal Process in the United States* 112 (New York: Free Press, 1977). Cf. Stephen J. Schulhofer and David D. Friedman, "Rethinking Indigent Defense: Promoting Effective Representation through Consumer Sovereignty and Freedom of Choice for All Criminal Defendants," 31 *Am. Crim. L. Rev.* 73, 86 (1993): "[I]f the Chief Defender values attorneys for their ability to move cases quickly and to persuade reluctant defendants to plead guilty, the accused might be better off making his own, poorly informed choice."

5. In many contexts, the Court has refused "to transfer from politically accountable officials . . . the decision as to which among reasonable alternative law enforcement techniques should be employed to deal with a serious public danger," and concluded that "the choice among such reasonable alternatives remains with the government officials who have a unique understanding of, and a responsibility for, limited public resources." *Michigan Dept. of State Police v. Sitz*, 496 U.S. 444, 453–54 (1990). The modern Court has declined to treat "probable cause" as a fixed and rigid requirement that the police must meet before privacy is invaded. Instead, it is a "practical, nontechnical conception" (*Brinegar v. United States*, 338 U.S. 160, 176 [1949]) that is "not readily, or even usefully, reduced to a neat set of legal rules" (*Illinois v. Gates*, 462 U.S. 213, 232 [1983]). The Court has insisted that the expertise of the officer at the scene be taken into account (*United States v. Ortiz*, 422 U.S. 891, 897 [1975]), and that he not be shackled by post hoc judicial second-guessing (*Illinois v. Gates*, 462 U.S. 213, 238 [1983]). Even if the police act without probable

cause, they need not fear the exclusion of evidence if they reasonably rely on a warrant; see *United States v. Leon*, 468 U.S. 897 (1984), and the warrant and probable cause requirements themselves are riddled with exceptions. See, e.g., *New York v. Burger*, 482 U.S. 691 (1987) (exception for administrative searches); *California v. Acevedo*, 500 U.S. 565 (1991) (exception for automobiles); *Skinner v. Railway Labor Executives' Ass'n*, 489 U.S. 602 (1989) (exception for "special needs").

6. In the quarter-century since *Miranda*, the Court has reversed only two convictions on the ground that post-*Miranda* custodial interrogation produced an involuntary statement, compared with twenty-three Supreme Court reversals on voluntariness grounds in the comparable time period immediately preceding *Miranda*. See Louis Michael Seidman, "*Brown* and *Miranda*," 80 *Cal. L. Rev.* 673, 744–45 and notes 239, 240 (1992).

7. See *Strickland v. Washington*, 466 U.S. 668, 689 (1984) (judicial review of counsel's performance should be "highly deferential" and "indulge a strong presumption that counsel's conduct falls within the wide range of reasonable professional assistance").

8. See, e.g., *Coleman v. Thompson*, 501 U.S. 722 (1991) (habeas unavailable after procedural default); *Teague v. Lane*, 489 U.S. 288 (1989) ("new rules" generally unenforceable on habeas); *Stone v. Powell*, 428 U.S. 465 (1976) (Fourth Amendment exclusionary rule generally unenforceable on habeas).

9. The most recent data, from 1993, indicate that the crime rate fell by 3 percent from the previous year, the second consecutive year of decline. The violent crime rate showed an annual decline of 2 percent. See Federal Bureau of Investigation, *Crime in the United States, 1993*, Uniform Crime Reports 11 (Washington, D.C.: Government Printing Office, 1993).

10. For the first six months of 1994, while the crime rate was declining, the number of prisoners grew by nearly forty thousand, the equivalent of fifteen hundred per week. In the last decade, the United States prison population has doubled on a per capita basis. See *State and Federal Prison Population Tops One Million*, U.S. Department of Justice Press Release, Oct. 27, 1994 (Washington, D.C.: U.S. Department of Justice, 1994).

11. *Id.*

12. See Pierre Thomas, "U.S. Prison Population, Continuing Rapid Growth Since '80s, Surpasses 1 Million," *Wash. Post*, Oct. 28, 1994, at 3.

CHAPTER 19

Our Unconstitutional Senate

Suzanna Sherry

In the race to the bottom that characterizes this part of the volume, I cast my vote for Article I, Section 3: "The Senate of the United States shall be composed of two Senators from each State. . . ." Indeed, were this provision not unequivocally enshrined in the Constitution itself (Article V), it would undoubtedly be unconstitutional, for, as the United States Supreme Court has recognized, it is in conflict with the most basic principles of democracy underlying our Constitution and the form of government it establishes.

The Court has held that "[l]egislators represent people, not trees or acres,"[1] and that "[t]he conception of political equality from the Declaration of Independence, to Lincoln's Gettysburg Address, to the Fifteenth, Seventeenth, and Nineteenth Amendments can mean only one thing—one person, one vote."[2] To hold otherwise would be to allow a vote to be "worth more in one district than in another" and would thus "run counter to our fundamental ideas of democratic government."[3] The Court has accordingly invalidated legislative districting schemes where the disparity in population between the largest and smallest districts entitled to the same number of legislators is as little as 1.07 to 1.[4] How, then, can a democratic nation tolerate a Senate in which the largest state has more than sixty-five times the population of the smallest and yet each has two senators? Moreover, the Court has waxed eloquent on the inequity of "minority control of . . . legislative bodies" in "a society ostensibly grounded on representative government."[5] What, then, should we conclude about a Senate in which slightly over 17 percent of the population elects a majority of the members?

An answer is that the provision, while indefensible, is harmless, because laws require the concurrence of the House of Representatives as well. Yet this argument forgets that the Senate has unique powers. On October 15, 1991, the Senate voted to confirm Clarence Thomas to the Supreme Court, by a vote of 52 to 48.[6] But the vote in the Senate conceals an exactly opposite split in the population at large. The delegations from twenty-two states split their votes, with one senator voting in favor and one against. Fifteen states voted entirely in favor and thirteen entirely against. Tallying the populations of each state (and allocating half the population of the split-vote states to each side) yields the conclusion that the senators voting in favor of Judge Thomas represented 48 percent of the population and the senators voting against him represented 52 percent.[7] A single change in vote, by Senator D'Amato from New York, for example, would have increased the margin to 56 percent against, without changing the result. If Senator Seymour of California had voted differently, the margin would have increased to 58 percent against, again without changing the result. (If both men had switched their votes, the percentage against would have increased to 62, and presumably Vice President Quayle would have cast the deciding vote in favor.) Justice Thomas still sits on the United States Supreme Court, despite the fact that the representatives of a majority of the population voted against him.[8]

The other standard defense of this otherwise unjustifiable provision is that it represents a necessary compromise between the large and small states: without it, we are told, the Constitution might never have been successfully written and ratified. While this may or may not be true, the circumstances of the 1787 Constitutional Convention reinforced the beliefs of the small states that they were entitled to equal representation, and made the ultimate compromise a foregone conclusion. Even before the convention began, the state delegations agreed that each state would have a single vote during the proceedings, regardless of its population. Moreover, when even that rule did not preclude a deadlock over whether to allocate representation by state or by population, the convention sent the matter to a Committee of Eleven, which consisted of one delegate from each of the states present at the convention. More ominous still, the committee consisted of many of the most able and vocal delegates from the small states and none of the most uncompromising firebrands from the large states.[9] The compromise—or concession, depending on one's point of view—was inevitable. We can only speculate on the results had the larger states been more insistent from the beginning.

Why did the large states agree to such a crippling and ridiculous situation? Because, at bottom, the delegates from the large states trusted those they viewed as likely to be sent to the Senate from the small states to represent the interests of the nation rather than of the individual states. The aristocratic Senate was never meant to be particularly representative of the population at large. As the nation became more and more democratic, however, the Senate became an ever more glaring anomaly. The Seventeenth Amendment repaired a small part of the problem, but the more egregious malapportionment remains.

NOTES

1. *Reynolds v. Sims*, 377 U.S. 533, 562 (1964).
2. *Gray v. Sanders*, 372 U.S. 368, 381 (1963).
3. *Wesberry v. Sanders*, 376 U.S. 1, 8 (1964).
4. *Karcher v. Daggett*, 462 U.S. 725 (1983) (invalidating congressional districts where maximum deviation was 0.7 percent). But see *Brown v. Thomson*, 462 U.S. 835 (1983) (upholding state legislative districts where maximum deviation was 8.9 percent).
5. *Reynolds v. Sims*, 377 U.S. 533, 565 (1964).
6. 137 Cong. Rec. S14704–5 (Oct. 15, 1991).
7. All calculations are based on the population according to the 1990 census, as recorded in *The World Almanac and Book of Facts: 1995*, at 376–77 (New York: Newspaper Enterprise Association, 1995).
8. This is not an isolated example. A minority of the population similarly prevailed in 1986, when Daniel Manion was confirmed to sit on the Seventh Circuit by a closely divided vote. A thorough historical search would undoubtedly turn up many other such incidents.
9. See Daniel A. Farber and Suzanna Sherry, *A History of the American Constitution* 128–29 (St. Paul: West Publishing, 1990).

CHAPTER 20

How to Violate the Constitution without Really Trying

Lessons from the Repeal of Prohibition to the Balanced Budget Amendment

Laurence H. Tribe

Shortly before the proposed Balanced Budget Amendment went down to defeat by a single vote in March 1995,[1] Kansas senator Nancy Kassebaum explained her reason for dropping her previous opposition to that much debated but still undelivered change in the United States Constitution.[2] It was not that the senator had overcome her doubts about the ability of the Balanced Budget Amendment actually to curb the evils of an ever increasing deficit. No, the reason was more subtle: "It may be like the Prohibition Amendment," she explained. "We may just have to get it out of our system." It was true that "[p]rohibition didn't stop drinking," but then it did not really wreck, or even permanently mar, the Constitution either.[3] After all, we repealed the Eighteenth Amendment when we ratified the Twenty-First, a little over a decade later.

The Eighteenth Amendment, it should be said, is nearly everybody's prime example of a constitutionally dumb idea. Dean John Hart Ely, for instance, uses it as Exhibit A in his case against constitutionalizing social or economic policies.[4] To my knowledge, however, few people have focused on how silly the Prohibition *Repeal* Amendment—the Twenty-First—was. Not that the *idea* it represented was silly. It was not. What could be sounder than getting rid of the Prohibition Amendment? The problem was not the idea but its implementation.

Before getting to the punchline—what was so dumb about the way the Twenty-First Amendment went about repealing the Eighteenth—let me say why the point seems worth pursuing. Lots of ideas make constitutional sense in the abstract. Protecting future generations from our own shortsighted proclivities to heap on a mountain of debt through a sort of taxation without representation is actually a pretty good idea.[5] But between the rhetoric and the reality, as they say, falls the shadow. Otherwise put, in constitutional matters, as in others, the devil is in the details. So one must look closely at the details before signing on to the whole package.

Consider, then, the details of the Twenty-First Amendment. Its opening section repealed the Eighteenth Amendment. So far, so good. Its closing section (Section 3) set a seven-year time limit on ratification. Again, a fine idea. In fact, the practice of setting such limits in advance actually dated back to the Eighteenth Amendment (before whose advent Congress had neglected to set any time limits at all on ratification of amendments, leading to such peculiar episodes as the ratification of the Twenty-Seventh Amendment over two centuries after its proposal to the States).[6] But consider Section 2, the inside of this constitutional sandwich. Here is the relevant part: "The transportation or importation into any State, Territory, or possession of the United States for delivery or use therein of intoxicating liquors, in violation of the laws thereof, is hereby prohibited."

Now there is one for the books! Notice that this language does not merely empower the states, notwithstanding the inhibitions of the Dormant Commerce Clause,[7] to bar transporting or importing intoxicants for local delivery or consumption. That was its evident objective.[8] In fact, reading the Supreme Court's decisions purporting to describe the Twenty-First Amendment,[9] one gets the distinct impression that it was rather ordinary—just a constitutional embodiment of the proposition that, provided the states not use their control over beer, wine, and spirits to violate unrelated constitutional provisions, they are free to erect barriers to the influx of alcohol, notwithstanding the principles of federalism that would normally tell the states that they must sink or swim together.[10]

Now this was not the first time an amendment's text missed its mark.[11] But this miss is a doozy. The text actually forbids the private conduct it identifies, rather than conferring power on the states as such. This has the singular effect of putting the Twenty-First Amendment on a pedestal most observers have always assumed was reserved for the rather more august Thirteenth Amendment, which is typically described as the *only* exception to the principle that our Constitution's provisions, even when they do not say so expressly,[12] limit only some appropriate level of *government*.

To repeat, Section 2 of the Twenty-First Amendment directly prohibits—talk about *prohibition!*—the conduct that it was apparently meant to authorize the states to prohibit, freeing them of some (but not all) otherwise applicable limits derived from the rest of the Constitution. As a result, not only does the amendment do more than its purpose required, it also does less. That is, it fails to specify that the states are authorized by it to do anything at all; that conclusion is evidently thought to follow by some sort of logical necessity. And just what it is they *are* authorized to do—to prohibit importation of liquor, yes; to use their liquor authority to distort the national liquor market, no[13]—is left largely to the constitutional imagination. Moreover, the two statutes enforcing the Twenty-First Amendment[14] necessarily rest for their underlying authority[15] not on anything added to the Constitution by the Twenty-First Amendment[16] but on the good old Commerce Clause of Article I, Section 8.

The upshot is that there are two ways, and two ways only, in which an ordinary private citizen, acting under her own steam and under color of no law, can violate the United States Constitution. One is to enslave somebody, a suitably hellish act. The other is to bring a bottle of beer, wine, or bourbon into a state in violation of its beverage control laws—an act that might have been thought juvenile, and perhaps even lawless. But *unconstitutional?*

The moral of my story is simple. Before voting for *any* amendment on the premise that we can always repeal it later, senators should make sure they have got their exit strategy—and, come to think of it, their entry strategy—mapped out in some detail. The Constitution may not be ruined by repeated hit-and-run attacks of the sort that Prohibition and its repeal entailed, but it may not emerge intact either. The cost-benefit calculus of each new adventure in constitutional tinkering had better include honest attention, first, to the details of what sort of enforcement the effort will entail[17] and, second, failing effective enforcement, to what glide path we can follow for leaving the new toy behind, if not for making it fly. In particular, when an amendment is proposed that conspicuously lacks any effective means of enforcement—as both Prohibition and the Balanced Budget Amendment did—think hard, before embarking on the flight, about how you plan to land. How, precisely, can the nation gracefully shut down those constitutional experiments that fizzle? And, perhaps a trickier matter, how can it safely unplug those that threaten to blow up the lab altogether?

NOTES

1. "Senate Rejects Amendment on Balancing the Budget," *N.Y. Times*, Mar. 3, 1995, at A1 (vote of 66–34, which became 65–35 when Majority Leader Robert Dole switched his vote so that he could bring up the measure again at any time).

2. Alan McConagha, "Inside Politics," *Wash. Times*, Jan. 17, 1995, at 5.

3. *Id.*

4. John Hart Ely, *Democracy and Distrust: A Theory of Judicial Review* 99–100 (Cambridge: Harvard University Press, 1980).

5. See *Constitutional Amendment to Balance the Budget: Hearings on S.J. Res. 9, S.J. Res. 18, S.J. 182, and Related Proposals before the Senate Committee on the Budget* 3, 102d Cong., 2d Sess. (June 4, 1992) (testimony of Prof. Laurence H. Tribe).

6. Sanford Levinson, "Authorizing Constitutional Text: On the Purported Twenty-Seventh Amendment," 11 *Const. Comm.* 101, 102–7 (1994).

7. The Constitution does not explicitly limit the states' ability to regulate matters affecting interstate commerce; rather, the requirement that state laws not discriminate against or unduly burden interstate commerce flows from the "negative implications" of the affirmative grant to Congress of power over this subject area in Article 1, Section 8. See Laurence H. Tribe, *American Constitutional Law* §§ 6-1 to 6-14 (Mineola, N.Y.: Foundation Press, 2d ed., 1988, explaining the doctrine.

8. See, e.g., *South Dakota v. Dole*, 483 U.S. 203, 218 (1987) (O'Connor, J., dissenting) ("history of Amendment" supports view that it was intended to restore absolute state control over liquor and that "the Federal Government could not use its Commerce Clause powers to interfere in any manner with the States' exercise [of this power]") (internal quotations omitted); *Healy v. Beer Inst.*, 491 U.S. 324, 349 (1989) (Rehnquist, C.J., dissenting) (amendment gave state "virtually complete control" over liquor importation and distribution, a "special power" that "primarily created an exception to the normal operation of the Commerce Clause") (internal citations and quotations omitted).

9. See, e.g., *Bacchus Imports, Ltd. v. Dias*, 468 U.S. 263, 275 (1984); *Craig v. Boren*, 429 U.S. 190, 206 (1976); *Hostetter v. Idlewild Bon Voyage Liquor Corp.*, 377 U.S. 324, 331–32 (1964).

10. See, e.g., *Baldwin v. C.A.F. Seelig, Inc.*, 294 U.S. 511, 523 (1935).

11. Take the Eleventh Amendment, for example. Read literally, it says nothing to limit federal jurisdiction over suits against a state by the state's *own* citizens, the typical context in which the amendment is invoked. Moreover, a powerful argument can be made that its text was intended only to restrict party identity as a basis for federal court jurisdiction. Tribe, *American Constitutional Law* § 3-25, at 175, note 8 (collecting commentary). To give sovereign immunity some life, however, the Supreme Court has basically ignored the Eleventh Amendment's language and construed the amendment as embodying or exemplifying the *concept* of state sovereign immunity. *Hans v. Louisiana*, 134 U.S. 1 (1890); *Pennhurst State School and Hospital v. Halderman*, 465 U.S. 89, 98 (1984) (construing *Hans*).

12. See, e.g., the Second, Third, and Fifth Amendments to the Constitution.

13. See *Healy v. Beer Inst.*, 491 U.S. 324, 337, 341–42 (1989); *Bacchus Imports, Ltd. v. Dias*, 468 U.S. 263, 274–76 (1984).

14. The first, the Federal Alcohol Administration Act, was adopted to "enforce the Twenty-First Amendment" by imposing licensing requirements on liquor distributors, as well as penalties for violating these requirements. 49 Stat. 978, ch. 814, § 3–4 (1935) (currently codified at 27 U.S.C. §§ 203–4 [1994]). The second imposes criminal penalties for violations of state liquor importation and distribution laws. See 62 Stat. 761, ch. 645, § 1 (1948) (currently codified, as amended, at 18 U.S.C. § 1262 [1994]).

15. See the Tenth Amendment (requiring such authority).

16. A draft version of the Twenty-First Amendment had actually included an additional clause providing that "Congress shall have concurrent authority to regulate or prohibit the sale of intoxicating liquors to be drunk on the premises where sold." S.J. Res. 211, 72d Cong., 2d Sess., 76 Cong. Rec. 4138, 4139 (1933). Despite certain judicial statements to the contrary, see *Arrow Distilleries, Inc. v. Alexander*, 109 F.2d 397, 401 (7th Cir. 1940), *cert. denied*, 310 U.S. 646 (1940), in its final version the amendment included nothing that could possibly serve as any source of authority for Congress to enact enforcing legislation.

17. For example, by stripping the federal courts of their power to hear any case or controversy arising under the Balanced Budget Amendment, the Nunn Amendment almost enabled the former amendment to pass, despite its rather strange (and dangerous) consequence for the balance of powers: the president would have been its sole enforcer, without fear of judicial intervention. Tony Mauro, "Nunn's Provision May Have Killed Amendment's Muscle, Experts Say," *USA Today*, Mar. 1, 1995, at 4 (quoting Laurence Tribe).

CHAPTER 21

The Whole Thing

Mark Tushnet

The question seems to me badly posed, for two reasons. It assumes that constitutional provisions "are" something-or-other, which can be laid against the metric by which we measure stupidity. But, as this reference to *United States v. Butler*[1] suggests, it is no longer clear to many of us that constitutional provisions have such a quality.

Consider, for example, someone who believes that the metric for stupidity is defined by the degree to which a policy advances the interests of some particular favored group. Perhaps at one time the First Amendment as then interpreted advanced those interests, because the major threats to the political program favored by that group came from government agents. The First Amendment was at that time not a stupid provision. As time passed, two things happened: (1) The group's political program changed, so that now the main threats come from nongovernmental actors. Even if nothing else occurs, the First Amendment, now less important to the group than before, is "more stupid" than it used to be. Perhaps, though, it does not cross some threshold of stupidity if it is merely less important. (2) The prevailing interpretation of the First Amendment changed, so that now it provides greater protection for the group's political adversaries than it did earlier. Now the First Amendment really might be the Constitution's most stupid provision, depending on how dramatic the changes in interpretation are.

Is that the most helpful way to describe what has happened, though? I can certainly imagine someone taking the position that the First Amendment, properly interpreted, is not stupid at all. For such a person, "the First Amendment" is just fine; the problems arise solely because it has been badly interpreted. In short, to identify any provision as stupid requires that one have a fairly strong theory of interpretation and interpretive error. It is not clear that such a theory is available.

Second, and for me more important, trying to locate a single provision as the most stupid may be misguided. At least I would like the opportunity to answer along these lines: "Most of Article I, much of Article II, a fair chunk of Article III, nearly all of Article VI, and many of the Amendments." It has occurred to me, though, that such an answer is equivalent to saying "Article V."

My concern is that the basic structure of our national government may be unsuitable for contemporary society. This is only a concern, not a firm conclusion, and in what follows I simply want to indicate lines of thinking that might be productive.

Consider the following propositions drawn from observations by political scientists interested in constitutional structures. Political systems with single-member districts in which the candidate who receives a plurality of the vote wins tend to have two-party systems, while those with multimember districts and proportional representation tend to have multiparty systems.[2] "Electoral laws that turn plurality preferences into legislative majorities are likely to be especially disastrous in highly divided societies."[3] "[P]arliamentary democracies tend to increase the degrees of freedom that facilitate the momentous tasks of economic and social restructuring facing new democracies as they simultaneously attempt to consolidate their democratic institutions."[4]

These observations suggest that the arguments for proportional representation and a parliamentary system are stronger than many United States constitutionalists, brought up in a presidential, plurality-winner system, think they are. Of course the particular historical circumstances of the United States may make those arguments unpersuasive. The United States is not a new democracy, for example, for which parliamentarism might be especially suitable. Social divisions in the United States may not be so severe as to require proportional representation as a partial solution. Two-party systems address social division by developing coalitions within the parties rather than through the multiparty governing coalitions that characterize systems with proportional representation. The former solution might be appropriate to the degree of social division that exists in the United States.

The Constitution creates a presidential system. To some degree it conduces to the adoption of plurality-winner electoral systems for Congress, and thereby to the development of a twoparty system. Creative constitutional interpretation and statutory design might overcome these apparent obstacles to the adoption of an alternative regime.[5] Nonetheless, the very weight of the existing electoral and political system may impede creative thinking about institutional, and therefore constitutional, design for the United States.[6]

What is the source of this "weight"? Of course, to some extent, it is history itself and the fact that the existing constitutional structures seem to many to be functioning reasonably well. Another source, though, might be the Constitution itself.

The weight of existing structures would be less, though it would not disappear, if it were easier to amend the Constitution. Perhaps some degree of institutional stability is required for a system to warrant the name *constitutional*; if so, this suggests that it should not be too easy to amend all of a constitution's provisions, or perhaps any of its basic institutional prescriptions. There may be room, however, between creating an amendment process that is too easy to use and sticking with the present strong supermajority requirements of Article V.[7]

But, if the Constitution were amended to alter the supermajority requirements for its own amendment, could the new process eliminate the equal representation of the states in the Senate?

NOTES

1. 297 U.S. 1, 62 (1936). ("When an act of Congress is appropriately challenged in the courts as not conforming to the constitutional mandate the judicial branch of the Government has only one duty,—to lay the article of the Constitution which is invoked beside the statute which is challenged and to decide whether the latter squares with the former.")

2. Maurice Duverger, *Political Parties: Their Organization and Activity in the Modern State* (London: Methuen, 1954).

3. R. Kent Weaver and Bert A. Rockman, "When and How Do Institutions Matter?" in R. Kent Weaver and Bert A. Rockman, eds., *Do Institutions Matter?: Government Capabilities in the United States and Abroad* 458 (Washington, D.C.: Brookings Institution, 1993).

4. Alfred Stepan and Cindy Skach, "Constitutional Frameworks and Democratic Consolidation: Parliamentarism versus Presidentialism," 46 *World Pol.* 1, 4 (1993).

5. Nothing in the Constitution appears to require that members of the House of Representatives be elected from single-member districts rather than on a statewide basis, for example. Perhaps Congress has the power to prescribe multimember districts and proportional representation for the House of Representatives, pursuant to its power to "make . . . Regulations" for the "Times, Places, and Manner of holding Elections" (Art. I, Sec. 4). But it seems to me awfully difficult to figure out a way

to devise a system of proportional representation in the Senate that is compatible with the requirements of (1) equal representation of each state in the Senate (Art. 1, Sec. 3 [and Art. V]), and (2) the staggered elections for the Senate (Art. 1, Sec. 3).

6. No one should have been surprised when politicians elected under a plurality-winner system were uncomfortable with the scholarship of Lani Guinier, which argues for moves in the direction of proportional representation.

7. Akhil Amar's suggestion that the existing Constitution accommodates a mechanism for constitutional amendment outside of Article V indicates that, even here, it might not be proper to call Article V "stupid." Akhil Reed Amar, "Philadelphia Revisited: Amending the Constitution outside Article V," 55 *U. Chi. L. Rev.* 1043 (1988).

CHAPTER 22

How Stupid Can a Coasean Constitution Be?

William N. Eskridge, Jr., and Sanford Levinson

The Constitution undoubtedly contains many unwise, even stupid, provisions, and many more that are trivial. Its assumption of severely limited government, concentrated in localities, has become increasingly unrealistic. Some of its best ideas, such as a system of checks and balances and an independent judiciary, work less well today than they did at the founding. The Slavery Clauses still mar the document, even if they have been superseded. Robin West has suggested that one reason to be ambivalent about activist judicial review is that the Constitution is a retrograde document.[1] Most of the essays in the first half of this volume can be read to support some version of West's argument. How stupid is the Constitution?

Not very, argues Daniel Farber: the Constitution we have is surprisingly smart.[2] Its worst provisions (the Slavery Clauses and Prohibition) have been explicitly repealed; its individual-rights protections are open-textured enough to accommodate the demand for rights by a changing polity; and the structural provisions have proved supple enough to provide a framework for workable democracy without being too rigid in the face of new political dynamics.

Most of the essays in the first half of this volume can be read to support Farber's argument. None of the contributors argues that the polity is in immediate danger because of stupid constitutional provisions. Even the two authors who focus on the Senate do not claim that its present structure threatens the polity with disaster.[3] Other contributors nominate provisions whose deleterious effect is either more speculative (the Good Behavior Clause, the Electoral College) or largely symbolic (the requirements that the president be native born and at least thirty-five years old). Most telling, a number of potential stupidities have been smarted up by highly dynamic interpretation. The apparent strictness of the Necessary and Proper Clause did not stand in the way of the Supreme Court's upholding the U.S. Bank, a fairly bold constitutional conclusion.[4]

Farber explains this unstupid state of affairs by reference to the Coase Theorem.[5] That theorem posits that apparently inefficient legal rules do not deter the creation of efficient regimes, because parties will simply bargain "around" the legal rules. The legal rules only impose transactions costs on private parties and affect the distribution of wealth or entitlement among the parties, but do not seriously impede people's ability to develop efficient private and public institutional arrangements. But it is not clear that bad constitutional provisions—as opposed to bad laws—can be bargained around easily. It took the bloody Civil War to undo the constitutional sanction of slavery, to take the biggest example. The One Senator, One Vote Clause of Article I, Section 3 cannot be amended out of the Constitution,[6] and any informal arrangements made around that clause would trigger vigorous protests from senators from states with small populations, today concentrated in the West and Great Plains.

Relatedly, the expenses of bargaining around the Constitution are potentially ruinous. Farber considers these worries nothing more than the unavoidable costs of a political system, but at some point costs become too high. If a company incurs excessive costs, it goes bankrupt. If a tennis player makes too many unforced errors, she loses the match. So, too, do nations rise and fall, perhaps through their own unforced errors and wanton imposition of social costs.[7]

The risks of constitutional stupidities multiply beyond easy calculation if the costs are suddenly sprung upon an unsuspecting polity through the detonation of constitutional landmines.[8] Several contributors are concerned that the Constitution contains landmines that are likely to go off in the future, with unpredictable but potentially grievous results. There are a good many possibilities: the Electoral College or even the House of Representatives might choose a president who is the runner-up in the popular vote,[9] a defeated president or Congress might make damaging commitments during the period between their defeat and the accession of the new office holders;[10] a tainted vice president might choose to exercise his apparent constitutional prerogative to preside over his own impeachment trial;[11] a coalition of aged Supreme Court justices might go on a constitutional rampage;[12] senators from the West might shut down the government by holding appropriations measures hostage to issues of parochial interest to the West but deleterious to the country as a whole;[13] or a president might defy Congress or the Supreme Court on matters ranging from investigations of presidential scandal to executive control of the public administration.[14] We might offer different predictions as to which of these (or other) landmines will detonate in our lifetimes, but it strikes us as foolhardy to believe that absolutely none will. If landmines go off, normal cost-benefit analysis is shattered in the explosion.

Our most important concern, based upon the various essays, is whether the eighteenth-century Constitution is well designed for the polity of the twenty-first century. As Frederick Schauer and Robert Nagel argue,[15] there are reasons to think not. The Constitution is libertarian and federalist in its orientation, while the country is now a centralized administrative state whose regulations pervasively affect our lives. If the administrative state has a key role to play in addressing our most vexing national problems, especially those associated with urban areas, that role will be played badly, or not at all, because of the domination of the Senate by rural and small town interests, the stiff requirements for enacting legislation, potential impediments from unresponsive judges, and fragmentation of administrative authority between state and federal governments. On the other hand, it is far from clear to us that liberty and federalism impede an energetic polity. Both of us believe that individual liberty as well as the commitment to diversity and localist politics captured by federalism at its best are positive goods. Yet they sometimes operate at cross-purposes, and it is sobering to notice that almost none of the polities constructing new constitutions for themselves are choosing to emulate the complex horizontal and vertical divisions of power that so distinguish the United States Constitution from its international counterparts.

In any event, Schauer's and Nagel's concerns suggest the persuasiveness of Stephen Griffin's and Mark Tushnet's answer to our inquiry:[16] Article V is the stupidest provision, because it makes the increasingly imperfect Constitution too difficult to amend.[17] Farber would be entitled to rejoin, consistent with the Coase Theorem, that the imperfect Constitution is often amended by practice and interpretation. Thus the political system has revised constitutional meaning in this century to allow Congress to delegate vast amounts of legislative authority to nonexecutive agencies,[18] the president to negotiate executive agreements that are treated as the law of the land,[19] the states to disrupt private contractual expectations,[20] and the courts to invalidate legislation because it deploys sex-based classifications, regulates commercial or indecent speech, or invades an individual's right to sexual privacy.[21] Any of these constitutional changes could have been effected through Article V amendments, such as the proposed Equal

Rights Amendment; failing that, the polity has internalized the changes anyway.

Farber's response presents some hard questions that we think are implicit in our challenge to identify constitutional stupidities. Our Coasean Constitution is a dynamic one, but only in response to ongoing negotiations among important groups in our polity. How stupid can such a constitution be? How far can "interpretation" operate to update an outmoded constitution? Mark Tushnet thinks that even the most creative interpretation cannot instantiate fundamental reforms such as a parliamentary system that unifies rather than fragments government, or proportional representation for the Senate. What if Akhil Amar and Bruce Ackerman are right, however, that the Constitution can be interpreted to render Article V only one of several means of amending it?[22] To the extent that Article V or some other barrier prevents constitutional "reform," how seriously do the unremediated imperfections mar the Constitution and actually harm the operation of the polity? To the extent that constitutional reform can proceed along lines of practice and interpretation, rather than amendment, can those informal, Coasean devices create a "Perfect Constitution"? Or do those devices in fact fail to head off tragic results and perhaps even carry their own tragic costs? These questions are explored in the second half of this volume.

NOTES

1. Robin West, "Constitutional Scepticism," 72 *B.U.L. Rev.* 765 (1992).

2. Farber, "Our (Almost) Perfect Constitution," chapter 6 of this volume.

3. Farber seems to believe that the structure of the Senate is the worst aspect of the Constitution but still concludes that "[o]n balance, . . . the Senate seems to have worked tolerably well." One of us mildly disagrees with Farber's point, arguing that the "sagebrush Senate" impedes serious state response to the problems of inner cities. William N. Eskridge, Jr., "The One Senator, One Vote Clauses," chapter 5 of this volume.

4. John Yoo, "*McCulloch v. Maryland*," chapter 38 of this volume.

5. Farber, "(Almost) Perfect," applying Ronald Coase, "The Problem of Social Cost," 3 *J. L. & Econ.* 1 (1960). For a brilliant application of the Coase Theorem in another context, see Daniel A. Farber, "The Case against Brilliance," 70 *Minn. L. Rev.* 917 (1986).

6. U.S. Const., Art. V.

7. See Mancur Olson, *The Rise and Decline of Nations: Economic Growth, Stagflation, and Social Rigidities* (New Haven: Yale University Press, 1982).

8. Drawing upon the learning of stupidity expert Forrest Gump, Jack Balkin, in the initial symposium we organized, likened the Constitution to a "box of chocolates," a pleasanter way to think about constitutional surprises. See J. M. Balkin, "The Constitution as a Box of Chocolates," 12 *Const. Comm.* 147 (1995). Because Balkin wrote a tragedy piece for the current volume, we (perhaps stupidly) excluded his earlier, Gumpian piece on stupidity.

9. See Akhil Reed Amar, "A Constitutional Accident Waiting to Happen," chapter 1 of this volume; Sanford Levinson, "Presidential Elections and Constitutional Stupidities," chapter 11 of this volume.

10. See Levinson, "Presidential Elections."

11. Michael Stokes Paulsen, "Someone Should Have Told Spiro Agnew," chapter 14 of this volume.

12. See L. H. LaRue, "'Neither Force nor Will,'" chapter 10 of this volume; L. A. Powe, Jr., "Old People and Good Behavior," chapter 15 of this volume.

13. See William N. Eskridge, Jr., "The One Senator, One Vote Clauses," chapter 5 of this volume; Suzanna Sherry, "Our Unconstitutional Senate," chapter 19 of this volume.

14. See Steven G. Calabresi, "An Agenda for Constitutional Reform," chapter 3 of this volume.

15. Robert Nagel, "The Last Cetrifugal Force," chapter 13 of this volume; Frederick Schauer, "The Constitution of Fear," chapter 17 of this volume.

16. Stephen Griffin, "The Nominee Is . . . Article V," chapter 8 of this volume; Mark Tushnet, "The Whole Thing," chapter 21 of this volume.

17. The Constitution has been radically amended only three times: in 1791 (the Bill of Rights was added as a result of promises made to secure ratification of the original Constitution); after the Civil War (the Reconstruction Amendments); and during the Progressive Era (the Sixteenth through Twentieth Amendments). Notwithstanding the country's rapid evolution since 1921, there have been no amendments of consequence, except for the repeal of Prohibition in Amendment Twenty-One.

18. See *Mistretta v. United States*, 488 U.S. 361 (1989), which allowed Congress to delegate the so-called sentencing "guidelines" that have transformed criminal justice in America to a hybrid body.

19. See *Dames & Moore v. Regan*, 453 U.S. 654 (1981), which enforced a non-treaty executive agreement to supersede the Foreign Sovereign Immunities Act.

20. See *Home Building and Loan Ass'n v. Blaisdell*, 290 U.S. 398 (1934), allowing state negation of private contract rights in an economic emergency, notwithstanding directive language of the Contracts Clause.

21. See *Virginia v. United States*, 116 S. Ct. 2264 (1996) (debate between majority and dissenting opinions over review of sex-based classifications); *Griswold v. Connecticut*, 381 U.S. 479 (1965) ("penumbral" right to privacy).

22. See Bruce Ackerman, *We the People: Foundations* (Cambridge, Mass.: Belknap Press, 1991) (theory of "constitutional moments"); Akhil Reed Amar, "Philadelphia Revisited: Amending the Constitution outside Article V," 55 *U. Chi. L. Rev.* 1043 (1988).

PART II

Constitutional Tragedies

What is the worst decision you would feel compelled to reach under your own favored theory of constitutional interpretation?

CHAPTER 23

Constitutional Tragedies and Giving Refuge to the Devil

Larry Alexander

My task, as I understand it, is the following: I am to assume that I am the sole justice on the United States Supreme Court, so that I can employ my pet theory of constitutional interpretation and have it be outcome-determinative. The question that I must then answer is what case or class of cases would present me with a tragic choice between proper constitutional jurisprudence and just outcome. What cases are "constitutional tragedies" under a regime of "Alexander's constitutional interpretation"?

It is a nice question, although I expect that many of those charged with answering it will duck or evade it. After all, they will say, if I really am Hercules[1] and what I say goes, then constitutional tragedies can be averted, especially if my theory of constitutional interpretation is of the "justice-seeking"[2] or "Constitution-perfecting"[3] kind. If the Constitution is "the best it can be,"[4] then, in my hands at least, it will never yield a tragic result. Only originalists or formalists will confront constitutional tragedies.

I believe the hypothetical response I just adumbrated is deeply mistaken. Constitutional tragedies are unavoidable even if we are Hercules and fully control constitutional methodology. Or at least this is what I shall argue.

The invocation of the concept of tragedy will undoubtedly conjure up those examples of the genre that seem most apt to the subject of legal tragedies. Sophocles' *Antigone*, of course, comes immediately to mind, and I believe it is indeed suitable to my task. I shall not use it, however, for two related reasons. First, Creon is a tyrant, and there is a danger that his tyranny will dissolve the tragedy by shifting all of our sympathy to Antigone. Second, the law that Antigone must defy is not one the wisdom or justice of which we can easily perceive.

Melville's *Billy Budd* is a better model for constitutional tragedies. Captain Vere is not an unsympathetic tyrant, nor is the necessity of an unbending rule regarding striking an officer beyond our modern comprehension. Nonetheless, I shall not use *Billy Budd* as my tragic model, because its very concreteness opens up the unwanted possibility that someone will gainsay the tragedy by gainsaying the necessity of the rule in question.

To close off the escape routes from constitutional tragedies, I need to avoid the concreteness of an *Antigone* or a *Billy Budd* and find a literary portrayal that is more abstract. My choice, which I regard as the greatest literary exposition of the tragedy inherent in law generally and thus in constitutions as a type of law, is a scene from Robert Bolt's *A Man for All Seasons*.[5] The scene occurs near the end of act 1 and involves Sir Thomas More, his wife Alice, his daughter Margaret, and William Roper, a suitor of Margaret. Richard Rich, who represents a mortal danger to More, is just leaving.

Roper:	Arrest him.
Alice:	Yes!
More:	For what?
Alice:	He's dangerous!
Roper:	For libel; he's a spy.
Margaret:	Father, that man's bad.
More:	There is no law against that.
Roper:	There is! God's law!
More:	Then God can arrest him.
Roper:	Sophistication upon sophistication!
More:	No, sheer simplicity. The law, Roper, the law. I know what's legal, not what's right. And I'll stick to what's legal.
Roper:	Then you set man's law above God's?
More:	No, far below; but let me draw your attention to a fact—I'm *not* God. The currents and eddies of right and wrong, which you find such plain sailing, I can't navigate. I'm no voyager. But in the thickets of the law, oh, there I'm a forester. I doubt if there's a man alive who could follow me there, thank God . . . *(He says this last to himself)*
Alice:	*(Exasperated, pointing after RICH)* While you talk, he's gone.
More:	And go he should, if he was the Devil himself, until he broke the law!
Roper:	So now you'd give the Devil benefit of law!
More:	Yes. What would you do? Cut a great road through the law to get after the Devil?
Roper:	I'd cut down every law in England to do that!
More:	*(Roused and excited)* Oh? *(Advances on Roper:)* And when the last law was down, and the Devil turned round on you—where would you hide, Roper, the laws all being flat? *(He leaves him.)*

> This country's planted thick with laws from coast-to-coast—
> man's laws, not God's—and if you cut them down—and you're
> just the man to do it—d'you really think you could stand up-
> right in the winds that would blow then? *(Quietly)* Yes, I'd give
> the Devil benefit of law, for my own safety's sake.

Roper: I have long suspected this; this is the golden calf; the law's your
god.

More: *(Wearily)* Oh, Roper, you're a fool, God's my god. . . . *(Rather bit-terly)* But I find him rather too *(Very bitterly)* subtle . . . I don't
know where he is nor what he wants.

Roper: My god wants service, to the end and unremitting; nothing else!

More: *(Dryly)* Are you sure that's God? He sounds like Moloch. But indeed it may be God—And whoever hunts for me, Roper, God or
Devil, will find me hiding in the thickets of the law! And I'll hide
my daughter with me! Not hoist her up the mainmast of your
seagoing principles! They put about too nimbly!⁶

The author intends our sympathies to lie with More, not Roper, and I am
sure that the author succeeds with most of you. He surely does with me.

It would be a mistake, however, to read More as not appreciating the
force of Roper's position. More is keenly aware of the paradoxical and
tragic nature of law. If we can chop down the trees of law to get at the
Devil, we leave ourselves with no refuge if the Devil turns on us. That is
More's case for law. On the other hand, if we leave the trees of the law
standing, then we may be unable to get at the Devil, who, like us, can seek
the refuge of the law. And although Roper's starchy rectitude and lack of
subtlety make him an unsympathetic character, he is surely correct that the
law's providing the Devil with refuge *is* a tragedy. It would be a mistake to
discount Roper's side of the argument, as More, whose life was endan-
gered, surely was aware.

That then is the paradox—and tragedy—of law, and of constitutions as
supreme law. We can have law only if the Devil can have it, too.

Now no constitutional theorist advocates outright chopping down the
"forest" of constitutional rules. In fact, however, those who endorse "justice-
seeking," "Constitution-perfecting," or other similar Dworkinian strategies
of constitutional interpretation⁷ in effect would "cut a great road through
the law." Under these theories, although the Constitution appears to be a
forest of rules, in actuality it is an open field. The "trees" of the law are nothing more than images created by a virtual-reality mask of language and historical fact. The Devil may appear to be hiding behind one, but as we approach it, the "tree" disappears and leaves the Devil in our clutches.

The same point applies to theories of constitutional interpretation that would have us "modernize" the Constitution, that is, chop down the real, but ancient, trees that are there and replant the constitutional field with newer varieties behind which the Devil cannot hide.[8] This approach, which is in reality nothing more than a "justice-seeking" or "Constitution-perfecting" approach differently described, unsurprisingly does not avoid the dilemma of its cohort approaches. The method of cutting and replanting is a method that the Devil too can employ. If our saw is strong enough to cut down the constitutional trees that shelter him, his saw can no doubt cut down the trees that shelter us.

Nor is the problem here a positivistic conception of law. Indeed, it is just such a conception—"man's laws, not God's"—that protects us from the Devil, even as it protects the Devil from us.

Consider a Constitution that merely said (or could be "interpreted" to say in essence) "Do what is just." Assume, moreover, as you are invited by the editors to do here, that you are the sole final decision maker regarding the Constitution's application. Indeed, assume further—this will be easy for some of you—that you are quite wise and knowledgeable and strongly motivated to be just. Could you not *then* go after the Devil—injustice—without fearing his going after you?

The answer is, of course, that you could not. For however Herculean you imagine yourself, you lack two godlike traits necessary for dissolving the paradox of law and averting the possibility of tragedy. To begin with, you cannot foresee all future issues and circumstances, which means that you will not be able to construct a set of ideal rules that will never have tragic consequences. Equally if not more important, you are not immortal. Someone else will rule after you, and that person will not be Herculean. He or she will not be as wise and as just as you. We cannot guarantee perpetual rule by angels.

The second problem is not so much one of motivation as of knowledge: what does justice truly require? The norm "Do what is just" is always processed by us as "Do what (I believe) is just." Even if we believe, as I surely do, that justice is independent of what we happen to believe it to be, no one can stand outside his beliefs about justice and have an alternative route of access to the true article.

Thus, because every decision claims legitimacy, not only for the substance of its result, but also for the methodology by which the result is reached, a nonpositivistic methodology is the source of legitimacy for subsequent decision makers acting on what *they* believe justice requires. It is of no use to claim that you have legitimated only what justice truly requires, and not mistakes, for no decision maker can separate what justice truly requires from what he or she believes it requires.

The rejection of positivistic conceptions of law and the Constitution frees the wise and just to pursue the Devil without impediment but at the same time unties the hands of those less wise and less virtuous. And the greater danger is the danger posed by the unwise. Some of the Devil's very best work is done by those with good intentions but an absence of wisdom.

A positivistic constitution—one of hard, unalterable rules—will give refuge to the Devil but also from him. A natural law constitution—one of broad, vague principles of justice—may usher in great victories over injustice, but those principles may tomorrow be otherwise employed. As More put it, "They put about too nimbly." Though, as I have explained on numerous occasions,[9] I ultimately side with More in his preference for a constitution of positivistic rules, both kinds of constitution are tragic.[10]

The conclusion must be this: no methodology capable of allowing us an unimpeded shot at the Devil can protect us from him, and no methodology capable of protecting us from the Devil will not also impede our pursuit of him. That is the tragedy of constitutional law and of all law. And that is why every Supreme Court decision that is a cause for great rejoicing is also a cause for great worry.

NOTES

1. See Ronald Dworkin, *Taking Rights Seriously* 105 (Cambridge: Harvard University Press, 1977).

2. See Christopher Eisgruber and Lawrence Sager, "Good Constitutions and Bad Choices," chapter 27 of this volume.

3. See James Fleming, "Constitutional Tragedy in Dying: Or Whose Tragedy Is It, Anyway?," chapter 29 of this volume.

4. See Ronald Dworkin, *Law's Empire* 53 (Cambridge, Mass.: Belknap Press, 1986).

5. Robert Bolt, *A Man for All Seasons* (New York: Random House, 1962).

6. *Id.* at 65–67.

7. See notes 2–4 above.

8. See Erwin Chemerinsky, *Interpreting the Constitution* 45–56 (New York: Praeger, 1985).

9. See Larry Alexander, "Incomplete Theorizing," *Notre Dame L. Rev.* (1997); Larry Alexander and Emily Sherwin, "The Deceptive Nature of Rules," 142 *U. Pa. L. Rev.* 1191 (1994); Larry Alexander, "The Gap," 14 *Harv. J. of Law & Pub. Pol'y* 695

(1991); Larry Alexander, "Law and Exclusionary Reasons," 18 *Philosophical Topics* 5 (1990); Larry Alexander, "Constrained by Precedent," 63 *S. Cal. L. Rev.* 1 (1989); Larry Alexander, "Pursuing the Good—Indirectly," 95 *Ethics* 315 (1985).

10. See Larry Alexander, "The Constitution as Law," 6 *Const. Comm.* 103 (1989).

CHAPTER 24

The Meaning of Constitutional Tragedy

J. M. Balkin

How should we understand the notion of constitutional tragedy? One approach views it as a matter of interpretive theory: constitutional tragedies occur when a favored method of constitutional interpretation produces regrettable results. A second approach focuses on constitutional evil: the possibility that the Constitution permits or requires serious and profound injustices, like slavery. Constitutional tragedy occurs when we cannot escape the possibility of constitutional evil.

The second approach is surely related to the first, since the avoidability of constitutional evil depends on the limits of constitutional interpretation. Optimistic interpreters might insist that constitutional evils are usually the result of improper readings of the Constitution. *Dred Scott v. Sandford*[1] was a wicked result, but it was also a bad interpretation. If we distinguish the history of interpretations of the Constitution from its best interpretation, could we not escape the problem of constitutional evil (and constitutional tragedy as well)?

Yet, resting our hopes on an ideal Constitution faces two problems. First, it begs the question of whether the Constitution, shorn of all bad prior readings and interpreted in its best possible light, will always lead to happy endings and never to unhappy ones. If it does, this may not prove the real advantage of our theory of constitutional interpretation. Rather, it may reveal a defect: that our theory is not, in fact, a theory of constitutional interpretation at all, but a free-floating disquisition on the right and the good.

Second, although individuals can imagine ideal constitutions, they do not have control over what the Constitution means. The Constitution is not simply the best interpretation of it judged from the perspective of a particular academic's mind. It is an ongoing political and social institution with a history that constrains its possible future growth and development. Even if an ideal Constitution could avoid all unhappy endings, it is by no means clear that the existing institution of constitutional law can do so. As an ongoing legal and political practice, the meaning of the Constitution is controlled by no single person, but is rather the product of ongoing political and theoretical struggle by judges and citizens, politicians and academics, over its meaning, scope, and direction. The institution of the Constitution is a joint project in which we Americans play roles of differing influence and importance. And each of us suffers the consequences of what we and others do in the name of the Constitution.

The belief that the best interpretation of the Constitution can avoid constitutional evil shares something in common with the belief that the Constitution means what a particular academic's vision of reason demands that it mean. Both beliefs are in a sense solipsistic; both forget that the meaning of the Constitution in practice—as a part of an ongoing tradition—is social and public. It is created through the interaction of people with conflicting views and ideologies, who in turn operate against the history of past readings of the Constitution and past decisions made in its name.[2] Even the justices of the Supreme Court are hemmed in by the political necessities of their time and by the work of previous justices. The problems that they encounter are set for them by the political configuration they face, by the doctrinal categories already in place, by the past deeds and misdeeds of the nation.

That is why I would like to offer a third perspective on the nature of constitutional tragedy, one that connects constitutional tragedy to the fortunes of a nation that lives under a Constitution it continually creates and recreates. Constitutional tragedy is what befalls us, as a nation, because of the Constitution we have collectively created for ourselves. In this process, the innocent are punished along with the guilty, the sins of the parents are visited upon the children. And still we go forward, unknowingly, sowing the seeds of later tragedies.

Tragedy means more than unjust results or unhappy endings. True, people often equate tragedy with misfortune; we often say that an accident is "tragic" because it is terrible and sad. But there is also a dramaturgical concept of tragedy and many theories about tragedy, ranging from those of the ancient Greeks to those of the present day. This dramaturgical sense of tragedy is about more than unhappiness; it is about the human predicament and the complicated relationship between our fates and our characters, between those aspects of our lives we can control and those that are beyond our knowledge and our abilities.

Aristotle tells us that tragedy is a story about a hero, usually of noble birth, who is undone through circumstances beyond his control. Often the hero's destiny has already been foretold. But the tragedy also occurs in part due to a tragic flaw in his or her character, a flaw that spurs the hero on to his or her eventual destruction. In a classical tragedy, we witness a reversal of fortune, a moment when the hero recognizes this reversal, and the hero's eventual defeat. In a well-made tragedy, the audience is edified by this event, experiencing a catharsis or emotional release.[3]

Aristotle pointed to the story of Oedipus as an example of tragedy. Oedipus's flaw is his arrogant self-confidence. He solved the riddle of the Sphinx, and thus he believes he can master all difficulties placed in his path. Because he is blinded by pride, he does not understand until too late that he has been undone by his own character and by circumstances beyond his control. In Sophocles' version, Oedipus's subjects come to him with yet another riddle: Thebes is suffering from a plague, and his subjects want to know why the gods are angry with them. Oedipus solves the mystery, but discovers that he is the cause, for he has killed his father and slept with his mother. At that point he puts his eyes out. Before he could see but was truly blind; now he is blind but truly sees.

If constitutional tragedy is of this kind, who is the tragic hero? Most examples of constitutional evil or constitutional injustice involve persons who suffer at the hands of others. Yet no matter how much we may empathize with the victims of constitutional injustice, these persons are not tragic heroes. For example, we do not attribute a tragic flaw to slaves suffering from constitutionally protected slavery. They did not suffer unhappiness because of some defect in their character. Contemplating their suffering, one sees no reversal of fortune, no hand of fate; and certainly one experiences no catharsis.

A second possibility is that judges are tragic heroes, and in particular, the justices of the Supreme Court. Imagining judges as heroes is flattering. It is flattering not only to judges but to academics, who often imagine themselves in the role of judges, shaping the meaning of constitutional law through argument and interpretation. But judges who interpret the Constitution are hardly tragic heroes. They may have to make "tragic" choices between unpalatable alternatives, but they are not necessarily undone by them. When judges hold that homosexuals have no constitutional rights that heterosexuals are bound to respect, the judges are not subsequently beaten up by drunken homophobes. When judges deny poor people rights of subsistence, the judges' homes are not seized, forcing them to live on the streets. Indeed, the salaries of federal judges are constitutionally guaranteed. They may be the most obvious vehicles of constitutional evil, but they are not the heroes of the story.[4]

To be sure, the courts—and particularly the Supreme Court of the United States—can squander their political capital by unwise decisions. They can create insoluble dilemmas for themselves by their previous holdings, and they can cause other political actors to hold them in contempt. But this is a far cry from the sufferings that Oedipus or Antigone underwent. Most Supreme Court justices die in their beds. True, they receive bushels of hate mail; they are regularly castigated in the press by unhappy litigants and activists. But they are also continually lauded and praised by the political and legal establishment, invited to inaugural balls and asked to speak at judicial conferences and bar association dinners. If they are fated to be subject to anything, it is to an almost unending stream of toadying. No matter what damage they may eventually cause to the country or suffer to their reputations, they hardly deserve the name of tragic hero.

Moreover, even after Supreme Court justices have squandered the Court's political capital, it has usually replenished itself with little effort. America has lived through *Dred Scott*, through *Lochner*,[5] through *Korematsu*,[6] and many other dark days, and still the Supreme Court is respected and revered and its opinions obeyed. This is at most the story of the ebb and flow of political clout; it is not the stuff of tragedy. At least not yet.

Neither the victims of constitutional evil nor the judges who perpetrate it are the proper heroes of constitutional tragedy. If there is a tragic hero to the story of the Constitution, it must be the American people as a whole. The American people, acting through the three branches of government, commit themselves to a disastrous course of action due to some defect in the national character, which leads eventually and unwittingly to great suffering and severe punishment. Because the American nation is the unwitting hero of its own constitutional tragedy, the hubris of one generation is often visited upon the next, and many innocents suffer. The forces of tragedy are indiscriminate in their application. They destroy not only the hero but often many others as well. Oedipus's sins were visited on his subjects, as well as on his children. Antigone's tragedy followed on that of her father.

From this perspective, the constitutional evil of slavery looks very different. It is the story of Americans making a deal with evil, what William Lloyd Garrison called a "Covenant with Death and an Agreement with Hell,"[7] then pretending it was not an evil—or if so, an evil that could be managed, assuaged, compromised away—until finally slavery provoked a crisis, leading to the deaths of hundreds of thousands of Americans. Only as Americans begin to fathom the blood and suffering they have brought upon themselves by their pact with Hell do they begin to recognize their mistake, their hubris, and their wrongheadedness. "A new birth of freedom" gradually emerges from this struggle, but at a terrible cost.

To a great extent, this is Abraham Lincoln's later interpretation of the Civil War. It is the interpretation that he offers in his Second Inaugural Address. This speech is the great recognition scene in the American tragedy of the Civil War. The crucial passage comes immediately before the most famous portion asking for reconciliation "with malice towards none, with charity for all":

> Fondly do we hope—fervently do we pray—that this mighty scourge of war may speedily pass away. Yet if God wills that it continue, until all the wealth piled by the bonds-man's two hundred and fifty years of unrequited toil shall be sunk, and until every drop of blood drawn with the lash, shall be paid by another drawn with the sword, as was said three thousand years ago, so still it must be said, "the judgments of the Lord are true and righteous altogether."[8]

One is tempted to see the Civil War as a constitutional tragedy of classical proportions, with America recognizing its mistake only when it is too late. But that is too tidy an interpretation. The tragedy still continues. The complete recognition has not yet arrived. America did not completely understand the evils of its ways. Slavery was not abolished until 1865; egalitarian and remedial measures were blunted; and the badges and incidents of slavery remain with us today.

Generations of white Americans would fail to understand the meaning of the Civil War and the depth of America's sins. Less than twenty years after the carnage, Justice Bradley would vote to strike down civil rights laws, uttering his famous statement that "[w]hen a man has emerged from slavery, and by the aid of beneficent legislation has shaken off the inseparable concomitants of that state, there must be some stage in the progress of his elevation when he takes the rank of a mere citizen, and ceases to be the special favorite of the law."[9] This is the sort of continuing blindness that eventually leads to new forms of tragedy.

Constitutional tragedy, then, is our country's blindness to the evils within it, evils it has wrought on itself and others, evils that later rise up and submerge it in misery and retribution. Constitutional tragedy is hubris, the hubris of a nation. We hope as a nation that the evil bargains we have entered into are not so terrible: that we can accept them, that we can live with them, that they will not ultimately consume us. We believe that we have the courage and the ability to deal with their consequences. We imagine that all injustices can eventually be undone, all conflicts harmonized, so that the bargain with evil, the pact with Hell we enter into today, will not be enforced against us in later years. We believe, in short, that we can escape full payment for our compromise with evil. Yet each clever action we employ to escape our fate simply brings it closer to fruition.

An oracle told Oedipus's father, Laius, that his house was cursed and that his son was destined to kill him. When Oedipus was born, Laius ordered Oedipus's feet pierced and left the child to die on Mount Cithaeron. The baby was found and raised by others he thought to be his parents, so that when Oedipus met his real father he did not recognize him. Believing that he could make everything right, Laius, like Oedipus himself, simply accelerated the course of events.

So too did the American nation deal with slavery, imagining that it could handle the evil within its breast by compromise, by clever parliamentary stratagem, by procedural device and legal maneuver. The antebellum generations thought themselves mature and competent statesmen and, like Oedipus, able to solve any riddle, resolve any difficulty. The cleverer they thought themselves, the more quickly they hastened the nation's day of reckoning, when it would become clear that no amount of trickery and no political compromise would forestall the inevitable calamity that awaited them and their children.

Yet this hubris is more than simple egotism. It also reflects the need to reduce cognitive dissonance.[10] Americans want to believe in the justice of their legal system; they want to treat their Constitution as an object of veneration. But accepting the reality of constitutional evil is dissonant with this belief. One cannot pledge one's faith to a deeply evil and unjust thing. To reduce dissonance, one must downplay the significance of constitutional evils, or one must convince oneself that the Constitution's defects can and will be remedied in good time. Belief in an ideal constitution is another way of reducing this dissonance: by separating the actual practice of constitutional law from the ideal Constitution of our imaginations, we can pretend that the former is an imposter, a sort of evil twin, who must and will eventually be unmasked and dethroned.

Thus, while the interpretive theorist wonders whether the Constitution produces only happy endings, it is perhaps more to the point to consider the psychological processes by which we convince ourselves that the constitutional evils around us are not truly evil, recasting them as unfortunate wrongs with which we can live. Many Americans actively defended slavery in 1850, asserting that it was a justifiable and honorable institution. Many progressive thinkers detested slavery but thought it was not as bad as the barbarisms of previous generations and that, in time, it would eventually pass away. The strategy of many antislavery progressives before the Civil War, including Abraham Lincoln, was to accept the southern states' right to slavery but to oppose its spread to new territories. Even after the war began, Lincoln sought to bring the South back into the Union with slavery intact. Only the depth of the tragedy changed his mind and the country's.

We now see slavery differently than the generation of 1850 saw it. Because slavery is a constitutional evil of the past, we can afford to be suitably shocked and horrified that our predecessors let it continue as long as they did. We can look with scorn upon slavery's apologists and with condescension upon the progressives willing to compromise with them. But is our position so different from theirs? The possibility of profound constitutional evil leads us, like them, to ever new strategies for allaying cognitive dissonance: we imagine that no evil existing today can be as bad as we now understand slavery to be. We are not the first generation to wish away the evils around us, nor will we be the last. The age of tragedy is still with us, and it is part of the tragedy that we do not understand this as a nation until it is too late.

Is there such a tragedy brewing today? Is there a blindness that we have taken upon ourselves? Are we engaged, even now, in the reduction of cognitive dissonance necessary to get ourselves through the day? If you ask me what it is, I would say that it is our indifference to poverty, and the overwhelming consensus of opinion, especially by so-called liberal constitutionalists,[11] that the Constitution does not protect the poor from the overreaching of the political process—even when the overreaching is due to an unholy alliance of spiteful demagogues, on the one hand, and spineless accommodators on the other. I would say that at this moment, we are, and have been for some time, brewing a terrible stew of despair, resentment, and hopelessness throughout our country, making it impossible for people to better themselves, to educate themselves, to free themselves from new forms of slavery, and to become full citizens of our country. Perhaps we will be fortunate and this scourge will pass away quickly, bloodlessly, happily, and without any reckoning to ourselves. Let us pray that it will. But let us also pray that we are not now engaged in the creation of a new constitutional tragedy that will punish our children for the sins that we commit today.

NOTES

1. *Dred Scott v. Sandford*, 60 U.S. (19 How.) 393 (1857).

2. Thus, we (the American people) do control the meaning of the Constitution, but we do so collectively, not individually. The meaning of the Constitution in practice does not reflect the excellent reasoning of any single person—no matter how stellar her academic credentials—but the give and take of political struggle and legal compromise.

3. Aristotle's is not the only theory of tragedy. Many scholars throughout history have offered accounts, including Hegel, Schopenhauer, and Nietzsche. But Aristotle's is the most famous and lasting analysis, and it connects best with what I have to say here.

A contemporary way of imagining tragedy is in terms of "tragic choices": equally unpalatable alternatives that one is led to by previous circumstance. In classical terms, this is a focus on the moment when the decision maker recognizes his or her situation and must act. A tragic choice, in other words, is another version of the recognition scene.

4. Judges do play a role in constitutional tragedies, but they do so only as part of a larger political system. They work within an existing political consensus about what is politically possible and impossible. They are hemmed in by the work of their predecessors; previous precedents and doctrinal categories shape their legal imaginations and push them in directions they might otherwise not wish to go. Judges often face difficult and unpalatable decisions when they interpret the Constitution. But these "tragic choices" are usually the result of previous actions, not merely by their judicial predecessors, but by the political culture as a whole. When Justice Story upheld the Fugitive Slave Law in *Prigg v. Pennsylvania*, 41 U.S. (16 Pet.) 539 (1842), he did so in part because the case was before him. And it was before him because of an entire history of conflict over the Constitution's previous bargain with slavery.

5. *Lochner v. New York*, 198 U.S. 45 (1905).

6. *Korematsu v. United States*, 323 U.S. 214 (1944).

7. Walter M. Merrill, *Against Wind and Tide: A Biography of Wm. Lloyd Garrison* 205 (Cambridge: Harvard University Press, 1963).

8. Abraham Lincoln, *Speeches and Writings, 1859–1865*, at 687, ed. Don E. Fehrenbacher (New York: Library of America, 1989).

9. *The Civil Rights Cases*, 109 U.S. 3, 25 (1883).

10. For a fuller discussion, see J. M. Balkin, "Agreements with Hell and Other Objects of Our Faith," 65 *Fordham L. Rev.* 1703 (1997).

11. See, e.g., Ronald Dworkin, *Freedom's Law: The Moral Reading of the Constitution* 36, 72 (Cambridge: Harvard University Press, 1996).

CHAPTER 25

The Tragic Case of
Capital Punishment

Gerard V. Bradley

There were 56 tragic constitutional results in 1995, and there have been 313 since 1976[1] when the Supreme Court upheld revised death penalty laws.[2] There is little reason to believe that capital punishment will expire any time soon: the 1995 total was the highest since 1957; with the retirements of Justices Brennan, Marshall, and Blackmun, no Supreme Court justice believes capital punishment is, in principle, unconstitutional.

Under the method of constitutional interpretation that I defend—a certain type of "originalism"[3]—capital punishment is all but certainly constitutional. It is, nevertheless, always immoral, at least in a developed society like the United States. In this paper I shall summarize my reasons for holding these two opinions, and then consider the options for someone, like me, who is conscientiously opposed to a practice that is constitutional.

Note well: in this paper I speak of "unconstitutionality" and "constitutionality" simpliciter. This caveat allows me to sidestep the important but secondary issue of what deference a court owes to a legislative judgment in favor of the constitutionality of, say, the death penalty. Since the Constitution neither explicitly nor by fair implication holds that death *shall* be imposed upon anyone, the relevant question is whether a death sentence authorized by a legislature—to keep it simple, let us say by Congress—and imposed by a court, may constitutionally be carried out.

Another caveat: our question has to do with capital punishment in itself; accidental features of the contemporary practice of it are not our concern. Some say, for example, that capital punishment in and of itself violates the prohibition on racial discrimination. In principle, though not in practice, there cannot be a contradiction between a sentence of death and the ban on racial discrimination. If reliable data indicates some racial bias in a particular sentence, resentencing is in order. If reliable evidence shows a system-

atic racial bias, then the system needs reform. If that bias appears to be in-
eradicable, then, all things considered, capital punishment may be declared
"unconstitutional" in the sense it was from 1972 to 1976 (the practice was
suspended, pending reform). In all these situations, though, capital punishment as such remains valid.

Procedural due process is sometimes thought to be a killer of death sentences. Because of the inherent fallibility of a humanly administered system
of justice, it is maintained, an innocent person might be executed. Just so,
and some innocents likely have been executed. But there is no reason why
that possibility should not, if it invalidates capital punishment, invalidate
other types of punishment. And an argument against all punishment of
criminals proves too much.

If we are to find a constitutional infirmity in capital punishment as such,
then we need a constitutional norm contradicted by some part of the description of capital punishment itself. There are two leading possibilities
which track the essential nature of executions: (1) death is an inherently disproportionate punishment for any crime, and, assuming there is some
norm of proportionality in the Constitution, capital punishment is unconstitutional; and (2) an individual's right to life is violated by a death sentence, and by "right to life" I mean some right not to be killed that is protected by the Constitution.

Anyway, here goes.

Is Capital Punishment Unconstitutional?

The original, unamended Constitution says nothing about capital punishment. The Framers, however, clearly believed in the constitutionality of imposing death as a punishment for certain crimes. The first Congress not
only instituted a death penalty for the crimes of murder, rape, and forgery[4]
but also prescribed particular rules governing appointment of counsel in
capital cases.[5]

The unamended Constitution says nothing about capital punishment,
and so it would seem to permit death sentences. Because there is no requirement that anyone be executed, the question is whether the unamended
Constitution contains a principle—of political morality or individual
rights—that could legitimately develop in a way incompatible with capital
punishment. Nothing within that document comes to mind.

What of the Bill of Rights, and the rest of the amendments to the Constitution? Leaving aside for the moment the Eighth Amendment, we see in

the Fifth Amendment's Grand Jury, Double Jeopardy, and Due Process Clauses some regulation of the death penalty. Even so, there is neither an explicit nor an undeniably implicit mandate or prohibition. These provisions contemplate use of the death penalty and further evince the ratifiers' belief in capital punishment's constitutionality. The same pattern, though muted, is evident in the Fourteenth Amendment: "due process" is a prerequisite to state "depriv[ation]" of "life," but in no event shall any state deny persons the "equal protection" of the laws. Again, though there is no command that the death penalty be imposed, there is certainly no clear-cut prohibition.

Some originalists would argue from all this information that capital punishment must be constitutional. Not according to the originalism I defend. One difficulty in others' originalisms is that constitutional meaning is sought in a snapshot of the world as it was, say, in 1790: if the Framers practiced something before, during, and after putting together a Constitution, then that practice must be constitutional. (This is often thought to be an unanswerable argument for the proposition that no originalist can defend *Brown v. Board of Education*, since the congressional proposers and state ratifiers of the Fourteenth Amendment were confirmed practitioners of segregated schooling.)[6] Justice Brennan depicted this approach pretty accurately in a 1985 speech: "In its most doctrinaire incarnation, this view demands that justices discern exactly what the Framers thought about the question under consideration and simply follow that intention in resolving the case before them."[7] Brennan had no difficulty dismantling this position.

The Constitution is not a collage of photographs of early national America. The Constitution is made up of principles whose practical import changes with time—as America changes—even as the principles remain the same. Many constitutional principles, historically recovered, are intrinsically dynamic. Others depend for their concrete application upon ever-changing contingent circumstances.

The First Amendment's Nonestablishment Clause is a good example of what I call a dynamic principle. Contrary to the prevailing judicial view, its plain meaning, historically recovered, is that the federal government may not deliberately discriminate among religious sects.[8] But what was sect-neutral in the almost wholly Christian America of 1790—like the Lord's Prayer—is sect-preferential in today's more diverse society. So certain public-school prayers which may have been constitutional in 1791 are not constitutional now.

There is no reason that anyone should hold a priori that capital punishment is immune to invalidation by a dynamic principle. The Eighth

Amendment contains what looks like a dynamic principle: *no* punishment which is "cruel and unusual"—the conjunctive—may be imposed. The Framers undoubtedly did not consider capital punishment "cruel and unusual." But that does not necessarily determine the question of constitutionality for us, for the defining characteristic of the class is not necessarily whatever the Framers counted as "cruel and unusual." Here we reach a very underdeveloped aspect of originalist approaches to constitutional interpretation: the legitimate development of doctrine. Let me therefore set up the problem in some detail.

I take it as axiomatic that no development of doctrine is legitimate if it contradicts the constitutional text. This axiom may create some apparent anomalies, but the alternative is to declare an unambiguous constitutional provision unconstitutional. The implications and ramifications of doing that are more troubling than the anomalies.

Some examples of anomalies engendered by my axiom: the Electoral College could not pass muster under the rule of one man, one vote; the limitation of the presidency to natural-born citizens is inconsistent with equal protection principles. To take the latter example, no convincing argument is available for the proposition that, say, a senator born abroad but brought here as an infant and since naturalized is unfit for the presidency.

Here is an example of illegitimate development, of the Court developing a principle to the point where "constitutional law" contradicts the text. For some time the Supreme Court has interpreted the Reasonableness Clause of the Fourth Amendment to include a "warrant preference": wherever possible, searches must be conducted pursuant to a warrant. Applied to so-called administrative searches—inspections pursuant to municipal housing codes, for example—we have now warrants on much less than probable cause, notwithstanding the express prohibition on them in the constitutional text.[9]

Now, some terms in our Constitution have no meaning whatsoever apart from that specified in the Constitution. The Electoral College is a good example: it is an entirely constructed device, invented by the Framers to solve a problem presented to them. Many constitutional terms, however, have (one might say) a double life: they have a theoretical or natural sense as well as a more restricted sense. And by "more restrictive" I here mean a limited, constructed usage. A good example of these possibilities is raised by the first sentence of Article II. Is the "executive" power vested there in the president just those powers thereafter specified, or does the president enjoy all the powers contained in a sound theory of "executive" authority? (To make matters interesting, Article I refers to the "legislative powers" specified "herein.") I do not know the answer to the question of "executive" power, because I do not know enough of the relevant history. But it requires no historical knowledge to assert and defend the view that whether the ratifiers intended the restricted (artificial, stipulated, conventional) or the unrestricted, natural sense intended is the decisive interpretive question.

I hold, characteristically as an originalist, that it is up to those who give life to an authoritative norm to show that they mean it to include all "natural," i.e., real, true, valid, examples of the kind. Put differently, the sense in which a term is used in the Constitution is stamped upon it by its originators, and that sense—itself a purely historical question—is authoritative, binding, and determinative, even two hundred years later.

It seems to me that "cruel and unusual" is not a term with an unrestricted meaning save perhaps for "disproportionate." Whether I am wrong about that is a philosophical question; and, in any event, I take up the question of whether death is a disproportionate punishment in the next section. I believe the historical evidence shows that the ratifiers of the Eighth Amendment intended the term to rule out certain sanguinary punishments then considered barbaric. The historical evidence suggests to me an artificial class of referents that could be, and was, so far as the framers were concerned, closed to new members.

Is Capital Punishment Inherently Disproportionate? Does It Violate the Criminal's Constitutional Right Not to Be Killed?

Let us focus initially on proportionality, which is, to start with, the aim of punishment. John Finnis provides this solid account of the aim of punishment:

> [T]he defining and essential (though not necessarily the exclusive) point of punishment is to restore an order of fairness which was disrupted by the criminal's criminal act. That order was a fairly (it is supposed) distributed set of advantages and disadvantages, the system of benefits and burdens of life in human community. The disruption consisted in a choice to take the advantage of following one's own preferences rather than restraining oneself to remain within that fair order (or, where the crime is one of negligence, an unwillingness to make the effort required to remain within the legally or morally required pattern of actions and restraints). Since freedom to follow one's preferences is in itself an important human good, the criminal's act of

self-preference was itself the gaining of an advantage over those who restrain themselves to remain within that legally and/or morally required pattern. So the essential point of punishment is to restore the disrupted order of fairness by depriving the criminal of his ill-gotten advantage. And since that advantage consisted at least primarily in (wrongful) freedom of choice and action, the appropriate means of restoring the order of fairness is by depriving the criminal of his freedom of choice and action.[10]

To better appreciate the aim or point of punishment, one should hold in the mind's eye a diachronic view of a society's interaction, a broad pattern of restraint, action, opportunity, established by custom, morality, and law. As Finnis suggests, public authority administers punishment so that, over a period of time, it is the case that no one is made a "sucker" by choosing to remain within the law's path for pursuing one's projects in cooperation with others.

The essential (but not exclusive) moral wrong in criminal behavior is the selfish and therefore unfair grab of more freedom than is one's due, more than others enjoy by virtue of their continued respect for the law. In suffering punishment, which as such need be no more than unwelcome deprivation of the liberty to do as one pleases, criminals lose this unjustified advantage over law-abiding citizens.

The important point is that punishment is not logically tied to any particular form or kind of unwelcome imposition. How malefactors should be punished—both as to kinds of deprivations imposed upon them and as to the extent of imposition of any one kind—is entirely a matter of specification, save that the scale of punishments should exhibit a rough coherence: larceny should be punished less severely than robbery (which is forcible larceny); robbery less severely than murder, etcetera. So, while we cannot say either that death is the only fit punishment for any type of crime, we cannot say that is necessarily disproportionate for at least the most serious crimes, and I think it is not. Thus far considered, capital punishment is not unconstitutional.

My view is that no one whosoever may intentionally kill another person. I have expressed the reasons for my view elsewhere.[11] Here I should like to add that I do not see how a death sentence may be carried out without violating that norm. That is not quite the no-brainer that the reader may imagine that it is. On a careful account of just what one intends—aims for, is going after—in one's activities, as opposed to what foreseeable effects one willingly accepts, it is at least not clear who precisely must intend death in the course of a capital proceeding. It might be that the hangman's act is specified by obedience to a valid order of some higher, competent authority (for example, a death warrant signed by the governor). But someone in this chain of action must be an executioner. I use "executioner" to identify whoever it is (governor, juror, judge, legislator) that, on the supposition that capital punishment is an intentional killing, actually intends the prisoner's death. To support capital punishment, then, is to support a system which requires someone to adopt the moral character of an intentional killer. For this reason, I hold that one must not support capital punishment.

Whether there is a constitutional norm prohibiting public authority from intentionally causing the death of any person is relatively easy to answer. The very extensive and long history of capital punishment, when no doubt about its nature as a species of homicide was expressed, shows as much. Indeed, the entire legal tradition seems to have accepted the liability of a certain class of criminals to state-imposed death. So, capital punishment is both immoral and constitutional.

Must I Work to Secure the Abolition of Capital Punishment?

That is, is there some unconditional positive obligation to work to eliminate this wrong? No, I *should* work to eliminate capital punishment, insofar as it is consistent with my other responsibilities, so, there is a conditional obligation to do so. Those other commitments, which include but are not limited to my other professional duties as well as my duties as husband, father, son, may be so great that I may rightly do very little to bring about the abolition of capital punishment. In no case, however, may I do anything which would constitute support for capital punishment. And it would constitute support for capital punishment to vote for a political candidate, say a governor, who was pro-death penalty *because* of his death penalty stance. My vote for a pro-death penalty governor, if it should ever come about, would have to be in spite of that stance, even if the candidate honestly believed in the permissibility of capital punishment and even if the death penalty actually reduces crime.

What options are available to someone, with views like mine, who becomes a judge in a death penalty state? The principles which shape the options are the same whether I am an appellate or a trial judge. Among those principles is *not* the principle that, in one common expression of it, an "unjust law is no law at all;" otherwise, there could never be a "tragic case," like capital punishment, where a valid law was unjust. Indeed, one can and should distinguish the law of a particular community from the requirements of natural justice in a way that is not suggested by the common expression. This limited positivism is a matter of separating what counts as law here or there from what is simply right, true, just; and such a distinction (woven throughout this paper) distinguishes what the law is from what anyone, all things considered, may—or must—do.

Included among the principles that shape the available options is the moral norm that prohibits lying, otherwise, the effect would be the same as if unjust laws were not laws: no tragic cases. For if lying were permissible for good or proportionate reasons, a judge holding my views probably could justify to himself some fabricated procedural defect in the capital proceeding, or a false assertion about the meaning of the death penalty statute or the Constitution, or both, to avoid imposing a death sentence. So, unjust laws are laws nonetheless though they do not bind in conscience the way just laws do, and if the judge's honest opinion about the relevant legal materials is that capital punishment is constitutionally permissible and authorized by statute in this jurisdiction, then that is it. The judge may not misstate the law to avoid the hard moral question, "May I give judgment in accord with the positive law?"

The alternatives to misstating the law are recusing oneself from the case or resigning one's office. Either move should be accompanied by a clear public statement of the reasons for doing so: the people who trusted one with judicial responsibility are entitled to be told why this exercise of the judicial office is one he cannot perform. The principles governing the decision whether to give judgment in accord with the positive law or to recuse or resign are these: one may never formally cooperate with capital punishment; one *may* materially cooperate where doing so is not unfair; and one must not give scandal—that is, one must not lead others into wrongdoing by an act, right in itself, which in its setting sets a bad example, *as if it were a wrongful act.* Note well: the norm against giving scandal excludes, without exception, acts which are *intended* to corrupt (by bad example) others. Because many acts which are obligatory (like testifying truthfully as a witness at trial) may (and often forseeably will) scandalize others, one must avoid giving scandal only insofar as it is consistent with one's other obligation. Given the paramount importance of the inviolability of human life, I would either resign my office or recuse myself from capital proceedings in order not to give scandal. My continuing in office would serve some good; but if recusal were not a practical possibility, permitting a replacement to discharge those responsibilities would make resignation the better choice.

But what is absolutely *required* of me? Cooperation of every sort must be distinguished from full involvement in wrongdoing. "Cooperation" is to be distinguished from acting in concert, as in, for example, a gang robbery, where each gang member performs acts which constitute parts of the act of robbery, and the group, in an important sense, is the actor. "Cooperation" refers to acts more or less distinct from others' wrongful acts but which are some way involved in and contributing to that wrongdoing. "Cooperation" is of two kinds. "Formal" cooperation is always wrong because there the co-operator agrees with, or intends, the wrongfulness of the primary actor's acts. "Material" cooperation, which is sometimes wrong, occurs when the cooperator's act facilitates another's wrongdoing in fact, but where the co-operator does not intend the wrong itself. The electrician who keeps the prison power plant operational facilitates electrocutions, but he surely need not intend them. He may well intend just to keep the lights on and the re-frigerators running, all to the benefit of the prisoners within, accepting (fairly, I think) the side effect of facilitating executions. The prison official charged with actually pulling the switch long enough to kill, cannot but in-tend to kill, even if, perhaps, he kills regretfully or reluctantly.

Can an appellate judge affirm a capital conviction without *formally* co-operating in the eventual execution? I believe so; the appellate judge could intend to consider the regularity of the proceeding below, comparing it to the positive law. But affirming the conviction facilitates execution—this is material cooperation. Is it unfair? I am not sure, but the need to avoid scan-dal is here, for me, decisive.

What of a trial judge? Can a trial court enter a judgment of conviction and impose a sentence of death without intending to kill, without intend-ing that the punishment of death actually be imposed? I think not. I think that no one who holds the views I do about capital punishment may preside over a capital trial.

NOTES

1. *N.Y. Times*, Dec. 6, 1996.

2. *Gregg v. Georgia*, 428 U.S. 153 (1976).

3. See Gerard V. Bradley, "The Bill of Rights and Originalism," 1992 *Ill. L. Rev.* 417 (1992).

4. See 1 Stat. 115 (1790).

5. See 1 Stat. 118 (1790).

6. See Earl Maltz, "*Brown v. Board of Education*," chapter 34 of this volume.

7. William Brennan, Jr., "The Constitution of the United States: Contemporary Ratification," 27 *S. Tex. L. Rev.* 433 (1986).

8. See Gerard V. Bradley, *Church-State Relationships in America* (New York: Greenwood Press, 1987).

9. See, e.g., *Camara v. Municipal Court*, 387 U.S. 523 (1967).

10. John Finnis, *Fundamentals of Ethics* 128 (Oxford: Clarendon Press, 1983).

11. See Gerard V. Bradley, "No Intentional Killing Whatsoever: The Case of Capital Punishment," in Robert George, ed., *Essays in Honor of Germain Grisez* (1997).

CHAPTER 26

Constitutional Tragedies:
The Dark Side of Judgment

Rebecca L. Brown

The anxiety that many feel over the role of an independent court in a democracy has eluded me. As a nation that values liberty, we should celebrate such an institution rather than apologize for it. After all, the Constitution does as much to limit the demos as to empower it, and neither goal should be understood as deviant. In short, judges should be allowed to judge.

Surely Felix Frankfurter had something like this view in mind when he called upon judges for "allegiance to nothing except the effort, amid tangled words and limited insights, to find the path through precedent, through policy, through history, to the best judgment that fallible creatures can reach in that most difficult of all tasks: the achievement of justice between man and man, between man and state, through reason called law."[1] Whatever it was that Frankfurter intended to inspire by these words, they artfully describe an approach to constitutional interpretation that entrusts the judge with the job of identifying the principles that inform our liberal democracy and applying them in the name of justice.

This is not the place to defend an approach to constitutional interpretation, but rather to confess its darkest secrets. We are asked to purge ourselves of the sin of hypocrisy by facing up to the worst consequence—tragedy, perhaps—that an honest application of our preferred approach could occasion. This was a thorny assignment for one who believes that a judge must place the avoidance of immoral or unjust results high on the scale of values to be served by constitutional decisions. So what types of tragedies could still arise? Is this interpretative approach really without a dark side?

Moved by the spirit of introspection and purgation that the project invites, I was forced to admit that there really are two kinds of bad things that could follow from this way of understanding the judge's role in interpreting the Constitution. I will refer to such situations as tragedies, although the question of whether they are, in fact, tragedies I lay to one side for the moment.

The first kind of tragedy ensues when judges exercise bad judgment; the other can arise even if judges exercise good judgment. In the first case, judges may do all the things one wishes them to do, but not well, not thoughtfully, not honestly, or not prudently. Any time a result depends on the peculiarly human capacity of judgment, the chance always looms that it will be used in a way that is not wise, just, correct, or good under whatever standard we use to evaluate the decisions. The fear of such errors is so acute in some theorists as to lead them to brand any system that allows for even the possibility of them as judicial tyranny.

An example of this type of tragedy is the infamous *Lochner v. New York*.[2] I cannot say that the process of reasoning that the Court used in that case was illegitimate or even necessarily misguided. Examined for what it actually says, the opinion does not reveal the excessive formalistic or mechanical analysis of which it has often been accused. In fact, by my metric the Court did quite well in several ways, which suggests that a result like *Lochner*—striking down on constitutional grounds an arguably progressive limitation on bakers' work hours—is a very real possibility.

What did the *Lochner* Court do right? First of all, it looked at the language of the Constitution, the Fourteenth Amendment's Due Process Clause. It examined the right articulated there, liberty, in light of its understanding of contemporary societal values—specifically, the right to make a contract to buy or sell labor. It concluded that this right had such an essential relation to the ideal of liberty in the eyes of the society of the time that such a right must be considered a facet of the liberty protected by the Constitution. It expressly reached an understanding of the constitutional precept of liberty as applicable to the current age.

This type of translation of basic constitutional principle to specific societal value is just what a court ought to do when interpreting the Constitution. This is the process by which the text of the Constitution is given life and breath through a long and eventful existence. It is important to remember that when *Lochner* was decided, the nation was still very much in the shadow of the Civil War, still under the influence of passionate antislavery rhetoric.[3] Especially under these circumstances, it seems absolutely appropriate that the Court should be particularly sensitive to the threats to liberty associated with restrictions on an individual's freedom to sell his or her own labor in an open marketplace. This is an example of allowing judgment to enliven an indeterminate text, using prevailing American commitments as informed by recent transformative national experience. This strength has a corresponding weakness, of course, in the possibility that the Court was a bit behind the times with this concern and had failed to appreciate that the society had moved on to a post–laissez-faire belief system.[4]

Another thing that the Court did right, in my view, was to begin its analysis with an assumption that legislation which is unreasonable (that is, without a reason) and impinges on liberty violates the Fourteenth Amendment.[5] Today, I suspect that many people would take issue with this assumption, the prevailing attitudes about popular preference tending to go in reverse: many believe that majoritarian institutions may make even unreasonable incursions into individual liberty *unless* the Court can specifically justify an interference with majority will. But since protection of rights is a dominant purpose of the Constitution, at least coequal with that of the maximization of popular preference, it is both legitimate and appropriate for courts to demand of majorities that they have some reason for interfering with the liberties of individuals. Although the standard applied in *Lochner* did not impose an especially onerous burden on the state, the requirement did have some bite: the state was required to show that the act had a "direct relation, as a means to an end, and the end itself must be appropriate and legitimate."[6] By asking the state to make such a showing, the Court was taking seriously its role as protector of individual liberty against arbitrary interference from the vicissitudes of the political process. This is an appropriate posture for a constitutional court to assume.

In examining the state's asserted purposes for its exercise of the police power, the Court found the proffered justifications unpersuasive. Notice that this was not a balancing of individual rights against state interests, such as that which characterizes much of the Court's later constitutional analysis. In *Lochner*, the Court examined state interests only for the purpose of deciding whether the act in question was, in fact, an exercise of the state's police power. The Court appeared to view the police power available to the states as a set of enumerated powers that entitles the state to legislate only in areas of morals, health, and safety. If a measure falls within none of those legitimate areas of power, then it is invalid under the Fourteenth Amendment, because, in such a situation, liberty is invariably impinged without appropriate reason.

The Court found that none of the justifications that would warrant state regulation of the baking industry—public health, workers' health, gross disparity in bargaining power between employee and employer, or safety concerns—supported the law in question. It could not, therefore, be considered an exercise of the police power at all. Without a valid invocation of the police power, the state had no basis for interfering with the individual's freedom to contract for labor. The case was an exercise in the examination of power, not of rights, and certainly not of "substantive due process." In considering the question of whether a state power exists—before ever considering whether an individual right restricts it—the Court was facing the right issue.

The Court expressed skepticism about the true purposes of the law at issue in *Lochner*. This skepticism has been proven justified by subsequent analysts, who have demonstrated that the law at issue in *Lochner,* despite its guise as a health regulation, was probably a rent-seeking, competition-reducing measure supported by labor unions and large bakeries for the purpose of driving small bakeries and their large immigrant workforce out of business.[7] One could take issue with the Court (as did Justice Harlan in dissent) on its interpretation of the facts before it, such as its conclusion that bargaining power between employees and employers was equal, or that bakeries did not pose substantial health risks to employees. Any one of these questions, if decided the other way, would have justified the law as coming within the domain of the state's legitimate police power. Yet reexamination in hindsight has suggested that if the law had survived, many bakers, especially immigrants whose language problems made other work hard to find, would have been left unemployed or struggling with significantly reduced wages because of the restriction on the number of hours they could work.[8]

When the Court found that the professed purposes of the law were unpersuasive and thus speculated that the law had been passed "from other motives," it did not articulate what it feared those motives might be. Yet the implication of its holding is that under the Fourteenth Amendment, state laws must have *some* articulable public purpose if they interfere with liberty. Society has subsequently become much more inured to the loss of public purpose in the legislative process and has acquiesced to some degree in the vision of legislation as a servant of private rather than public interests. But perhaps if the *Lochner* demand for some genuine public legislative purpose had survived, our acceptance of the public choice model might not have taken such firm hold. Ironically, by checking the political process as it did, the *Lochner* Court actually took a stand *in favor of* the integrity of majority rule, by implying that no uncorrupted representative government would freely pass a law that had no public purpose. (An ironically Elysian argument—ironic because of Ely's clear antipathy to *Lochner*.) The Court did not profess any role in overseeing the legislative process but did assume the task of testing its products against a low, but meaningful, standard of rationality. This, again, is an appropriate understanding of the Court's role in a democracy.

The *Lochner* majority exercised judgment, and did so with appropriate concern for the protection of individual liberty. Some theories of the Constitution purport to rule it out, to show that no right-thinking person could regard the case as anything other than a blunder of major proportion. My theory cannot. But to say that *Lochner* is logically compatible with a regime of judicial judgment is not to pay it tribute as a paragon of jurisprudence. An admitted danger of such a regime—perhaps actualized in *Lochner*—is that judges may misdescribe rights, endowing individuals with more insulation from public values than they should have and thereby frustrating progressive social change. Some critics have suggested that *Lochner* was not an exercise in genuine rights protection at all, but rather a covert effort to impose conservative social values on a progressive populace. The problem with an account of the judicial role that recognizes the necessity of independent judgment arises both in trying to tell the difference between the two and in preventing the dishonest approach even when it is recognizable. Thus, I must acknowledge that a decision like *Lochner*, even if one believes the more cynical account of the Court's motivation, is well within the possibilities of my approach to constitutional interpretation. If *Lochner* is a tragedy, then, it is one that I must own, as I must also own the possibility of more *Lochners*—cases in which individual rights may be too generously fortified against the powers of the state, and maybe even for nefarious reasons.

That is my first category of tragedies. But one might fairly ask whether this type of error, if error it be, can honestly be considered a tragedy in our system. All constitutional theorists must allow for the possibility of error. Errors could be made either by incorrectly protecting individuals from state interference or by incorrectly failing to protect them. Yet the latter type of error seems easily the more tragic. The institution of slavery,[9] state-enforced racial segregation,[10] incarceration of the innocent,[11] involuntary sterilization,[12] exclusion from the practice of a profession,[13] and criminalization of consensual intimacy[14]—all represent the ignominy of a free society's occasional failure to recognize a basic liberty. While they are not tragic in the classical sense, in that they are not brought about by a flaw in the victims themselves, they certainly raise serious concerns about the deep and irreparable cost of such error both to individuals and to the values of a society that tolerates their victimization. When an individual right is mistakenly denied, it is the *state* that wrongly is permitted to exploit the individual, and thus the harm is of the gravest nature and magnitude.

On the other hand, a judicial error the other way—by occasionally recognizing a right that should *not* be protected—does not have the same impact on state treatment of individuals. There are those who believe that failure of a polity to achieve its legislative goals because of constitutional impediment may be a grave wrong. Proponents of this view argue that if a court is not reined in, it may erroneously strike down legislation, such as the law in *Lochner*, that prevents *private* exploitation of individuals—and thus wreak tragedy.

This argument is at bottom a suggestion that when the courts err in the direction of individual rights, they may protect one individual right, but at the same time make it impossible for the state to protect another. Abortion is probably the best example of this. The assisted suicide issue, discussed by other authors in this volume, also raises similar concerns in that (the argument for tragedy goes) failure to prohibit that act actually threatens the individual with the harm of overreaching or manipulation by others.

These examples do show that erroneously recognizing a right can also work harm, and in that sense they are counterexamples to the claim that decisions like *Lochner*, even if mistakes, are not generally tragic ones. But the examples are significant, because they actually accept the premise that the most grievous societal wrong happens only when an individual is not adequately protected by law. Once one accepts that premise, it seems to me one must, as a logical matter, choose an approach to constitutional interpretation that tends to err on the side of greater, rather than less, protection for individuals—agreeing that there may be times when it is necessary to argue in specific cases about how to define the individual whose right is at stake (such as in the abortion case) or how best to protect the individual (such as in the assisted suicide case). But the latter disagreement should not detract from my fundamental point about tragedy: *Lochner* is not as bad as *Plessy*.

I acknowledged at the outset that there are two kinds of tragedy under a judgment-centered Constitution: tragedies born of bad judgment (of which *Lochner* is an example) and tragedies born of good judgment. The latter threatens not merely individuals but the nation. In a world of judgment-centered constitutional interpretation, judges would no longer deny, but would candidly declare, a commitment to protecting the values that they identify as inherent in our democratic structure and embodied in the text of the Constitution against incursions even by large popular majorities. They would also confess that the task of interpretation involves the imprecise, open-ended attempt to articulate the concepts of our forebears in meaningful contemporary terms. But this admits to some indeterminacy in the Constitution, and it is possible that the majorities whose will was examined, and in some cases thwarted, by this process would grow to perceive the incursions as arbitrary. Many thoughtful and persuasive scholars have speculated about the loss of prestige and power that a judiciary could suffer on this account. The judge who openly admits to making choices among possible interpretations presents the gravest danger of this type of decline.

I view this possibility as a tragedy in the true sense of the word, Greek-style. For it comes from a serious commitment to the idea that the Court is the repository of principle in our democracy and has the job of protecting the fundamental liberties that our civilization recognizes to be universal. Yet in that core commitment lie the seeds of the destruction of the Court's ability to do that very job. In the classical pattern, the fatal flaw of the hero, the judiciary, may be its own hubris in assuming the role of guardian of principle, which ultimately could cause its very strength to become its downfall.

Just as in the classical tragedies, the problem and the solution are intimately intertwined. The classical antidote for hubris is *sophrosyne,* or moderation. Similarly, the Court's role must be understood correctly, recognizing that judgment is not the same as unfettered discretion and that some indeterminacy is not the same as meaninglessness. An essential component of judgment is the recognition of appropriate constraint in the historical and sociological inquiry that is interpretation.

NOTES

1. Felix Frankfurter, "Chief Justices I Have Known," in Philip Elman, ed., *Of Law and Men* 138 (New York: Harcourt Brace, 1956).

2. 198 U.S. 45 (1905).

3. William E. Nelson, "The Impact of the Antislavery Movement upon Styles of Judicial Reasoning in Nineteenth Century America," 87 *Harv. L. Rev.* 513, 547–66 (1974).

4. Indeed, this seems to be one of the concerns animating Justice Holmes in his dissent. See *Lochner*, 198 U.S. (1905) at 75 (Holmes, J., dissenting).

5. See Richard A. Posner, *Law and Literature* 285 (Cambridge: Harvard University Press, 1988).

6. *Lochner*, 198 U.S. (1905) at 57.

7. Bernard H. Siegan, *Economic Liberties and the Constitution* (Chicago: University of Chicago Press, 113–25).

8. *Id.*

9. See *Dred Scott v. Sandford*, 60 U.S. (19 How.) 393 (1856).
10. See *Plessy v. Ferguson*, 163 U.S. 537 (1896).
11. See *Korematsu v. United States*, 323 U.S. 214 (1944).
12. See *Buck v. Bell*, 274 U.S. 200 (1927).
13. *Bradwell v. State*, 16 Wall. (83 U.S.) 130 (1873).
14. *Bowers v. Hardwick*, 478 U.S. 186 (1986).

CHAPTER 27

Good Constitutions
and Bad Choices

Christopher L. Eisgruber and Lawrence G. Sager

Compared to many, we are optimistic about the Constitution and generous in our view of the capacity and authority of constitutional judges. In our view, the Constitution aims at justice and sponsors an active partnership among framers, legislators, judges, and other political actors. For their part, judges are invited and required to exercise considerable independent moral judgment in the course of filling in the abstract liberty-bearing provisions of the Constitution with concrete legal doctrine. Judges bring valuable, institutionally secured abilities to this undertaking, and overall, we believe, our practice is reasonably well suited to the project of identifying and implementing the basic requirements of political justice. This is the justice-seeking view of our constitutional arrangements.[1]

But nothing in this Constitution-affirming, judge-crediting picture is inconsistent with the possibility of constitutional tragedy. On the contrary, we believe that constitutional tragedy is so prolific in prospect as to make the choice of the worst among the many possible bad outcomes academic and uninteresting. Even constitutional optimists must recognize that judges lack the authority to redress many species of catastrophically bad public choices.

Here is a sampler of some of the bad public choices a good constitutional judge would have to leave standing:

- The waging of a cruel, unjust, and madly self-destructive war
- The pursuit of an economic policy likely to leave us in a state of material and cultural devastation
- Planning choices likely to deplete the land, poison the water, and cripple our cities
- Regulatory structures and tax regimes that legalize and subsidize the production of addictive substances and stimulate gambling

- The maintenance of an economic structure that entrenches vast inequalities of wealth and well-being (though this last, as we shall see, is more complex than the foregoing examples from the vantage of our constitutional practice)

Heated constitutional controversy distorts perspective. To the partisans in contemporary debates over euthanasia, gay rights, the rights of criminal defendants, affirmative action, single-sex education, and educational vouchers, it might sometimes seem that judicial power is plenary. But the reach of the constitutional judiciary is finite indeed, and almost no one holds otherwise. Almost no one believes, for example, that the Supreme Court should control military policy, regulate banks, or preside over fiscal or developmental policy generally. And as our little list suggests, the prospect for tragedy in these precincts is boundless.

Our Constitution thus requires judges to permit much that is awful. This emphatically is not because of defects in the Constitution: even the best imaginable constitution would deny a conscientious judge the capacity to save us from tragedies of this sort. What places so much of our political life outside the reach of the constitutional judiciary (and would do likewise under the best of constitutions) is this: a justice-seeking constitution must include broad space for and commitment to the popular political process. It must do so not in opposition to or dominance of the enterprise of political justice, but as part of the requirements of political justice. Our constitutional tradition recognizes the need for such broad democratic space, and it would be much the worse if it did not.

Two important propositions follow. First, the domain of constitutional justice is more limited than the domain of full political justice, and certainly more limited than the domain of best outcomes generally. Some important questions—for example, the relative value of park land, art museums, and athletic facilities—depend in principle on the aggregate wishes of the members of our political community. Other important questions may not in principle depend upon popular will but may still be properly assigned to the popular political process in a well-functioning democracy. Many questions that may fall under the rubric of political justice, for example, are fact-specific, time-dependent, and/or legitimately subject to competing priorities. It is neither appropriate nor sound as a matter of social strategy to extend constitutional justice to matters such as these. To function effectively as the political conscience of a democratic people, a constitution's liberty-bearing precepts must be spare, durable, and relatively nonnegotiable.

Second, the domain of *judicially enforceable* constitutional justice is more limited still. Some matters of constitutional justice come wrapped with questions of strategy and responsibility that belong to the popular political process. Take the possibility that persons are constitutionally entitled to economic arrangements such that, if they work hard on their own behalf, they will be able to provide themselves and their families with minimally decent food, shelter, education, and medical care. We believe that something like this right to minimum welfare is contained within the Constitution. But what, for these purposes, is the precise content of "minimally decent"? Should benefits be provided in cash or in kind, by direct public subsidy or private commercial entities? What unit of government—local, state, or federal—should bear responsibility? And, crucially, how should the costs of meeting this obligation be distributed?

Judges regularly face hard choices, and well-established constitutional doctrines have compelled judges to undertake heroic measures, including the supervision of schools, prisons, and hospitals. The justice-seeking judge's job description makes such undertakings necessary under extreme circumstances. But direct judicial enforcement of the right to minimum welfare would be institutionally more ambitious by several orders of magnitude, and correspondingly less appropriate.

So there are some aspects of constitutional justice that will not be fully or directly enforceable by judges. For good reason, they will be judicially "underenforced." However, once the popular political process has put in place programs which respond to these underenforced demands of constitutional justice, the judiciary may well have a role in protecting access to these constitutional entitlements. Again, the right to minimum welfare provides an example. In *Plyler v. Doe*,[2] the Supreme Court considered a constitutional challenge to the exclusion of illegal immigrants from public schools in Texas. By the time *Plyler* was decided, the Court had retreated from the fundamental rights strand of its equal protection analysis, on the understandable ground that if government did not owe persons a particular benefit in the first place, it was hard to see how the distribution of that benefit among nonsuspect classes could transmute it into a constitutional entitlement. Under conventional equal protection doctrine, that left available only the possibility that the minor children of illegal immigrants were a suspect class. But that proposition was one to which the Court was firmly opposed. Bereft of doctrinal resources, the Court nevertheless pressed on and found the exclusion unconstitutional. The structural puzzle of *Plyler* evaporates if we recognize that there is a constitutional right to an adequate education: on this reading, the right is judicially unenforceable in the first instance, but it is within the competence of the constitutional judiciary to insist that every child have fair access once a system of public education has been put in place.

Our emphasis on democracy as the source of constitutional tragedy may suggest a bimodal constitutional view of political decision making, in which a carefully crafted judiciary is error-free, while a carelessly assembled popular political process lurches along at constant hazard. Surely not. Our Constitution, like any good constitution, shapes the institutions of popular politics with the goal of ensuring that capable people are put in office and that the persons in office use their talents well. But no such institutional strategy is foolproof, and disasters of the sort we have catalogued could well occur.

If we bracket the demands of democracy and imagine a constitution foolish enough to create the Ultra Court, a court with final authority over every political choice, the prospect of catastrophic error remains, of course. Presumably, this undemocratic constitution would structure the Ultra Court with considerable care, in order to encourage the selection of the best possible judges and to create a milieu of decision making conducive to sound judgment. But, of course, bad judges might be chosen, and even superb judges might on occasion make wretched decisions. The Ultra Court could unleash devastating consequences on the political community it oversees. (Strictly, this would not be a "constitutional tragedy," since it has the form of a judge reaching the wrong decision rather than reaching the right decision with awful results; but that turns out to be a quirk in the structure of the idea of constitutional tragedy, a quirk of little importance to the members of the relevant political community, who face disaster in either event.)

We can generalize: means, by their very nature, bear an instrumental relationship to ends (otherwise they would simply *be* ends). Accordingly, they can fail. Constitutions are means to the end of good government, and they can never escape the vulnerability of their instrumental status.[3] Plato had a formula for perfect government: recognize great people in their infancy; protect them from the corrupting influence of their less-than-perfect parents; and give these paragons absolute power when they reach maturity.[4] Plato, however, could found his perfect city only in words. Real political communities must content themselves with more practical and more fallible mechanisms of governance. Well-formed communities must be democratic, and democratic communities must leave substantial areas of choice to representative institutions. Neither the best of judges nor the best of constitutions can save a democratic people from their own folly or deeply flawed sense of justice.

NOTES

1. The justice-seeking view of our constitutional practice is explored in Lawrence G. Sager, "The Betrayal of Judgment," 65 *Fordham L. Rev.* 1545 (1997); Lawrence G. Sager, "Justice in Plain Clothes: Reflections on the Thinness of Constitutional Law," 88 *Nw. L. Rev.* 410, 415 (1993); Lawrence G. Sager, "The Incorrigible Constitution," 65 *N.Y.U. L. Rev.* 893 (1990).

2. 457 U.S. 202 (1982).

3. For an illuminating meditation on this theme, see Sotirios A. Barber, *On What the Constitution Means* 40–50 and passim (Baltimore: Johns Hopkins University Press, 1984).

4. Plato, *The Republic*, ed. Allan Bloom (New York: Basic Books, 1968).

CHAPTER 28

Jocasta Undone

Constitutional Courts in the Midst of
Life and Death

Marie A. Failinger

For American constitutional judges, tragedy does not often present itself as Greek. Neither the ancient tragedy of the city-state felled by the gods[1] nor its more modern form, the Oedipal character who inexorably follows his tragic flaw toward doom for his people, is likely to be the stuff of judicial review. Of course, judicial commentators have accused various justices or benches of the Supreme Court of Oedipal hubris, of moving without humility to destroy the constitutional Progenitor of the Court, the people's will, most notably in *Dred Scott*[2] or *Roe v. Wade*.[3]

Yet, even if one might rightly claim that federal judges display hubris in proceeding as if they can single-handedly resolve a constitutional crisis writ large, these cases must fairly be described as non-Oedipal. The tragic form in constitutional dramas is quite different: not one but many choruses of the interested pour out a tragedy generated by a morally divided polity—in *Dred Scott* and *Roe*, divided on the moral definition of human being—each side urging that its reading of the American narrative prevail, while the disinterested cringe, hoping in vain that the tragic consequence will be averted. In many of our constitutional crises, the Oedipal actor does not take center stage. Rather, the courts are asked to rescue the protagonist, the American polity, from its own tragic flaw, one it lacks common ground to resolve. And when they try, we spend our time censuring their rescue attempts, rather than remembering who it was that slew Oedipus's father to begin with.

One form of constitutional tragedy increasingly confronting the federal courts poses the most difficult case in the debate over constitutional interpretation: the case in which a judge cannot escape doing momentous harm to individuals, no matter how he or she rules. (Such a tragedy is daily judicial fare for the nonfederal bench; as just one example, any decision in a contested custody case is virtually certain to cause some harm to the child's security and relationships.) Federal courts also often decide similar cases,[4] where the constitutional conflict is not between the individual and the state treasury or community peace but between the rights or well-being of some individuals against the rights or well-being of others.

If the harms on both sides are sufficiently great,[5] I would argue, such a conflict is more truly tragic than the Coverian moral-formal dilemma of judges, whether they are deciding whether to return fugitive slaves,[6] uphold abortion rights,[7] or resist a death sentence.[8] As difficult as moral-formal struggle must be, the judge can resolve the dilemma—which is, after all, within *his* conscience[9]—by the simple, if personally sacrificial, act of resignation.[10] Resignation does not remove the need for judgment, nor absolve the first judge fully from the consequences of a subsequent decision even in the proximate-cause sense; but it does lessen the risk of a continuing moral-formal crisis, since the successor judge's moral views are likely to differ from the first judge's.

While some of these "rights versus rights" tragic conflicts are occasioned by "first-order" decisions to create scarcities in crucial goods such as medical care,[11] two truly tragic, nonscarcity dilemmas come to mind: assisted suicide[12] and capital punishment.[13] Both are truly tragic, because the judge must decide between commensurably bad outcomes. In capital punishment challenges, he decides between death and death—between the certain death of the convict and the possible deaths of innocents who may be killed in the absence of a capital punishment regime that deters other murderers. In assisted suicide pleas, she decides between death and suffering so immense, which radiates so beyond the sturdy walls of the human shell,[14] that even a physician who cannot imagine its whole destructive fury is willing to lay aside his first ethical principle to acknowledge that its horror is equivalent to the death of a living, spirited human person. These are important dilemmas precisely because they partially avoid the commensurability debates of other tragic conflicts, such as whether violation of a woman's autonomy and bodily integrity or even health is comparable to the destruction of a human fetus.[15]

Each of these tragic choices depends upon the acceptance of a causal proposition: If we *do* permit A to kill himself with a physician's help, then B (who is elderly), C (a mentally impaired person), and D (a physically deformed/child) will die at the hands of physicians against their will (or without informed choice). If we *do not* kill A (a murderer), then B, C, and D will die at the hands of other murderers, who would have been deterred from their brutality had A been put to death.[16] Perhaps the easiest way to avert the tragedy for a judge is to reject the causal analysis: she could assume that physicians will not kill profoundly disabled patients, and that killers will not be deterred by the execution of others.[17] Of course, this is precisely when the argument against judicial intervention becomes complicated. On the one hand, judges are doing what judges do every day, determining the existence of a factual causal relationship (A's drunken driving caused B's paralysis). On the other, in this constitutional setting, they are doing precisely the sort of investigation and prediction which legislatures are called upon to do in passing social legislation.[18] Indeed, the judgment that a court can *know* that act X does not cause result Y smacks more of hubris than substitution of values, precisely because even most courts acknowledge that they cannot "prove" values (or even get close), they can only affirm them.[19] Since the assertion of causation, especially the sort of global causation that these propositions entail, conveys the sense that it is provably "correct," and yet is immensely difficult to "prove," it might better rest with those who have the most access to the largest range of information, the legislative and executive branches.

A second option we might pursue is to distinguish between active and passive intervention, as in the assisted suicide cases, suggesting that action, such as injecting poison into the patient, is morally complicitous, but inaction, such as failing to resuscitate, is morally neutral. In the assisted suicide cases, this argument says that the actor causes the death if he actively intervenes, but nature or God causes the death if he passively stands by. But the active-passive distinction does not instruct the judge in our constitutional dilemmas. In the conservative view, the "passive" approach is for the court to let the judgment of the legislature or executive stand, to withdraw from deciding whether the state may deny death to the would-be suicide;[20] or to refuse to intervene in the executive's killing of the capital murderer. In this view of judicial nonintervention, the judge refuses to overrule the state's ban on physician-assisted suicide, so that the incapacitated sufferer must await his natural death; similarly, the judge watches impassively as the state moves toward poisoning or electrocuting one of its citizens.

Yet in these cases where the state must take life or permit it to be taken— that is, cannot avoid that life is being taken—the "passive" response under a traditional due process approach is to conceive of the state as a whole as the actor, rather than just the judge. If the state as a whole is to be truly passive in choosing which lives will be taken, a court would have to stop any state intervention at all in this morally problematical act—morally problematical precisely because we cannot predict "causation" with any certainty, no matter who we are. In this traditionally liberal understanding of state passivity, the murderer will not be killed, and the terminally ill patient will be able to enlist a physician to help him die. Even considering the standard exception to the liberal nonintervention paradigm—the state can prevent A from harming B—the state may not intervene: in either case, there is nothing approaching certainty that we can avoid any harm to C (a future target for murder or euthanasia) by the actions we take (killing murderer A) or prevent (refusing patient A's request for assisted suicide). The level of certainty that the state's action can prevent future deaths is not even close to the likely prevention we effect when police arrest an attempting murderer, one justification for punishing attempts.

More importantly, we should reject the active-passive distinction in such constitutional cases, because it creates precisely the tragic illusion of which both Oedipus and the Calabresian formula[21] warn us. If the court can convince itself that it *did nothing*, or that it helped the state to do nothing, it can preserve the illusion that a "morally debasing outcome" is averted in the short run; but ultimately, the value tensions which provoked the court case will surface, perhaps in a much more destructive way.[22] Calabresi and Bobbitt, borrowing from the classical Greek definition of tragedy, warn of the "prospect of insuperable moral difficulty, a nightmare of justice in which the assertion of any right involves a further wrong, in which fate is set against fate in an intolerable necessary sequence of violence."[23] *Dred Scott* is such a tragedy of not-doing, both in the sense that it pretends to judicial passivity before a constitutional text, and in the sense that it withdraws all government intervention before a privately created property arrangement.

Following the causal approach, a judge might argue that, given the constitutional value placed on life and liberty, he should put his money on what he knows will certainly happen and avoid the inexorably horrible outcome. If as a judge, I pass on a capital punishment appeal, an individual is certain to be put to death; if I save him, some future victim *might* die, but we cannot know that for certain. Similarly, in the assisted suicide case, if I let the state have its way, a human being will bear suffering that cannot even name itself for weeks, perhaps months or years; if I acknowledge a liberty right, some physicians *may* kill innocent, unwilling patients in the future, but I do not know that for sure. This is also a risk assessment, except that the risk of harm if the judge refuses the individual is much more certain than if the judge acts to help him. However, at least in a utilitarian formulation, we should want to measure not just the amount of risk but the potential harm:

in the capital case, for instance, we have the nearly certain risk (allowing for pardons) that one person will die against the much less probable risk that many, many people will die if he is not executed.

Yet the person who wishes to die and the person who has killed another are staring the judge in the face, one human being pleading for mercy from another human being, while the potential victims of the potential murderers and doctors are not directly confronting the judge in their humanity. The confrontation of the Other cannot be dispositive in judicial decisions, or most murderers would have to receive mercy because their victims are not in front of the court to appeal to their own suffering and loss of life. But in a case of causal uncertainty, the appeal of the person standing before the court, in his frailty and his magnificence, must count for something. If not, why do we bother with a court system which demands that the decision maker confront those human beings contending in the case at all?

A fourth judicial option in the constitutional tragedy is to place responsibility with the person whose action is necessary to cause the death that is the tragedy. In this view, the judge cannot take responsibility for what everyone else might do in the future—indeed, the judge might insist that even the legislature cannot take such responsibility in truly critical cases, such as life-and-death decisions. Rather, we must put the responsibility where it most clearly lies, on the stranger or doctor who kills, and define the state's duty as serious watchfulness for those circumstances where the probability of death is so certain that we feel justified in intervening to prevent it, as in the case of attempted murder or perhaps child abuse.

Such a solution, of course, carries the most risk, because it depends on individuals accepting the moral demands placed upon them by the community. Perhaps more frightening in a liberal state, it demands that the community maintain a most nonliberal watchfulness over those who are in a position to create tragedy, such as health care providers and potentially violent persons.

Strangely enough, in the cases of both assisted suicide and capital punishment, the courts have resisted the option of locating the responsibility in the person whose act is most proximate to the tragic consequence.[24] One does not know whether to attribute this resistance to the fact that constitutional judges are ever more risk-averse as the potential for physical and emotional violence escalates in a society at once more diverse and tied together with exceedingly narrow threads of a moral bond. Or perhaps one should speak of governmental hubris—the assumption that legislators or even judges can indeed prevent a tragedy (the killing of innocents) whose making is quite outside their hands, a tragedy that depends upon many people (doctors, murderers, others) rejecting the specific moral expectations of their community. Or maybe this resistance to locating responsibility with the true actor can be attributed to the judges' accurate sense that there really are no community moral expectations in the United States anymore, and that Americans are resorting to self-interest, passion, or idiosyncratic moralities to guide their lives.

If, however, the responsibility were relocated to the actor, the court would recognize that by intervening in a capital case, it can prevent a death, while only the future killer has the immediate power to prevent the death of his victim. Similarly, in the case of assisted suicide, the court can by its permission end the suffering of a dying patient, but the state cannot prevent a later doctor from killing, or assisting the death of, a deformed, mentally disabled, or incompetent person, a reality which is all too clear from the prevalence of illegal physician-assisted suicides noted in the *Compassion in Dying* case.[25]

In cases involving truly tragic consequences, where life is pitted against life or an equally critical value, the courts and their coequal branches must ask two important questions. Can any of our governmental institutions— courts, legislatures, executive entities—actually prevent the future tragedies posed in the assisted suicide or capital punishment cases? Or are they indeed out of their hands except for those who come before them, day by day? And if they cannot prevent them, and therefore must measure case by case, how can we measure the value of two constitutional goods against each other when two claimants ask for protection or care, as two failing patients each ask the doctor for a dead man's heart? Do we really care about death (and life) as an ultimate value, as we have increasingly suggested that we do in our society, or is life (or death) a value which we find interchangeable with many other values, including liberty, property, even checks and balances?

On such incommensurables, interpretivist approaches to the Constitution are unlikely to help. First of all, it would be difficult to unpack what Madison and his colleagues might have believed about human consciousness of death and suffering. The social understanding of what individual human life, death, and suffering mean and cost, in particular, has undergone profound transformation in modernity. About these issues, moderns share more with each other—whether they are conservative or liberal, traditionalist or progressive—than with their forebears. Nor will a structuralist approach be dispositive. Legislative deference is an unlikely solution, for legislatures do not talk in meaningful ways about the nature of suffering or the definition and value of human life. Judges, unfortunately, are no better, as the assisted suicide and capital punishment cases show. None of them takes up the question of what it means to us as a community for an individual person to live or to die.

Such cases—cases involving tragic, terrible consequences that we are not yet competent as a society to define and value through the institutions of law—may indeed be beyond law. Not just beyond the judiciary, but beyond law itself. There simply may be daily tragic events to which no legal artifact, no statute, no regulation, no judicial opinion, engaging or withdrawing from the fray, can possibly contribute anything useful in our present circumstances. And yet there may also be dilemmas so momentous for the human community that no institution claiming moral authority or acting as a critical social bond—which surely law does in America—can possibly turn a blind eye to them.

Embedded in these constitutional cases about life and death is the Oedipal tragedy of our limited Constitution, which is rather Jocasta's tragedy. Jocasta never intended that the son she bore should become her husband, yet she unwittingly married him because her people needed a king. Similarly, what we have created law *not* to be is what it *must* be for us to be Americans—a people free from a social tradition. We must have our Oedipus, our moral order, in that law borne not to be a moral order, and we must have no other for our king. And yet, as constitutional courts are surely bound to unmask and lament, in demanding that law assume in our culture the moral kingship it was not birthed to be, we are undone.

NOTES

1. In Aeschylean tragedy, for example, the previously innocent protagonist is faced, because of a Flaw in the Universe, with a fatal choice for his people, or he is tricked, tempted or driven by the gods into a situation which, sometimes fueled by his own hubris, cannot be resolved without tragedy. H.D.F. Kitto, *Greek Tragedy* 10, 20, 31–32 (New York: Doubleday, 1939); Albin Lesky, *Greek Tragedy* 62–63 (London: E. Benn, 1979).

2. See, e.g., James U. Blacksher, "Dred Scott's Unwon Freedom: The Redistricting Cases as Badges of Slavery," 39 *Howard L.J.* 733, 688 (1996).

3. See, e.g., William W. Van Alstyne, "Closing the Circle of Constitutional Review from *Griswold v. Connecticut* to *Roe v. Wade*: An Outline of a Decision Merely Overruling *Roe*," 1989 *Duke L.J.* 1677, 1681; Michael Stokes Paulsen, "Accusing Jus-

tice: Some Variations on the Themes of Robert M. Cover's *Justice Accused,*" 7 *J. Law & Relig.* 33, 36 (1989).

4. Of course, many historically important constitutional cases, such as the fugitive slave cases, might be so characterized. The fugitive slave cases can be reframed as rights-versus-rights conflicts: if the slave remains free, the owner suffers a severe economic loss; if the slave is returned, he suffers a host of harms, only beginning with his loss of liberty. We might distinguish these harms using retributive theory: as the person at fault in occasioning the dilemma (by buying another person), the slaveowner should suffer harm. Or we might distinguish them on commensurability grounds: the economic loss of one slave is hardly tragic, as it is simply not tantamount to the degradation of slavery.

5. Not all "rights versus rights" conflicts are immediately tragic. For example, it is difficult to argue that the Post Office ban on Kokinda's solicitation so profoundly harmed him, or prevented harm to those offended by him, as to be termed "tragic." See *United States v. Kokinda*, 497 U.S. 720 (1990).

6. See, e.g., Robert Cover, *Justice Accused: Antislavery and the Judicial Process* 197–259 (New Haven: Yale University Press, 1975).

7. See Paulsen, "Accused Justice," 74–81.

8. See, e.g., Ori Lev, "Personal Morality and Judicial Decision-Making in the Death Penalty Context," 11 *J. Law & Relig.* 637, 639–48 (1994–95).

9. The moral-formal dilemma has usually been posed as one that pits the demand of an objective, nonpersonal morality against those of an objective, nonmalleable law. It seems more precise to understand the dilemma as a personal (or group) interpretation of morality, even if that interpretation is conscientious and morally correct, against a positivist interpretation of law. If the moral position were truly objective in the sense of being empirically provable or representing a popular consensus, the initial dilemma would be unlikely to arise, since the law would reflect something of the opposing moral views, or a good judge would be more reluctant to find a conflict and would read the moral and formal demands as complementary. Even if the dilemma were cast as a choice between the clear demands of morality and those of positive law, however, a subsequent judge—Holmes and Rehnquist come to mind—might be clear about the relative priority of positive over moral law (or even moral over positive law) and so not find himself in such a quandary.

10. Cover himself called for judicial resignation in an earlier work on judicial responses to draft resister prosecutions. Robert M. Cover, "Atrocious Judges: Lives of Judges Infamous as Tools of Tyrants and Instruments of Oppression," 68 *Colum. L. Rev.* 1003, 1005 (1968)

11. Guido Calabresi and Phillip Bobbitt, *Tragic Choices* 20, 153–54 (New York: Norton, 1978). For instance, a first-order decision to ration health care forces a decision maker to trade off extraordinary treatment to save one patient against access to ordinary care to others. The first-order choices that occasion these dilemmas are truly Oedipal, created by the hubris of the American polity about its ability to man-

age the created world and its resources in a morally beneficial fashion and its blindness to the role of its own self-interest in shaping such programs.

12. See, e.g., *Compassion in Dying v. State of Washington*, 79 F.3d 790 (9th Cir. 1996) (en banc) (holding that assisted suicide prohibition for terminally ill patients violates the Due Process Clause), *reversed sub nom. Washington v. Glucksberg*, 117 S.Ct. (June 26, 1997) (holding no due process violation); *Quill v. Vacco*, 80 F.3d 716 (2d Cir. 1996) (holding that law prohibiting assisted suicide for terminally ill patients violates the Equal Protection Clause), *reversed*, 117 S. Ct. (June 26, 1997) (holding no equal protection violation).

13. See, e.g., *Gregg v. Georgia*, 428 U.S. 153 (1976).

14. For an eloquent description of the inexpressibility of pain and the inability of any other to share a person's pain, see Elaine Scarry, *The Body in Pain: The Making and Unmaking of the World* 3–19 (New York: Oxford University Press, 1985).

15. The abortion debates would more closely approximate these choices in two cases: if the proposed federal ban on partial-birth abortions does not exclude cases where the mother's life is at stake, and if abortion funding is not available at all for women whose pregnancies seriously imperil their lives or health. See, e.g., *Harris v. McRae*, 448 U.S. 297 (1980) (holding that the Hyde Amendment, which prohibits abortions in health-threatening but not life-threatening circumstances, does not violate the Due Process Clause). Of course, we might properly have such a debate about the relative value of death and unbearable suffering in our constitutional community, a debate which I believe would bear significant fruit in terms of the type of tragedy that Jack Balkin identifies in "The Meaning of Constitutional Tragedy," chapter 24 of this volume.

16. The theory of general deterrence poses the more inescapable case, since one can always achieve specific deterrence of A through incarceration, although specific deterrence poses a similar commensurability problem: a court must decide whether lifelong incarceration is worse than death. However, a retributive move can defeat the tragedy: even if incarceration is equal to or worse than death, the killer who is at fault should suffer the harm rather than the innocent victim-to-be.

17. Similarly, in a death case, the judge could accept a variety of retributive arguments, e.g., that the murderer is receiving what he is entitled to as a moral person. See, e.g., Jeffrie Murphy, *Retribution, Justice and Therapy* 82–90 (Boston: D. Reidel Publishing, 1979).

18. See, e.g., *Minnesota v. Clover Leaf Creamery Co.*, 449 U.S. 459 (1981)(although the Minnesota legislature may have made the factually incorrect determination that paperboard milk cartons are more environmentally damaging than plastic, they are constitutionally entitled to do so).

19. Similarly, this causal guestimating smacks more of hubris than substitution of the facts of a case (A is lying rather than B), because there are ways to test the veracity of claims about what someone did in the past or present, even though we may ultimately make a mistake.

I do not mean to import into this discussion the modern dichotomy between facts and values, which suggests that values are mere preferences, personal tastes which cannot be "known" because they are not empirically demonstrable, while facts can be certainly known through scientific methodology, and therefore are a more reliable basis on which to make public decisions. The difference, I suggest, is comparatively slight.

20. While many of those requesting assisted suicide can choose other means to die, they are no more legal. More importantly, some potential suicides argue that legalizing assistance will give them the opportunity to live as long as they can, while criminalizing assistance forces them to choose death before they are ready, since they must kill themselves while they are still physically able to. *Compassion in Dying,* 79 F.3d at 834–35.

21. Calabresi and Bobbitt, *Tragic Choices* 20–25.

22. *Id.* at 18–22.

23. *Id.* at 18, quoting William Arrowsmith, "The Criticism of Greek Tragedy," in Robert W. Corrigan, ed., *Tragedy: Vision and Form* 332 (San Francisco: Chandler Publishing, 1965).

24. Indeed, constitutional courts tend to resist this option perhaps more than other courts. For example, the constitutional doctrines of hate speech and incitement assigns joint criminal responsibility for violence to the person who speaks and to the one who actually commits the violence. One version of the obscenity doctrine locates responsibility for violence against women in the filmmaker or the book author, though a viewer or reader would be the potential violator.

25. *Compassion in Dying,* 79 F.3d at 811.

CHAPTER 29

Constitutional Tragedy in Dying:
Or Whose Tragedy Is It, Anyway?

James E. Fleming

[W]e are ourselves authors of a tragedy, and that the finest and best
we know how to make. [O]ur whole polity has been constructed as
a dramatization of a noble and perfect life; that is what we hold to
be in truth the most real of tragedies.
—Plato, *Laws*

What is a constitutional tragedy? How does it differ from or relate to an
imperfection in the constitutional document (for example, the imperfect
provision for affirmative liberties, which has led to decisions like *Dandridge
v. Williams, San Antonio v. Rodriguez, Harris v. McRae,* and *DeShaney v. Winnebago County*)?[1] A failure of the constitutional order (for example, the failure to generate the civic virtue necessary for citizens to affirm basic liberties, which might lead to a breakdown of the wall of separation between
church and state)?[2] A decision in constitutional law that has horrible consequences for the lives of particular citizens or groups and for the way of life
of the polity (for example, *Dred Scott v. Sandford, Plessy v. Ferguson,* and *Korematsu v. United States*)?[3] A decision that has disastrous consequences for
interpretive method and for the development of doctrine in important
areas (for example, *Slaughterhouse Cases* and *Bowers v. Hardwick*)?[4] A decision that makes a travesty of our constitutional order (for example, *Buckley
v. Valeo*, which reduces our political system from a fair scheme of equal participation to a veritable electoral marketplace of ideas)?[5] Finally, how does a
constitutional tragedy differ from or relate to a constitutional stupidity (for
example, the fact that the entire Bill of Rights did not apply to the states
from the beginning)?

162

However we answer these questions, it seems clear that we have no dearth of constitutional misfortunes, and I fear that we also have no adequate account of them.[6] Without purporting to answer these questions, I shall conceive constitutional tragedy in three senses. First, it would be tragic if the Constitution were to allow or require terrible evil or grave injustice, and if fidelity to the Constitution were to mandate complicity in such evil or injustice. The most glaring example would be the original Constitution's protection of slavery, and the complicity exacted from judges and other officials who enforced the fugitive slave laws.[7] Second, it would be tragic if the Constitution were wrongly interpreted to sanction a terrible evil or grave injustice, when in fact the Constitution, rightly interpreted, allows or requires a good outcome or "happy ending."[8] For example, we might speak of *Plessy v. Ferguson* and *Bowers v. Hardwick* as constitutional tragedies in this sense. Finally, some cases present "tragic issues" or necessitate "tragic choices." Justice Frankfurter characterized the first flag-salute case as "an illustration of what the Greeks thousands of years ago recognized as a tragic issue, namely, the clash of rights, not the clash of wrongs," and he conceived the Supreme Court's responsibility as being "to reconcile two rights in order to prevent either from destroying the other."[9]

Applying these three definitions, I shall argue that it was a constitutional tragedy for the Supreme Court to hold that the Constitution does not protect the right to die, including the right of terminally ill persons to physician-assisted suicide,[10] thereby overruling the Ninth Circuit decision in *Compassion in Dying v. Washington*[11] (to say nothing of the Second Circuit decision in *Quill v. Vacco*.)[12] First, such a holding entails that the Constitution sanctions a grievous wrong, a horrible form of tyranny: allowing the state to impose upon some citizens, against the grain of their conscientious, considered convictions about dying with dignity, what they regard as a ruinous, tragic ending of their lives.[13] Second, such a decision represents an awful interpretive tragedy, for the Constitution, rightly interpreted, does not permit this dreadful evil but to the contrary requires the "happy ending" of allowing citizens to author their own tragic endings. Finally, the question of whether the Constitution protects the right to die evidently presents a tragic issue as Frankfurter conceived it, for it involves a clash between two fundamental values: persons' right to autonomy in making certain important decisions for themselves and the state's authority to promote respect for the sanctity of life. The character of our polity will be defined by how we reconcile or destroy those values. Both proponents and opponents of protecting the right to die believe that it would be a tragedy if the other side were to prevail. Thus, no matter which way the Court had resolved this clash, its decision would be bewailed as a tragedy. This fact confirms that the right to die is the stuff of which constitutional tragedy is made. In this essay, I shall focus on the first two senses of constitutional tragedy.

Tragedy in Dying

It was tragic for the Supreme Court to hold that the Constitution does not protect the right to die, including the right of terminally ill persons to physician-assisted suicide. First, the state's proscription of physician-assisted suicide is tantamount to conscription of terminally ill persons into involuntary servitude.[14] The state commandeers those persons' bodies, lives, and deaths into service in fostering its conception of how to honor the sanctity of life. It exposes its dangerous presupposition that ultimately persons do not own themselves but are "mere creatures of the state" or of God.[15] What is more, the state exacts such service in the face of those persons' conscientious, considered convictions about how to lead their own lives and deaths, and indeed about how to respect the sanctity of life.[16] Thus, the state attempts to use terminally ill persons' bodies, lives, and deaths as pulpits for preaching a message or viewpoint about sanctity which they themselves conscientiously reject.

In effect, the state tries to impose a sentence of life imprisonment, or imprisonment in life, upon terminally ill persons who wish to end their own lives. To be sure, the state seeks to justify this evil, requiring this undignified sacrifice and unspeakable suffering, in the name of a supreme good or ultimate value, promoting respect for the sanctity of life. That effort does not redeem the evil, but to the contrary makes it more terrible and tyrannical. It shows that the state's asserted power to promote respect for the sanctity of life by prohibiting physician-assisted suicide is "an injury got up as a gift," an intolerable evil disguised and imposed as a supreme good.[17]

Second, the state's prohibition of physician-assisted suicide usurps citizens' power to make certain important decisions for themselves. Elsewhere, I have argued that the right to die is among the basic liberties that are essential to deliberative autonomy (as distinguished from deliberative democracy): such rights reserve to persons the power to deliberate about and decide how to live their own lives, with respect to certain matters unusually important for such self-government, over a complete life, from cradle to grave.[18] Put another way, these basic liberties are significant preconditions for persons' development and exercise of deliberative autonomy in making certain fundamental decisions affecting their destiny, identity, or way of life, and they span a complete lifetime. Decisions concerning the timing and manner of a person's death are among the most significant decisions for deliberative autonomy that a person may make in a lifetime. If the Constitution does not reserve such decisions to persons, it betrays its "promise" of a "rational continuum" of liberty.[19] A Constitution that does not protect the right to die, paradoxically, is not worth living under and not worth dying for.

These claims about conscription and usurpation suggest that the Constitution, now interpreted not to protect the right to die, is woefully imperfect from the standpoint of a vigorous conception of deliberative autonomy. Does this amount to a constitutional tragedy? It is tragic because it entails that the Constitution sanctions a terrible evil, a horrible form of tyranny: allowing the state to impose upon some citizens, against the grain of their conscientious, considered convictions about dying with dignity, what they regard as a ruinous, tragic ending of their lives. The Constitution permits the state to do this at the crucial moment when terminally ill persons are seeking to author the final chapters of their own personal tragedies.

The noble protagonists in this constitutional tragedy are citizens who have the courage to use their own deliberative reason and to take responsibility for their own lives and for their own judgments about how to respect the sanctity of life. The tragic flaw of these protagonists—the characteristic that is both their greatness and their downfall—is their autonomy, their daring to live autonomously rather than as mere creatures of the state or of God. They seek to exercise their deliberative autonomy, to give their tragedies a good, dignified, and noble ending, to write their own final chapters in character with, or so as to maintain integrity with, their conceptions of a good life—to die, as to live, with dignity.[20] The state, however, wishes to usurp their authorship of their own tragedies, to conscript them as mere players in its own tragedy about the sanctity of life. Thus, the state refuses to "[v]ex not [their] ghost[s]" as they lie terminally ill, at death's door.[21] Instead, it prolongs their pain and exacerbates their anguish, in effect maintaining wards of would-be cadavers as monuments to its view of the sanctity of life.

Most problematically, the state asserts, at terminally ill persons' ultimate moments of self-authorship, that they are not in fact the authors of their own lives and tragedies. The state proclaims that it is the author of their lives, at least of their tragedies. It basically says to them what the Athenian Stranger (on behalf of the state) says to the tragedians in Plato's *Laws*: "[W]e are ourselves authors of a tragedy, and that the finest and best we know how to make. [O]ur whole polity has been constructed as a dramatization of a noble and perfect life; that is what we hold to be in truth the most real of tragedies."[22] But in our constitutional democracy, citizens are not mere creatures of the state or of God, nor are we mere players in the state's tragedy, its "dramatization of a noble and perfect life." Rather, we citizens are the authors of our own tragedies, "the finest and best we know how to make." The state is not authorized to act as the master tragedian.[23] We must ask: "Whose tragedy is it, anyway?"[24] In our constitutional democracy, the answer is: "It is each citizen's, not the state's."

Interpretive Tragedies with Bad Endings

Furthermore, a holding by the Supreme Court that the Constitution does not protect the right to die represents an awful interpretive tragedy, for the Constitution, rightly interpreted, does not permit this dreadful evil but, to the contrary, requires the "happy ending" of allowing citizens to author their own tragic endings. Have I resisted answering the question for this volume, which is whether the Constitution, rightly interpreted, is woefully imperfect in the sense that it permits terrible evil, or requires a tragic ending?[25] Have I succumbed to the temptation of interpreting the Constitution as if it were a "perfect Constitution"[26] rather than a tragic Constitution? More generally, do I aspire to interpret the Constitution so as to give every potential tragedy a "happy ending"? Raising these questions leads to another aspect of constitutional tragedy, which I shall call interpretive tragedies with bad endings.

First, it is an interpretive tragedy if the Constitution is wrongly interpreted to sanction a terrible evil or grave injustice, when in fact the Constitution, rightly interpreted, allows or requires a good outcome or "happy ending." It is notable that when constitutional scholars lament dreadful cases that have sanctioned grave injustice, such as *Dred Scott*, *Plessy*, *Korematsu*, and *Bowers*, they ordinarily do not say that those cases were rightly decided, and that the Constitution requires such injustice. Instead, they typically argue that the cases were wrongly decided, and that the injustice could have been averted, if only the Court had rightly interpreted the Constitution (e.g., if only the dissenters' interpretations had prevailed). Indeed, a dreadful outcome is, if anything, more tragic if the wrong could have been avoided and a good outcome was available. In short, when the Constitution is interpreted to allow or require evil or injustice, the tragedy is often that the Constitution was wrongly interpreted, not that it was rightly interpreted.

Second, it would be a shame if constitutional scholars were to say that such interpretive tragedies could not have been avoided, or even to revel in the evil or injustice that the Constitution might be interpreted to allow, in order to avoid being charged with believing that we have a "perfect Constitution" that always provides a "happy ending." (Indeed, it would be unfortunate if our willingness to profess that the Constitution is imperfect and sanctions terrible evil were used as the measure of our fidelity to the Constitution.)[27] Our Constitution is indeed imperfect in many ways, as suggested above in the introduction. But we should strive to interpret it so as to mitigate its imperfections and to avoid interpretive tragedies with bad endings. We should aspire to interpret the Constitution so as to make it the best it can be.[28] That is, we should embrace what I call a Constitution-perfecting theory of interpretation, such as Ronald Dworkin's moral reading of the Constitution, which proudly aims at "happy endings" rather than reveling in the Constitution's imperfections or in the evil that it might be interpreted to permit.[29]

Finally, interpretive tragedies with bad endings, such as holding that the Constitution does not protect the right to die, dramatically highlight that the Constitution is imperfect to the extent that it leaves such significant basic liberties as the right to die hanging so precariously, twisting in the political winds, so vulnerable to becoming the latest casualty in the constitutional cultural wars. We have a constitution of principle rather than a constitution of detail.[30] Our constitution of principle does not specifically enumerate all the basic liberties that are necessary to secure the preconditions for social cooperation on the basis of mutual respect among free and equal citizens in our constitutional democracy, such as the right to die.[31] Yet if those basic liberties are not honored, the outcomes of the political processes are not trustworthy. Under our constitution of principle, the protection of those basic liberties ultimately depends upon the civic virtue, reasonableness, and civility of the citizenry. It would be a tragedy for our constitutional order if the citizens were to prove too corrupt, unreasonable, and uncivil—too untrustworthy—to live up to its commitments and aspirations by honoring the right to die.

NOTES

1. *Dandridge v. Williams*, 397 U.S. 471 (1970); *San Antonio v. Rodriguez*, 411 U.S. 1 (1973); *Harris v. McRae*, 448 U.S. 297 (1980); *DeShaney v. Winnebago County Dept. of Social Services*, 489 U.S. 189 (1989).

2. There already are cracks in the wall, but it has not yet collapsed.

3. *Dred Scott v. Sandford*, 60 U.S. 393 (1847); *Plessy v. Ferguson*, 163 U.S. 537 (1896); *Korematsu v. United States*, 323 U.S. 214 (1944).

4. *Slaughterhouse Cases*, 83 U.S. 36 (1872); *Bowers v. Hardwick*, 478 U.S. 186 (1986).

5. *Buckley v. Valeo*, 424 U.S. 1 (1976).

6. In giving an account of a constitutional tragedy, one might also ask how it compares with a literary tragedy. It might seem promising to draw upon formulations of the elements of tragedy in Greek, Elizabethan, or modern drama. See, e.g., A. C. Bradley, *Shakespearean Tragedy* (London: MacMillan, 2d ed., 1905); Raymond Williams, *Modern Tragedy* (London: Chatto and Windus, 1966). But that effort is stymied by the lack of agreement about what those elements are and by the difficulty of translating from those genres to the discourses and dilemmas of constitutional law.

7. See Robert M. Cover, *Justice Accused: Antislavery and the Judicial Process* (New Haven: Yale University Press, 1975).

8. I believe that the term "happy ending" comes from Sandy Levinson. For an application of the term, see Ronald Dworkin, *Freedom's Law: The Moral Reading of the American Constitution* 38 (Cambridge: Harvard University Press, 1996). It may seem jarring to speak of "happy endings" in the context of an analysis of the right to die, including the right of persons to author their own tragic endings. By "happy ending," I refer to the notion that the Constitution, rightly interpreted, is consistent with what justice or sound political philosophy requires. By no means do I intend to suggest that persons' tragic endings will be happy.

9. Letter from Felix Frankfurter to Harlan Fiske Stone regarding *Minersville School District v. Gobitis*, in Walter F. Murphy, James E. Fleming, and Sotirios A. Barber, *American Constitutional Interpretation* 1166–68 (Westbury, N.Y.: Foundation Press, 2d ed., 1995); *Minersville School District v. Gobitis*, 310 U.S. 586, 594 (1940). Frankfurter was wrong to conceive that case as illustrating a clash of rights; as Justice Robert H. Jackson effectively retorted in the second flag-salute case, "The sole conflict is between authority and the rights of the individual." *West Virginia v. Barnette*, 319 U.S. 624, 630 (1943). Still, Frankfurter's formulation of a "tragic issue" may be helpful in thinking about what constitutes a constitutional tragedy. For the idea of "tragic choices," see Guido Calabresi and Philip Bobbitt, *Tragic Choices* (New York: Norton, 1978).

10. This essay speaks as of May 1, 1997, before the Supreme Court handed down its predictable and regrettable decisions rejecting the right of terminally ill persons

to physician-assisted suicide. Washington v. Glucksberg, 117 S.Ct. 2258 (1997); Vacco v. Quill, 117 S.Ct. 2293 (1997). I have not revised the essay in light of those decisions, with the exception of the addition of a reference to a piece about the decisions by one of the co-editors of this book (see note 24). I plan to criticize those decisions in subsequent work.

11. 79 F.3d 790 (9th Cir. 1996) (en banc), *reversed sub nom. Washington v. Glucksberg*, 117 S.Ct. 2258 (1997). I shall put to one side all of the difficult issues concerning whether there are crucial distinctions between the right to die conceived as the right to refuse unwanted medical treatment and the right to die conceived as the right to physician-assisted suicide. I believe that Judge Reinhardt convincingly showed that many proffered distinctions of this sort, although familiar, are distinctions without a difference. *Id.* at 820–24. I also believe that Reinhardt persuasively argued that state interests, such as avoiding the involvement of third parties and precluding the use of arbitrary, unfair, or undue influence, do not justify a total ban on physician-assisted suicide, although they do justify the creation of procedural safeguards. *Id.* at 825–27, 832–33. In a related essay, I take up some of these matters. See James E. Fleming, "Constitutional Tragedy in Dying: Responses to Some Common Arguments against the Constitutional Right to Die," 24 *Fordham Urban L. J.* (1997).

12. 80 F.3d 716 (2d Cir. 1996), *reversed*, 117 S. Ct. 2293 (1997).

13. See Ronald Dworkin, *Life's Dominion* 217 (New York: Knopf, 1993). See also Ronald Dworkin, Thomas Nagel, Robert Nozick, John Rawls, Thomas Scanlon, and Judith Jarvis Thomson, "Assisted Suicide: The Philosophers' Brief," reprinted in *N.Y. Rev. Books*, March 27, 1997, at 41.

14. Cf. *Planned Parenthood v. Casey*, 505 U.S. 833, 928 (1992) (Blackmun, J., concurring in part, concurring in the judgment in part, and dissenting in part) (arguing that "[b]y restricting the right to terminate pregnancies, the State conscripts women's bodies into its service"). I realize that some will object that the state does not compel terminally ill persons to do anything, much less conscript them into involuntary servitude. In particular, they may contend that the state does not forbid such persons from committing suicide; it simply prohibits them from getting physicians' assistance in doing so. But that claim does not defeat the analogy to involuntary servitude, any more than a similar claim would defeat the analogy between involuntary servitude and the forced continuation of a pregnancy. It would be absurd to say that the Constitution protects the right of women to decide whether to terminate a pregnancy, but does not protect the right to physician-assisted abortion (as if the right to abortion embraced only self-performed abortion). It would be equally problematic to say that the Constitution protects the right of terminally ill persons to decide whether to terminate their lives, but does not protect the right to physician-assisted suicide (as if the right to die encompassed only self-performed suicide). As for the tirelessly repeated claims that there is a fundamental difference between "passive" and "active" euthanasia, I

have nothing to add to Judge Reinhardt's powerful rejection of those claims. *See Compassion in Dying*, 79 F.3d at 820–24.

15. See *Pierce v. Society of Sisters*, 268 U.S. 510, 535 (1925) (stating that "[t]he child is not the mere creature of the state"). For a recent assertion to the contrary, see Stephen L. Carter, "Rush to a Lethal Judgment," *N.Y. Times Mag.*, July 21, 1996, at 28 (approvingly stating that the laws in England and America that prohibited suicide "reflected a strong belief that the lives of individuals belonged not to themselves alone but to the communities in which they lived and to the God who gave them breath"). See also Michael J. Sandel, "Last Rights," *The New Republic*, April 14, 1997, at 27.

16. See Dworkin, *Life's Dominion* 217.

17. Cf. Catharine A. MacKinnon, "Privacy v. Equality: Beyond *Roe v. Wade*," in *Feminism Unmodified* 93, 100 (Cambridge: Harvard University Press, 1987) (arguing that the right of privacy may readily prove, for women, to be "an injury got up as a gift"). Similarly, Judge Reinhardt criticized the district court decision invalidating Oregon's Death With Dignity Act because it "treats a *burden* [prohibition of physician-assisted suicide] as a *benefit* and a *benefit* [the right to physician-assisted suicide] as a *burden*." *Compassion in Dying*, 79 F.3d at 838 (criticizing *Lee v. State of Oregon*, 891 F. Supp. 1429, 1438 [D. Or. 1995]).

18. James E. Fleming, "Securing Deliberative Autonomy," 48 *Stan. L. Rev.* 1, 9 (1995).

19. *Planned Parenthood v. Casey*, 505 U.S. 833, 848–50, 901 (1992) (joint opinion).

20. See Dworkin, *Life's Dominion* 199–213.

21. William Shakespeare, *The Tragedy of King Lear* act 5, scene 3, at 314–16 (cited in *Compassion in Dying*, 79 F.3d at 821).

22. Plato, *The Laws*, trans. A. E. Taylor, book 7, at 817b, in Edith Hamilton and Huntington Cairns, eds. *The Collected Dialogues of Plato* (Princeton: Princeton University Press, 1961).

23. See *Meyer v. Nebraska*, 262 U.S. 390, 401–2 (1923). ("[T]he ideas touching the relation between individual and state [in Plato's ideal commonwealth, which 'submerge the individual and develop ideal citizens'] were wholly different from those upon which our institutions rest.")

24. I allude, of course, to Brian Clark, *Whose Life Is It, Anyway?* (Chicago: Dramatic Pub. Co., 1974). But Sandy Levinson recently has written, "In answer to the question asked by playwright Brian Clark some years ago, *Whose Life Is It, Anyway?*, almost no one is truly willing to say, 'The person's own, to do with as he or she wishes.'" Sanford Levinson, "The Court's Death Blow: Is the Supreme Court's Decision on Assisted Suicide to be Lauded or Condemned?," *The Nation*, July 21, 1997, at 28, 29.

25. The program for the 1997 Annual Meeting of the Association of American Law Schools states the topic of the panel on "Constitutional Tragedies" as follows:

"A constitutional 'tragedy' is a decision that is required by a proper interpretation of the Constitution but that is otherwise much to be regretted and therefore tragic in its combination of inevitability and ill consequences. A dozen eminent scholars of constitutional law will set forth the most tragic result their constitutional methodology would yield."

26. See Henry P. Monaghan, "Our Perfect Constitution," 56 *N.Y.U. L. Rev.* 353 (1981).

27. See James E. Fleming, "We the Exceptional American People," 11 *Const. Comm.* 355, 368 (1994) (criticizing Bruce Ackerman, *We the People: Foundations* [Cambridge: Harvard University Press, 1991] for "kneel[ing] before the altar of Henry Monaghan's 'Perfect Constitution'").

28. See Ronald Dworkin, *Law's Empire* 176–275 (Cambridge, Mass.: Belknap Press, 1986); Ronald Dworkin, *A Matter of Principle* 146–66 (Cambridge: Harvard University Press, 1985).

29. For the idea of a "Constitution-perfecting" theory, as distinguished from a "process-perfecting" theory, see James E. Fleming, "Constructing the Substantive Constitution," 72 *Tex. L. Rev.* 211, 214–15 (1993); Fleming, "Deliberative Autonomy" 29. I mean "perfecting" in the sense of interpreting the Constitution with integrity so as to render it a coherent whole, not in Monaghan's caricatured sense of "Our Perfect Constitution" as creating a perfect liberal utopia or an "ideal object" of political morality. See Monaghan, "Our Perfect Constitution." For the idea of the "moral reading of the Constitution," see Dworkin, *Freedom's Law* 1–38; see also James E. Fleming, "Fidelity to Our Imperfect Constitution," 65 *Fordham L. Rev.* 1335 (1997). For a work that seems to revel in the evil that the Constitution might be interpreted to permit, see J. M. Balkin, "Agreements With Hell and Other Objects of Our Faith," 65 *Fordham L. Rev.* 1703 (1997).

30. See Dworkin, *Life's Dominion* 119, 126–29.

31. See Fleming, "Substantive Constitution" 290; Fleming, "Deliberative Autonomy" 20. 80 F.3d 716 (2d Cir. 1996), *reversed*, 117 S. Ct. (June 26, 1997).

CHAPTER 30

Dramatic Jurisprudence

Gary Jacobsohn

"The facts of this case are undeniably tragic." So began Chief Justice William Rehnquist's opinion for the Supreme Court in *Deshaney v. Winnebago County Dept. of Social Services*.[1] The reference was to the sad story of young Joshua Deshaney, a child beaten into a life-threatening coma by his father. Adding to the poignancy of the tale, as well as to its constitutional significance, was that this horrible act might have been prevented had the local child-welfare agency intervened more aggressively on the basis of its knowledge of the father's previous abuse of his son. But the tragic dimensions of the case also encompass the Court's own involvement, culminating in its unwillingness to provide the boy and his mother the relief they had sought under the Due Process Clause of the Fourteenth Amendment.

Chief Justice Rehnquist went out of his way to explain that this denial entailed a painful choice. "Judges and lawyers, like other humans, are moved by natural sympathy in a case like this to find a way for Joshua and his mother to receive adequate compensation for the grievous harm inflicted upon them."[2] But there are limits, he suggested, to how far sympathy should extend, and clearly they are exceeded when judges are required to subordinate legal obligations to the demands of compassion. In this sense judges and lawyers are not like other humans, or at least they have been disciplined to react differently. To which Justice Harry Blackmun responded in dissent: "Faced with the choice, I would adopt a 'sympathetic' reading, one which comports with dictates of fundamental justice and recognizes that compassion need not be exiled from the province of judging."[3] For him the tragedy of the case is evident in his memorable exclamation, "Poor Joshua!"[4]

From the perspective of dissenters, Rehnquist's law/sympathy opposition constituted a false dichotomy. Their claim in effect was that prevailing Fourteenth Amendment doctrine can readily accommodate both human compassion and judicial responsibility. Why compound Joshua's tragedy with judicial failure to do the right thing, which in this case would mean alleviating some of the burdens flowing from the violence perpetrated against him? While the condition of the victim ensures that any outcome in this sordid matter must unavoidably be tinged with sadness, the Court nevertheless had it within its power to contribute to a happier ending. That it refused to do so deepens the tragedy of *Deshaney*, both in the most obvious sense—Poor Joshua!—and in a more abstract jurisprudential sense that speaks *dramatically* to the role of the Supreme Court. It is to this latter application that I turn my attention.

While Joshua Deshaney is not to be confused with any of the tragic heroes of classical drama, the interpretive alternatives that confronted the judges in this case, as in many others, can readily be analogized to some of the conceptual attributes of tragedy and comedy. Indeed, the fact that judges have always had to assess the appropriate limits of judicial discretion and the desirability of achieving a fit between law and morality in the absence of a natural convergence of the two makes them prominent players in a kind of theater of jurisprudence. Scholarly debate about these matters often centers on infelicitous oppositions such as interpretivism and noninterpretivism, or originalism and nonoriginalism, all of which involve sharp disagreements about the character and scope of creative adjudication. However much distorted they are in colloquial use, the formal structures and patterns of tragedy and comedy are at their core devoted to similar oppositions, involving vexing and often torturous agonizing over the individual's capacity to exercise meaningful choice in the conduct and regulation of human affairs. Indeed, constitutional contestation might be construed as a struggle between tragic and comic models of juridical behavior.

Consider what happens in the development of comic and tragic plots. In the case of comedy, Northrop Frye observes that typically "a young man wants a young woman, . . . his desire is resisted by some opposition, usually paternal, and . . . near the end of the play some twist in the plot enables the hero to have his way."[5] Comic resolutions are achieved through the overcoming of obstacles; since this often involves the triumph of the son's will over the father's, "the older members of almost any society are apt to feel that comedy has something subversive about it."[6] Frye indicates that "the movement of comedy is usually a movement from one kind of society to another."[7] Most people in the audience see in this movement the ascendance to a decidedly better social state, even if the happy ending produced by the comic resolution is, as Frye puts it, "brought about by manipulations."[8] In a similar vein, Louis Kronenberg points out that "[c]omedy is not just a happy as opposed to an unhappy ending, but a way of surveying life so that happy endings must prevail."[9]

Often the relevance of all of this to jurisprudential reflection is rather explicit in the actual comedic narrative detail. Thus the action in comedy—Shakespeare is a particularly good example—is sometimes occasioned by the hardships of a cruel or irrational law, such as the law of killing Syracusans in the *Comedy of Errors* or the law of compulsory marriage in *A Midsummer Night's Dream*.[10] But in the narrative flow of the play, these laws become obstacles to be evaded or broken, necessary preconditions for the achievement of the inevitable happy ending. This of course contrasts with the predicament of the tragic hero, who, situated within "a world-view [where] nature is seen as an impersonal process which human law imitates as best it can,"[11] is unable to escape the necessary consequences of his actions. "Whether the context is Greek, Christian, or undefined, tragedy seems to lead up to an epiphany of law, of that which is and must be."[12] So in *Oedipus Rex* nature's balance is restored through interventions—what the Greeks referred to as *nemesis*—proceeding impersonally and independently of the motivations that may have inspired the original disturbance to the natural order of things. Poor Oedipus!

In constitutional theory the triumph of the son's will over the father's is accomplished through a clever transvaluation of constitutional meaning intended to convince the audience that parental authority has not in fact been undermined but only clarified through subsequent interpretation. Thus fathers may lay down a *concept* of fairness that they expect to have honored by their offspring, but as to any specific *conception* of fairness, that becomes a matter for the children to resolve, in a way that may or may not conform to paternal expectations.[13] A concept may be understood as embodying a moral principle, the application of which may yield different results, or conceptions, depending on the circumstances and context in which it occurs. It becomes the role of the Supreme Court to "revise these principles from time to time in the light of what seems to the Court fresh moral insights."[14]

One perhaps would not expect that judges who put this theory into practice would be more candid than politically unaccountable academics in expressing what is really going on here, but in Justice William Brennan we have someone who confounds such logic. Thus for him, "[e]ach generation has the choice to overrule or add to the principles of the framers."[15] The critical question is "What do the words of the text mean in our time?"[16] Precisely because the views of the fathers on such matters as the death penalty no longer speak for *our* community, we are not bound by their specific dispensations. Filial piety is fine, but not if it serves to deprive us of the results we expect, which in the case of contemporary constitutional adjudication translates into a more expansive claim of individual rights against the state.

Justice Brennan and Ronald Dworkin are practitioners of the genre of comedic jurisprudence. Theirs is the Constitution of happy endings, with judges exercising creativity in the pursuit of acceptable outcomes. However it may be manifested—through tendentious interpretations of language and intent (e.g., the argument that equal protection means equal concern and respect) or deliberate mischaracterizations of community mores (e.g., the claim that contemporary morality condemns capital punishment)—the agreeable judicial resolution is often brought about by a manipulative technique that resonates with genuine comic flair. Imaginative interpretative devices are placed in the service of a transformative agenda whose goal is the melding of constitutional language and present needs. Through acts of "contemporary ratification" (Brennan's term to describe his method), obstacles that lay in the path of our desires are overcome, and the realization of the society to which we aspire is *comically* advanced.

Of course there are those who will find in these efforts an unfortunate subversion of the liberal constitutionalism of the Founding Fathers. Some may even feel this way in spite of their temptation to acknowledge the moral appropriateness of specific judicial outcomes brought about by these methods. They will perhaps see themselves as a uniquely situated audience, finding irony in places not even intended by the authors of what has just transpired. They are the practitioners of the tragic jurisprudential vision, "the antithesis of the popular vision, in its comprehension of complexity, incongruity, and paradox."[17] So the happy ending experienced by the audience at large is filtered through a perceptual screen that produces an altogether different reaction, a bittersweet recognition that the pleasure of the moment has been purchased at a high cost, namely, erosion in the structural foundation of liberal democracy.

To protect these foundations, constitutional theorists such as Herbert Wechsler and Raoul Berger demand rigorous judicial adherence to norms of objectivity derived from neutral principles and/or original intent. Text and history supply the resources for judges to become in essence the impersonal voice of the Constitution. Justice Antonin Scalia, for example, sees the main advantage of originalism to reside in its capacity to check the dangerous proclivity of judges to mistake their own predilections for law.[18] Indeed, even most originalists (Berger is the outstanding exception) are in the end "faint-hearted," unable finally to accept some of the harsher conclusions flowing from their investigations.[19] Thus they conceal their concessions—as in the case of Robert Bork's defense of *Brown v. Board of Education*—in such arguably disingenuous strategies as raising the level of generality of the principles to which the Founders were committed. One must avoid at all costs making personal judgments, for as Chief Justice Rehnquist has observed, "[t]here is no conceivable way in which I can logically demonstrate to you that the judgments of my conscience are superior to the judgments of your conscience, and vice versa."[20]

Such moral skepticism is not a necessary component of the tragic jurisprudential vision, but the insistence on abiding by the results of impersonal adjudication most assuredly is. Justices Rehnquist and Scalia can perhaps take heart in Herbert Muller's observation that there is "a saving irony" in tragedy's promotion of "a spirit of compassion [in] the knowledge of irremediable evils and insoluble dilemmas."[21] Justice Blackmun's plea for compassion in *Deshaney* is in effect met with tragic jurisprudence's counterclaim: there is no judicially prescribed constitutional remedy for every evil, and the sooner we all realize that, the sooner we will cultivate the humility that is the necessary predicate for genuine compassion.

But if the limitations of the comedic jurisprudential model inhere in its failed sense of irony, then the defects of the tragic model are bound up in its exaggerated sense of law's determinacy. Long before the Crits revealed (with, to be sure, their own gross exaggerations) the indeterminacy of constitutional language and intent, no less than James Madison spoke of an "*unavoidable* inaccuracy" in the terms and objects of any legal document; hence they must be "considered as more or less obscure and equivocal, until their meaning be liquidated and ascertained by a series of particular discussions and adjudications."[22] If there is a message for us in Madison's assessment, it is perhaps that judges are not so omniscient as to be able to claim the mantle of objectivity that is required of tragedy's guiding force. It is one thing to accept the tragic revelations in the last scene of a classical drama as somehow necessary to the fulfillment of nature's mandate. But just as judges need to be careful in claiming certainty on behalf of *moral* judgments that lead to happy endings, so too must they exhibit restraint in the deference they are willing to extend to others on the basis of their assertions of unambiguous *legal* meanings.

It is no surprise, then, that all of this should lead me finally to tragicomedy, a genre that "is able to accommodate both the serious deterministic world of tragedy and the humorous, indeterministic world of comedy."[23] Occasionally a play—Shakespeare's *Measure for Measure* is among the most notable examples—deals explicitly with matters of legal interpretation, and "the fanatical worship of the letter [of the law] is shown to conflict with the genuine principle of equity."[24] Such particular demonstrations, while relevant to the argument here, concern me less than the distinctive structural attribute of the genre, the admixture of tragic and comic features, "the co-existence of amusement and pity, terror and laughter."[25] As translated for the constitutional stage, the judicial actors who follow a tragicomic script must strive for an accommodation between necessity and manipulation, between the obligation to find the law and the temptation to make it.

Constitutionalism is not about happy endings, but rightly conceived it should be about a happy ending, namely, the preservation of a decent polity, respectful of human personality and committed to popularly inspired change. Its failure from time to time to guarantee uplifting constitutional and political outcomes is a necessary part of that project, as the idea of limits is essential for a life worth living. The tragicomic approach to interpretation, much like Shakespeare's "problem" plays, defies easy categorization, but in its potential for balancing limits and possibilities, seems appropriate to the role of judging in a constitutional democracy. So Joshua Deshaney's loss is in itself no proof of constitutional failure; on the other hand, it may represent a failure of judicial imagination, given the degree of interpretive freedom manifest in the ambiguities surrounding the state action doctrine. Somewhere between the rigid dichotomies of Rehnquist's tragic approach and the sentimentalism of Blackmun's comic intervention may be found an answer worthy of the outgoing drama of constitutionalism.

To the matter, then, of what the worst thing a committed constitutionalist would be required in a constitutional case to uphold, one may ask, What is the worst constitutional result that could follow from the application of a tragicomic understanding of the judicial role? One answer is that the result, whatever it might be, would not be as problematic as the worst that is possible through the application of the tragic and comic alternatives. Thus, for the latter, *the worst* would be the result that secured the maximum amount of immediate happiness on the basis of a decision possessing only a minimal plausible grounding in constitutional text and history. Such a result might call into question the very possibility of legal restraints on the judiciary; therefore a committed constitutionalist would have to experience profound sadness amidst the likely euphoria of the moment. In the case of the former, it would be a result that would stimulate a maximum of disgust among decent people, in the absence of a convincing demonstration of historical and textual inevitability rooted in the relevant constitutional materials. Such a result might inspire grave doubts in the capacity of the legal order to approximate justice, undermining its ability to sustain people's abiding commitment to constitutionalism.[26]

The logic of tragicomic jurisprudence requires that it may on occasion culminate in results that will be seen as tragic. That will occur whenever the available sources for constitutional judgment speak unambiguously in a way that would render all efforts to achieve a happy ending simply comic, which is to say, baldly manipulative. Whatever one's views on the death penalty, for example, there will surely be times when its application will strike one as unjust. The tragicomic approach will seek to minimize such applications, by, say, admitting as relevant for constitutional consideration the extant patterns of racial bias in particular jurisdictions. But these considerations can take one only so far, beyond which the desire to avoid an abhorrent ending is achievable only by a willful act of judicial power. To avoid the truly unhappy ending to which the accumulation of such willful acts must lead, one must be ready to accept these occasional examples of injustice, taking comfort perhaps in the fact that the only real alternatives to the tragicomic solution will in the end culminate in something much worse.

NOTES

1. 489 U.S. 189, at 91 (1989).

2. *Id.* at 202.

3. *Id.* at 213 (Blackmun, J., dissenting).

4. *Id.*

5. Northrop Frye, *Anatomy of Criticism: Four Essays* 163 (Princeton: Princeton University Press, 1957).

6. *Id.* at 164.

7. *Id.* at 163.

8. *Id.* at 170.

9. Louis Kronenberg, *The Thread of Laughter* 3 (New York: Knopf, 1952).

10. Frye, *Anatomy of Criticism* 166. Frye notes that the "resemblance of the rhetoric of comedy to the rhetoric of jurisprudence has been recognized from the earliest times." *Id.*

11. *Id.* at 208.

12. *Id.*

13. Ronald Dworkin, *Taking Rights Seriously* 13–38 (Cambridge: Harvard University Press, 1977).

14. *Id.* at 137.

15. William J. Brennan, Jr., "The Constitution of the United States: Contemporary Ratification," in Walter F. Murphy, James E. Fleming, and Sotirios A. Barber, *American Constitutional Interpretation* 239 (Mineola, N.Y.: Foundation Press, 2d ed., 1995).

16. Brennan, "The Constitution of the United States" 240.

17. Herbert J. Muller, *The Spirit of Tragedy* 1 (New York: Washington Square Press, 1965).

18. Antonin Scalia, "Originalism: The Lesser Evil," in Murphy, Fleming, and Barber, *American Constitutional Interpretation* 235.

19. *Id.* at 233.

20. William H. Rehnquist, "The Notion of a Living Constitution," in Murphy, Fleming, and Barber, *American Constitutional Interpretation* 248.

21. Muller, *The Spirit of Tragedy* 287.

22. *Federalist* No. 37 (Madison), at 229, ed. Clinton Rossiter (New York: New American Library, 1961).

23. George L. Geckle, introduction to Geckle, ed., *Twentieth Century Interpretations of Measure for Measure: A Collection of Critical Essays* 12 (Englewood Cliffs, N.J.: Prentice-Hall, 1970).

24. Ernest Schanzer, "Measure for Measure," in Rolf Soellner and Samuel Bertsche, eds., *Measure for Measure: Text, Source, and Criticism* 249 (New York: Houghton Mifflin, 1966).

25. John Orr, *Tragicomedy and Contemporary Culture: Play and Performance from Beckett to Shepard* 1 (Ann Arbor: University of Michigan Press, 1991).

26. So, for example, I would find deeply disturbing any effort on the part of the federal government to use the tax structure to further widen and entrench the enormous gap between rich and poor in this country. While tragic and tragicomic opinions might very well come to the same conclusion on the constitutionality of such a policy, I can imagine justices of the tragicomic persuasion appealing to certain structural attributes of the constitutional order that establish limits to the authority of the federal government effectively to establish a plutocracy. Such arguments might hold out some hope to the victims of the policy that their fate is not sealed by the coincidence of political power and insatiable greed.

CHAPTER 31

Constitutional Farce

Pamela S. Karlan and Daniel R. Ortiz

Tragedy? We thought very hard. What is the most repugnant substantive result that a conscientious judge would feel compelled to support in interpreting the Constitution? We had no trouble coming up with awful outcomes. But each time we did, we found that without too much difficulty we
could work up colorable constitutional arguments against them. That is no
credit to our genius. The range of permissible constitutional arguments
now extends so far that a few workable ones are always available in a pinch.
Indeed, faced with this bounty we soon had to ask ourselves if there are *any*
significant substantive results—repugnant or otherwise—that a conscientious judge would have to support.

What has happened? Clearly tragedy was once a vibrant constitutional
genre. Robert Cover, for one, wrote famously of how tragedy framed the
central constitutional issue of the antebellum period: slavery.[1] But would
those jurists who felt constrained to uphold slavery even as they anathema-
tized it find tragedy even possible today? We think not; that is a loss. A legal
culture without the possibility of tragedy is a smaller one. In the rest of this
essay, we want to explore why we have lost tragedy in this traditional sense
and to explore one somewhat diminished sense in which it may survive.

The Battle of Genres

The decline of tragedy reflects in part the growing capaciousness of constitutional doctrine itself, particularly of those doctrines that protect individual freedoms. Once the "last resort[s] of constitutional argument[s],"[2] doctrines drawn from the Equal Protection and Due Process Clauses have now
become well-functioning, primary catch-alls. Faced with what she believes
a true evil, a judge can easily convince herself that it violates one or the other
(or both!) of these constitutional provisions.

Indeed, the very methodology of substantive due process makes the creation of a tragedy real work. Every step of the inquiry offers an easy out to the troubled jurist. The two central steps, in fact, practically invite the judge to find the apparent evil constitutionally prohibited. The first step, identifying whether the infringed interest constitutes a "fundamental right,"[3] requires that the troubled judge actively resist doctrine in order to make tragedy possible. Although the formulation varies somewhat from case to case, this step asks the judge whether the infringed interest is "so rooted in the traditions and conscience of our people as to be ranked as fundamental."[4] In other words, fundamental rights are those that our history and basic values recognize and protect.[5] In order to find himself bound in a tragedy, then, a judge genuinely troubled by a particular governmental action would have to believe that his culture did not sufficiently value an interest he himself found very important. But that would require the judge to recognize that his valuation of the personal right was idiosyncratic—that he, but not others, thought it worthy of protection. Although that is possible—a judge can admit that society disagrees with him about the importance of some individual interests—the more awful he believes their infringement, the less likely he is to think that society stands anywhere other than behind him. Only the greatest self-abnegator could do this, and he, of course, would see the tragedy as merely personal—hardly the stuff of crisis we were asked to worry over.

The other central stage of the due process inquiry presents the same difficulty. Once an interest is deemed fundamental, this stage requires the judge to ask whether the state has a compelling reason to infringe it.[6] If the state does not, the action is prohibited. But think what it means for a judge to find an infringement compellingly justified. If a judge thinks the state action that necessary, the infringement would be sad, but not tragic—at least in the legal sense. The substantive result, painful though it might be, would be compelled by unavoidable policy choices, not by the Constitution.

We must make one point clear. A judge who applied substantive due process doctrine in these ways would not be exploiting it or manipulating it strategically. Our point is not that the indeterminacies of constitutional doctrine allow a judge, equipped with only a minimum of creativity, to escape tragedy. Rather, we believe that in these circumstances a judge has to resist doctrine actively in order to make tragedy even possible. In other words, a judge has to work very hard to maintain the tragic condition. But a judge who found tragedy only through such active resistance to doctrine would be perverse. How deeply could she really be committed to ideals she had to work so hard to frustrate?

This capaciousness of doctrine reflects an even deeper threat to tragedy: the metastasis of a new genre of constitutional interpretation. Like history, the scholarly conversation about constitutional constraints has been expressed "the first time as tragedy, the second time as farce."[7] Perhaps the sheer accumulation of constitutional interpretation made this inevitable; as the Big Ideas get taken, scholars are forced to scurry around looking for as-yet-unadvanced positions to stake out. There is a reason that the most novel claims have remained unvoiced for so long, and it is not always because our scholarly forebears lacked vision.

Recent constitutional theory is a wonderful playground. It is sunny, fun, and playful, not to mention inclusive and diverse. But it is also often ridiculous, because the academy's professional reward structure has far deviated from the courts'. Bored by the workaday world of judicial constitutional interpretation and free from its pragmatic and political constraints, we academics reward outrageous interpretive moves, ones that a court would hardly countenance. So we find a Yale school of textuo-structuralism in which misplaced commas loom large,[8] in which the Fourteenth Amendment is not really an amendment while the New Deal is,[9] or in which the Thirteenth Amendment's prohibition of slavery provides the best source for a constitutional right to reproductive autonomy.[10] Its adherents are the Madonnas of constitutional interpretation. Flouting conventional practice with style is enough for praise; novelty and sheer technical virtuosity win academic garlands. Luckily, Rule 11 does not reach beyond the courthouse door.

This type of constitutional interpretation may thrill, but it is ultimately empty. It is a form of farce. Like that genre, it requires a huge suspension of disbelief, a mind unworried by the accumulation of improbable coincidence, and leaps of logic. And, above all, it demands aesthetic, not moral or political, appreciation. We admire this type of interpretation for its highly developed and elaborated artificiality, not for the purchase it gives us on real life. As consumers, we reward those producers not for changing our lives but for appearing to defy legal gravity. The result, however, should disappoint us. Instead of presenting a deep confrontation between the legal and moral orders, as does tragedy, farce presents only a brief professional diversion. We may smile at the cleverness of argument, but the world in the end remains unchallenged and unchanged. Farce's reward consists in the avoidance of pain and conflict, not in their resolution. Like Romans at the circus, we temporarily place the real workaday world aside.

Great danger lies this way. While farce has its place—we are not against escapism—farce's dominance makes tragedy impossible. The more promiscuously we can interpret, the more we can escape serious legal engagement with moral issues. Such interpretation may appear to reconcile law and morality, but any reconciliation is shallow. Farce does not so much change the world as release us from the real and painful responsibility of reforming it.

Consider an argument which is not far-fetched by present standards of constitutional interpretation: that the First Amendment prohibits and has always prohibited slavery. It is bold, clean, simple, and outrageous. Do you like it? The only problem is that it would have offered less comfort to slaves than to slaveholders. To the extent abolitionists spent their time making arguments like this, the institution of slavery was assured. For only by confronting the real problem, that the Constitution took the wrong position on slavery, was real reform possible. The First Amendment argument, though dazzling, would have been a cheap diversion, whose virtuosity the slaveholders especially would have appreciated.

And much of contemporary judicial discussion seems farcical as well. Over the last five years, for example, the Supreme Court has tied the reapportionment process up in knots.[11] In trying to articulate when race has played an unacceptably large role in redistricting, the Court has found itself reduced to observing, as it once did with obscenity, that although it cannot articulate a standard for other actors in the process to follow, it knows racial biasing when it sees it.[12] The Court's opinions substitute florid descriptions and pictures for analysis.[13] At the end of the day, things are so crazy that Justice O'Connor finds herself specially concurring in her own opinion.[14]

We have ended up with scholars and judges who resemble nothing so much as Polonius's description of the players-within-the-play in *Hamlet*: "The best actors in the world, either for tragedy, comedy, history, pastoral, pastoral-comical, historical-pastoral, tragical-historical, tragical-comical-historical-pastoral, scene individable, or poem unlimited: Seneca cannot be too heavy, nor Plautus too light. For the law of writ and the liberty, these are the only men."[15]

The Tragedy of Necessity

Whatever *Hamlet*'s virtues as dramatic tragedy, there has to be more to *constitutional* tragedy. The constitutional stage is positively littered with indecisive princes, but while modern doctrine may be contradictory, or confused, or downright unfortunate in any number of respects, much of it lacks the grandeur that tragedy seems to demand. Tragedy requires *heroes*, not simply players who strut and fret their way across an empty stage.

It is in their very largeness, their insistence, in Sir Isaiah Berlin's formulation, on taking responsibility for the life of society, that individuals become heroic and assume the potential for tragedy. So too in the case of doctrine. And thus we looked for our tragedy in grand action, rather than in a pinched choice of evil when good could not be done.

Oedipus Rex is the classic illustration of this idea of tragedy as a consequence of necessary heroic action: some bold step must be taken, but it leads down a path toward disaster. Oedipus had to kill the stranger at the crossroads, but this necessary confrontation set in motion a course of events that led to pain and sorrow. Ironically, tragedy here may come quite close to farce. Charlie Black's description of "the failure to recognize kinship as the prima materia of tragedy"[16] is also true, when you think about it, of bedroom farce, which depends on the characters' failing to see their relationships to one another.

As voting-rights scholars, we return to the decisive crossroads of our field: the road the Supreme Court took into the political thicket. In our view, the doctrine of one person, one vote is tragic stuff.

The Reapportionment Revolution that begat one person, one vote was surely heroic in its sweep. It is hard to think of another Supreme Court decision that remade any governmental institution as decisively or immediately as the Supreme Court's announcement in *Baker v. Carr*[17] that it would entertain claims of legislative malapportionment under the Equal Protection Clause, or its announcements in *Wesberry v. Sanders*[18] and *Reynolds v. Sims*[19] that congressional districts and state legislative districts had to have equal populations. Before the Reapportionment Revolution, reactionary factions from underpopulated backwaters had barricaded themselves into power. Having captured control of many states' legislatures and congressional delegations at the turn of the century, they had made it impossible for democratic politics to dislodge them. One person, one vote broke the logjam, and its requirement to keep apportionments current mandated decennial reallocation of legislative seats, creating at least a possibility for majoritarian and progressive politics.[20]

One person, one vote was heroic too in its grand simplicity. Unlike other Warren Court revolutions—for example, in criminal procedure and racial justice, where the Court found itself imposing complex regulatory regimes on recalcitrant police and education authorities—the Reapportionment

Revolution was an immediate, and smashing, popular success. The elegance of the slogan "one person, one vote" allowed the Court to hide from the nation, and from itself, the contingency and contestability of its political choices.[21] One person, one vote quickly came to seem a fundamental, and traditional, principle of democracy.

Finally, one person, one vote was heroic in its aspirations. Chief Justice Warren—the author of *Brown v. Board of Education*[22] among other heroic achievements—called *Reynolds* his most important opinion, "because it insured that henceforth elections would reflect the collective public interest— embodied in the 'one-man, one-vote' standard—rather than the machinations of special interests."[23] The Court thought that one person, one vote would ensure not just democratic control over the legislative branches but also republican virtue.

But the very things that made one person, one vote heroic also sowed the seeds of its later undoing. One person, one vote was so simple that the man on the street could understand it, and even a judge with only elementary-school mathematics could monitor it.[24] But it was also so simple that advances in redistricting technology could completely outflank its defense of majoritarian control.[25] It was the Maginot Line of democratic accountability. Rigid application of one person, one vote swept away many traditional constraints on outrageous gerrymandering, since compliance with its rigid mathematical requirements often meant splitting political subdivisions or ignoring natural boundaries between areas.[26] The equipopulous gerrymander is a staple of current redistricting. It results in many incumbents today being very nearly as entrenched as their pre-*Baker* counterparts. And the grotesque shapes associated with gerrymanders undermine public confidence in the fairness of the political system altogether. Endless manipulability, as *Hamlet* reminds us,[27] is deeply destabilizing.

At the same time, one person, one vote's insistence on the fundamentality of individual rights in the political system set the stage for the current "tragical-comical-historical" assault on race-conscious districting. To borrow Charlie Black's phrase, one person, one vote fails utterly to recognize kinship. That is, current doctrine fails to see that voters are more than fungible, atomistic ballot-casting monads; they enter the political process as members of richly textured, overlapping communities.[28] By denying the centrality of group membership, both to creating individuals' political preferences and to organizing their participation in the electoral process, one person, one vote made it possible for the Supreme Court to see "the simple command that the Government . . . treat citizens as individuals,"[29] rather than a fair allocation of political power among competing groups as the core of equal protection in redistricting.

And that is tragic in the everyday meaning of the term. The upshot of one person, one vote, is that today the Supreme Court denies African Americans the ability to participate in a political process that respects their claim to group recognition, all in the name of a kind of deracinated individualism. The Court's initial incursion into the political thicket convinced it that the judiciary, and not the political process, even once it had been freed of the stranglehold of malapportionment, should continually regulate the fundamental rules of political engagement. In short, one person, one vote has encouraged the Court's hubris. And we all know what often comes after hubris.

NOTES

1. Robert M. Cover, *Justice Accused: Antislavery and the Judicial Process* (New Haven: Yale University Press, 1975).

2. *Buck v. Bell*, 274 U.S. 200, 208 (1927).

3. *Bowers v. Hardwick*, 478 U.S. 186, 189–92 (1986).

4. *Michael H. v. Gerald D.*, 491 U.S. 110, 122 (1989) (opinion of Scalia, J.) (quoting *Snyder v. Massachusetts*, 291 U.S. 97, 105 [1934] [opinion of Cardozo, J.]).

5. *Id.* ("Our cases reflect 'continual insistence upon respect for the teachings of history [and] solid recognition of the basic values that underlie our society'") (quoting *Griswold v. Connecticut*, 381 U.S. 479, 501 [1965] [Harlan, J., concurring in judgment]).

6. *Roe v. Wade*, 410 U.S. 113, 154 (1973).

7. Karl Marx, *The Eighteenth Brumaire of Louis Bonaparte* (1852), in Robert L. Tucker, ed., *The Marx-Engels Reader* 594 (New York: Norton, 1978).

8. See Akhil Reed Amar, "Our Forgotten Constitution: A Bicentennial Comment," 97 *Yale L.J.* 281 (1987).

9. See Bruce Ackerman, *We the People: Foundations* (Cambridge, Mass.: Belknap Press, 1991).

10. See Andrew Koppelman, "Forced Labor: A Thirteenth Amendment Defense of Abortion," 84 *Nw. U. L. Rev.* 480 (1990).

11. See Pamela S. Karlan, "All over the Map: The Supreme Court's Voting Rights Trilogy," 1993 *Sup. Ct. Rev.* 245; Pamela S. Karlan, "Still Hazy after All These Years: Voting Rights in the Post-*Shaw* Era," 26 *Cumb. L. Rev.* 287 (1996).

12. See *Shaw v. Reno*, 509 U.S. 630, 646 (1993) (quoting *Karcher v. Daggett*, 462 U.S. 725, 755 [1983] [Stevens, J., concurring] [(quoting *Jacobellis v. Ohio*, 378 U.S. 184, 197 (1964) (Stewart, J., concurring)]). The very citation apparatus is reminiscent of the Keystone Kops piling out of a miniature car.

13. See *Bush v. Vera*, 116 S. Ct. 1941, 1954–55 and 1958–59 (1996) (opinion of O'Connor, J.) (colorful descriptions of challenged districts); *id.* at 1965–67 (maps); *id.* at 1982 n. 18 (Stevens, J., dissenting) (parodying the "obligatory florid description[s]" in Justice O'Connor's opinion); *Miller v. Johnson*, 115 S.Ct. 2475, 2484 (1995) (colorful description of challenged district); *id.* at 2496 (map); *Shaw v. Reno*, 509 U.S. at 630, 635–36 (colorful description of challenged districts); *id.* at 658 (literally colorful map).

14. See *Bush*, 116 S. Ct. at 1968 (O'Connor, J., concurring).

15. *Hamlet*, act 2, sc. 2, ll. 396–404.

16. Charles L. Black, Jr., "My World with Louis Armstrong," 95 *Yale L.J.* 1595, 1599 (1986).

17. 369 U.S. 186 (1962).

18. 376 U.S. 1 (1964).

19. 377 U.S. 533 (1964).

20. See Lani Guinier and Pamela S. Karlan, "The Majoritarian Difficulty: One Person, One Vote," in E. Joshua Rosenkranz and Bernard Schwartz, eds., *Reason and Passion: Justice Brennan's Enduring Influence* 207, 219 (New York: Norton, 1997).

21. See Jan G. Deutsch, "Neutrality, Legitimacy, and the Supreme Court: Some Intersections between Law and Political Science," 20 *Stan. L. Rev.* 169, 243–49 (1968).

22. 347 U.S. 483 (1954).

23. G. Edward White, *Earl Warren: A Public Life* 337 (New York: Oxford University Press, 1982).

24. See *Avery v. Midland County*, 390 U.S. 474, 510 (1968) (Stewart, J., dissenting) (complaining that apportionment "is far too subtle and complicated a business to be resolved as a matter of constitutional law in terms of sixth-grade arithmetic").

25. See Samuel Issacharoff, "Groups and the Right to Vote," 44 *Emory L.J.* 869, 883 (1995); Samuel Issacharoff, "Judging Politics: The Elusive Quest for Judicial Review of Political Fairness," 71 *Tex. L. Rev.* 1643, 1702 (1993); Pamela S. Karlan and Daryl J. Levinson, "Why Voting Is Different," 84 *Calif. L. Rev.* 1201, 1207 (1996); Richard H. Pildes and Richard G. Niemi, "Expressive Harms, 'Bizarre Districts,' and Voting Rights: Evaluating Election-District Appearances after *Shaw v. Reno*," 92 *Mich. L. Rev.* 483, 569–75 (1993).

26. See Richard Briffault, "Race and Representation after *Miller v. Johnson*," 1995 *U. Chi. Legal F.* 23, 43–44; Pildes and Niemi, "Expressive Harms," 573–74.

27. See *Hamlet*, act 3, sc. 2, ll. 355–61:

Hamlet: Do you see yonder cloud that's almost in the shape of a camel?
Polonius: By th' mass and 'tis, like a camel indeed.
Hamlet: Methinks it is like a weasel.
Polonius: It is back'd like a weasel.
Hamlet: Or like a whale.
Polonius: Very like a whale.

28. See T. Alexander Aleinikoff and Samuel Issacharoff, "Race and Redistricting: Drawing Constitutional Lines after *Shaw v. Reno*," 92 *Mich. L. Rev.* 588 (1993); Pamela S. Karlan, "The Rights To Vote: Some Pessimism about Formalism," 71 *Tex. L. Rev.* 1705, 1712–13 (1993).

29. *Miller v. Johnson*, 115 S. Ct. 2475, 2486 (1995) (internal quotation marks omitted).

CHAPTER 32

Constitutional Merry-Go-Round
The First Time Tragedy, the Second Time Farce

Theodore J. Lowi

When the Gods wish to punish us they answer our prayers.
—OSCAR WILDE

May your wishes be fulfilled.
—ANCIENT CHINESE CURSE

If there ever was a case for originalism, it is the separation of powers. The Framers were unmistakably clear in their intent, and they repeated themselves often, just to be sure their offspring would get the message. "Separation of powers" as a label was never used. But the principle itself was referred to, early and often. Madison, who is responsible for the Notes of the Debates at the Philadelphia Convention, took many occasions to repeat the principle, especially in several of his essays for *The Federalist*:

> No political truth is certainly of greater intrinsic value, or is stamped with the authority of more enlightened patrons of liberty than that . . . [the] accumulation of all powers, legislative, executive, and judiciary, in the same hands, . . . may justly be pronounced the very definition of tyranny.[1]

> After discriminating . . . the several classes of power, as they may in their nature be legislative, executive, or judiciary, the next and most difficult task is to provide some practical security for each, against the invasion of the others. What this security ought to be is the great problem to be solved.[2]

> In order to lay a due foundation for that separate and distinct exercise of the different powers of government, . . . it is evident that each department should have a will of its own. . . . The great security against a gradual concentration of the several powers in the same department consists in giving to those who

administer each department the necessary constitutional means and personal motives to resist encroachments of the others. The provision for defense must in this, as in all of the cases, be made commensurate to the danger of attack. Ambition must be made to counteract ambition.[3]

The separation of powers was designed for two purposes: (1) to prevent the legislative branch from dominating the system and (2) to make it difficult for the national government to make policy decisions at all.

Despite its clarity, original intent was overturned or disregarded as soon as the First Congress opened its doors. Congress immediately made Secretary of Treasury Alexander Hamilton its own agent, an American chancellor of the exchequer. Some would think of him as prime minister. It was Congress, not the president, whose command produced Hamilton's three great reports that would virtually set the national agenda for the next several decades.[4] And the original enactments of the new national government were large decisions, fundamental decisions, and essentially congressional decisions, including such monuments of public policy as the Jay Treaty, the Bank of the United States, the assumption of state debts, the Judiciary Act, the first national excise taxes, the payment of claims for war services, explorations and surveying, and, above all, the adoption of the amendments that became the Bill of Rights.

In other words, America was moving fast, given the average speed of constitutional development, toward realization and institutionalization not of the separation of powers but of its opposite, the fusion of powers—on the classic Westminster model. The presidency was not unimportant under Washington or Adams, but it was part of a Congress-centered government in which both of the popular branches (and the third branch as well) were under the control of a single party, the Federalists. Little of this bore any resemblance to the Constitution's design, except perhaps in maintaining separate names for the three branches.

Constitutional development continued in the same direction after the Jeffersonian/Republican revolution of 1800. The so-called Era of Good Feelings (1808–28) was a smile put on the face of one-party domination of the national government, but it established once and for all the important democratic principle of loyal opposition, and it also gave America the first intimation of genuine party government—which means one-party government, with occasional alternation of which party governs.

This period also produced more than a mere intimation of the direction and nature of constitutional development. If the test of institutionalization is succession and continuity under different regimes, fusion of powers was being institutionalized. Quite contrary to the intent of the Framers, the presidency was drawn further and further into congressional domination. Congress not only controlled the legislative agenda, but it also literally controlled selection of the chief executive himself. First, it controlled the system of nominating candidates for president (King Caucus). It also controlled the system for electing the president, because if there were at least three serious candidates, the election would undoubtedly end up in the House, given the great difficulty of producing the absolute majority of electors required by the Constitution. Why else would the original Article II provide that in the absence of an absolute majority of electors the House should choose "from the five highest on the List" (changed to the top three by the Twelfth Amendment)? The presidency was not merely drawn into the sphere of congressional influence. The presidency itself had become politically dependent on the legislature—just as the Founders had feared and had tried to head off by constitutional design—because Congress had become the actual constituency of the presidency. That is real-life fusion of the parliamentary kind.

Development of the fusion of powers would probably have become complete and irreversible if there had not been a sudden change in the party system, following the end of the Era of Good Feelings. Two historically important changes produced the Jacksonian Revolution: (1) the replacement of King Caucus with the convention as the presidential nominating system, and (2) the replacement of the probability of ultimate House election of the president with the undermining of the Electoral College itself by the simple practice of pledging electors. These two developments took presidential selection completely outside of Congress and gave the presidency a popular base totally and completely independent of Congress. In the process, the separation of powers was saved by the very institution publicly reviled by virtually every Founder, including Madison (the one possible exception is Aaron Burr). The separation of powers was not only saved from oblivion but strengthened by virtue of its consonance with the new two-party system, despite the fact that it was only a by-product of that system. In other words, the parties were not following any intent of the Framers. The presidency was simply strengthened in relation to Congress as a coincidental or accidental consequence of winning elections.

Although the presidency was strengthened in relation to Congress, Congress of course remained the dominant institution, literally the First Branch, throughout the nineteenth and into the twentieth century. By 1888, Woodrow Wilson could entitle his textbook *Congressional Government*.[5]

And by the time he had abandoned political science and had become president of the United States, Wilson had expressed his yearning for a British variant of republicanism by defining the presidency as an office of "stewardship," and even by proposing that responsible party government could best be established by removing the minority party members from the congressional committees. Nevertheless, despite a century of congressional domination, the presidency—thanks largely to the workings of the party system—could maintain enough independence and exercise enough "checks and balances" to approach a reasonable approximation of its original intent.

The Roosevelt Revolution was more than anything else a constitutional revolution, in that it permanently altered federalism, turned national government on its head (or finally on its feet?), and put the president at the center and Congress at the periphery, changing the characterization of the American System in all succeeding textbooks from "Congressional Government" to "Presidential Government." Yet the Roosevelt Revolution did not overturn or replace the separation of powers in the form in which it had prevailed for the previous century. Even as late as 1960, Neustadt's salutary formulation served quite well as an approximation of original intent and of operating reality: "separated institutions sharing power."

But just about the time Neustadt's formulation was becoming the coin of the constitutional realm,[6] realities were undermining it. A Second Constitutional Revolution was breaking out, one that would nationalize civil rights and establish welfare benefits as not quite a constitutional right but at least a constitutionally protected entitlement. These changes would in turn destroy the two-party system as we had known it—not by giving us a multiparty system (more's the pity) but by altering the form of party government from alternating one-party rule to rule by two permanent majority parties.

There is no mystery as to how this has happened, but the consequences of it have not yet been made clear and very much need to be. The Second Constitutional Revolution was a set of "wedge issues" that produced, through several sledgehammer blows, a severing of the South from the Democratic Party. This did not, however, produce the electoral realignment that most political scientists were expecting and predicting—and hoping for, as a condition favoring continuation of party government as we had come to know it. Instead, with an incomplete electoral realignment and an almost complete ideological realignment, we got, inter alia, what came to be called divided government. It is difficult to say when the term was first used or who gets credit for coining it, but here is a case, unlike obscenity, where we can define it as well as see it. Between 1946 and 1998 (the end of the 105th Congress), thirty-two of the fifty-two years—almost 62 percent— were years of divided government. (This includes the first six Reagan years, when Republicans controlled the presidency and the Senate but not the House of Representatives.) Of the thirty years between 1968 and 1998, twenty-four were years of divided government, giving that epoch a score of 80 percent. And in the eighteen years since the election of Ronald Reagan, sixteen of them, or 89 percent, were years of divided government.

At first, divided government did not seem to matter very much. Presidents continued to turn out the proposals, and Congress continued to pass important legislation, most of it in response to presidential initiatives, but much in response to their own. And we continued to appraise the national system in the terms set by Neustadt in 1960. But when you look closer at the past eighteen years, there is another sense in which divided government matters a great deal. There is another pattern entirely, and we have to consider it a culmination of new alignments and new institutional adjustments, not the mere turn of a cycle.

This new direction of development deserves a better name. "Divided Government" is no longer a proper name for the phenomenon, because it fails to convey anything beyond the statistical fact of its existence. What we need is a new name that can capture and convey to the mind's eye a conception of its constitutional significance. My tentative label for it is "Absolute Separation of Powers."

For the first time in our history we now have the "separate and independent branches" that the Framers envisioned so clearly. It not only accords with the architecture they designed but also produces the consequences they had hoped it would produce. So now, after two hundred years, we have given the Founders what they wanted. But they do not have to live with the Absolute Separation of Powers; we do.

In order to appraise the Absolute Separation of Powers, we need to define the phenomenon and explore a bit further how we got to where we are. For that, we have to look back again at the parties and party government. As we saw earlier, American government in the nineteenth century was one-party, with the parties alternating command. But that is no longer the case. What we have now—and have had for long enough to consider it institutionalized—is dual-party government, with each party nested in one of the branches. This is better understood not as party government or as two-party government but as duopoly government. Each party expects to control one of the branches, and each party therefore operates as a majority party. After a while, each begins to think like a majority party, and that is a special kind of mentality. In fact, it is a highly anti-innovation type of mentality, comparable to the same situation in a duopolistic or oligopolistic economy. With a guaranteed position, or market share, there is a strong tendency to be risk averse. "We must be doing something right." "If it ain't broke, don't fix it!" "Don't quit while you're ahead." In other words, long-standing majority parties are not only noninnovative but also anti-innovative. As in the economic sphere, when there are just two or three providers in a political market, they can easily know each other's basic interests without collusion and can cooperate without conspiracy. They can compete in a so-called bipartisan manner by picking specialized areas of competition—such as party (brand) loyalty, negative advertising, and research innovation—without trying to go the whole way through vigorous, all-out market (electoral) competition that might harm the competitor but risks harming oneself as well. Each competitor has a vested interest in the other—and also a vested interest in keeping additional competitors out of the competition altogether.

From this perspective, we can also see that when each party is nested in a separate branch (it does not matter very much which branch) and as long as the probability remains high that each party will have a sanctuary, each will win a piece of the government. From another, complementary perspective, each branch now has its own popular base independent of the other. Whereas in 1832, the party system gave the presidency a popular base independent of Congress, the party system today gives Congress a popular base that is no longer tied to small geographical constituencies. Geography or territoriality had always been the very essence of republican government in the United States. State territories frame the Senate (whether elected by state legislatures, as was the case until 1912, or by state popular vote since then). But this has been equally true of the House, particularly after 1842, when Congress tried by law to stamp out at-large election of entire state congressional delegations and any other method of representation except the single-member district, which was expected to be a system of geographical representation, with each district being compact, contiguous, and as close as possible to equal in population. That formality still exists, and geographic representation still has a formal reality with a certain amount of substance to it. But that substance is now not only decreasing but is being subordinated to the more diffuse constituencies defined by regional and national public opinion and by campaign finance. Note, for example, the decreasing percentage of campaign money that comes from within the home district of a member of Congress or even from the state of its senators. Moreover, the population of the United States is now so loose and homogeneous that an increasing proportion of districts are artificial, no matter how the lines are drawn. As of now, therefore, the same principles of politics and representation govern the presidency, the Senate, and the House. There is no longer the "mixed regime" that used to inform all hopes of republican government.

Now we can go back to the earlier question of whether we can actually live with the legacy of the Absolute Separation of Powers intended by the Framers and visited upon us in this most recent epoch of constitutional history. At first glance, it would appear that there are two answers, falling along strictly party lines. Republicans, who as a general rule take pride in being loyal to original intent, would answer "yes" in this specific case as well. Republicans have continually pledged allegiance to Ronald Reagan's belief that "government is the problem, not the solution." Republican liberals (that is, those Republicans who embrace the traditional free-market ideology that has made up the core of the Republican party since its founding) have made common cause with the genuine communitarian and Christian conservatives that make up their right wing to stigmatize the national government, and they have been so successful that their own liberal tradition has had to be closeted as the "l word." If the Absolute Separation of Powers has rendered the national government virtually incapable of governing (or more precisely, incapable of making substantial, substantive policy decisions), that allows the Republicans to claim in effect that their campaign pledges have been honored. Republicans pursued a policy-of-no-policy all during the 1980s, when they held the White House, and continued in that vein when they lost the presidency in 1992 and gained the Congress in 1994.

Democrats would seem to be ready to give the "no" response, loud and clear, to the question of living with the Absolute Separation of Powers, because for most of this century the Democratic Party has both governed and won elections by governmental innovation. However, their adjustment to duopoly has led them to a contrary position, embracing the Absolute Separation of Powers. President Clinton has become a model Republican, contributing significantly to a consensus in favor of the Absolute Separation of Powers. Let's look at the record.

1. First, during the past eighteen years—nay, during the past twenty-five years—there has been little to no innovation in government at the national level. That is to say, there have been almost no genuine, significant substan-

tive decisions expressed in statutes that have featured the two branches in a lawmaking relationship of truly shared power. The only exceptions of any substantive character involving both branches in genuine lawmaking have been laws aimed at downsizing existing programs without actually terminating any. Note well that in over sixty years, only two major New Deal agencies have been terminated. The Civil Aeronautics Board was abolished by, of all people, President Carter, and the Interstate Commerce Commission, after a fifteen-year effort on the part of the Republicans to get rid of it, was finally abolished under President Clinton. Only three or four other programs have been substantially gutted, for example, agriculture price supports, telephone and cable regulation, and entitlements within Aid to Families with Dependent Children. But even here, change came at the very tail end of the Republican era and left the agencies in place in case later decisions "upsize" the programs. In all other actions, downsizing has been the essential direction of both the major parties, and this downsizing has been at the margins, not addressing the substance. Here is the way the libertarian British journal *The Economist* put it in their bottom-line assessment at the end of the first year of the 104th Congress and the Contract with America: "So it seems like a revolution. But what are the revolutionaries actually doing? . . . They are consolidating . . . the New Deal, which they so roundly deplore. . . . By squeezing budgets without eliminating functions, the Republicans are asking the government to deliver on every promise ever made [but] with less and less money."[7]

Even the historic tax reform laws of 1981 and 1986 were essentially downsizing at the margins—though admittedly the margins were pretty big at first. On the other hand, upsizing began almost immediately, with new brackets and new loopholes. And even if one grants for the sake of argument that the tax reform laws of the 1980s were substantive and therefore exceptional, this is more than counterbalanced by the fact that annual deficits mushroomed after 1981, that their rate of increase grew larger all during the 1980s, and the largest share of the growth in the annual deficits was attributable to the incapacity of the current system of national government to make the substantive decisions to cut whole domestic programs and whole agencies, whole bomber wings and whole military bases.

This actually gives us an operational definition of innovation, literally and concretely establishing the difference between innovative and incremental, between substantial and marginal. Substantive or substantial change requires considering and debating a program or agency from a zero base, even if the decision is finally made to keep the program and only amend the law creating the program. Incremental or marginal decisions are decisions to cut percentages without bringing the nature or future of the program or agency into question. Cutting at the margins involves no genuine policy decision and no genuine sharing of powers between the two separated institutions of presidency and Congress. In sum, the last eighteen years presents an incapacity. This is not deadlock or gridlock. It is essentially a government of bookkeepers.

This mentality was reinforced by two major pieces of legislation, one in 1974 and one in 1985, that required, in effect, that policy decisions would not be policy decisions at all but bookkeeping decisions made at the margins of each governmental activity. The 1974 Budget and Impoundment Control Act was adopted by a Democratic Congress against a Republican president, to provide Congress with its own source of budget information and power to compete with the Office of Management and Budget (OMB)—to answer OMB item by item with mind-numbing budgetary figures on each and every governmental activity. Through a process called "reconciliation," new congressional budget committees were given the power to establish budget resolutions that set advance spending targets for agencies and large categories of agencies; these resolutions would require Congress and the Executive Branch to limit spending within those broad categories. Reconciliation pushed almost every policy decision into a budgetary process—to the advantage of the bookkeeping mentality.

This was reinforced by the 1985 Gramm-Rudman-Hollings legislation establishing mandatory deficit reduction figures that would produce a balanced budget by 1991. Any year the established deficit targets were not met, OMB would have to make automatic cuts across the board with a formula set by law to reduce the budgets of all governmental activities at a given percentage: the cuts occurred at the margins, even if the margins were to be felt as large ones. As one authority put it, these two reforms "moved budgetary gimmickry from the sidelines to the center stage." Some say the 1974 and 1985 decisions contribute to the enhancement of presidential power, and others say that it restored to Congress more powers to retaliate, thereby maintaining the balance between the two branches. Either way, the debate between the two branches was forced and formalized toward the budgetary margins, and the alterations of relative power between the two branches would have to be considered incremental at every step of the way.

2. A second manifestation of the Absolute Separation of Powers is the recent and growing tendency of both branches to take actions that do not require the other branch at all. These are actions of a lawlike character and

effect and status, but do not require the two independent institutions to share power. The most important and long-lasting of these is the Reagan approach to deregulation, through the imposition of a new presidential oversight process. One of Reagan's first actions after taking office was Executive Order 12291, issued February 17, 1981, giving OMB the authority to review all proposals by executive branch agencies for new rules and regulations prior to their being printed in the Federal Register and taking on the force of law. Reagan established within OMB an Office of Information and Regulatory Affairs (OIRA) "to provide for presidential oversight of the regulatory process." This process was to be implemented by subjecting every proposed rule with an estimated annual impact of $100 million or more to a cost-benefit test. President Bush went even further than Reagan by making his own vice president, Dan Quayle, head of the regulatory review process. All the while, Congress was not taxed with having to make any substantive regulatory decisions. (In 1996, Congress appeared to reenter the substantive regulatory arena with passage of the Small Business Regulatory Enforcement Fairness Act, which required all agencies to submit each final rule to Congress for sixty legislative days, during which it can be rescinded by joint resolution. But of course this is a paper tiger, because Congress already has more than enough powers to negate regulations, before or after issuance, and the president can veto a joint resolution, which then requires a two-thirds vote. Marginal stuff.)

Some re-regulation was to have been expected from a Democratic administration, and some has taken place. But it is of greater significance that the level of such regulatory activity requiring the participation of both branches had reached such a low level of frequency by 1996 that there was talk of replacing the "batting average" measure of presidential success with a new measure based upon the ability of president or Congress to keep regulation from happening.

Even though Democrat Clinton was still more likely than a Republican president to propose some re-regulation, there is ample evidence that he, like his Republican predecessors, prefers the independent route. The best recent example is his sending Vice President Gore to the AFL-CIO winter meeting in February 1997 to announce the issuance of new guidelines requiring companies doing business with the government to maintain good relations with their workers and the unions that represent them. The government could reject hundreds of millions of dollars worth of contracts and contract bids from companies that do not have a satisfactory record of employment practices. This was denounced as a blatant political payoff for labor support in the 1996 presidential election, and so it must have been. But the fact remains that he could have paid unions off just as well with a legislative proposal to this effect and could have gotten political credit for it even if Congress had rejected it. Other examples of presidential actions independent of Congress in 1996 alone include strict new EPA standards for solid particles emitted by power plants, automobiles, oil refineries, etcetera; similar standards for ozone; termination of Reagan-era approval of property owners draining wetlands of up to ten acres; an executive order establishing a 1.7 million–acre national monument in Utah; unilateral termination of a program that had permitted logging in old-growth forests.

3. A direct extension of the tendency to take actions that do not require participation by the other branch is the Bully Pulpit ploy, the announcement at the highest possible rhetorical level of relatively trivial actions, promises, or expectations that convey the impression of effectiveness. A favorite example is President Clinton's commitment to putting school children in uniforms. Other national guidelines for improving education have the same character: grading school and teacher effectiveness; computerizing classrooms; setting the goal of having each child reading a book by the age of eight; a "citizen army" of a million volunteer tutors to make sure children can read by the age of eight. There are still other Clinton extensions of what George Bush had called the "thousand points of light." Ironically, most of these—the Republican and the Democratic ones—are efforts to set national standards that would have to be implemented virtually entirely by local and state agencies and budgets.

4. A fourth type of evidence indicating the institutional consequences of the Absolute Separation of Powers is what can only be called "Tie Us to the Mast": constitutionally and legally self-imposed preventatives or self-imposed decision rules that make action virtually impossible. These can also be seen as Congress's effort to find a means of action independent of the president, as the president has found means of taking action independent of Congress. One of the best of these is a rule that has existed for a long time but has come into significantly increased usage in the past decade: the so-called filibuster rule. There has been a considerable increase in both the use and threat of filibuster, to such an extent that Senate leadership would be loathe to bring up a bill for a vote unless they were fairly certain they had the sixty votes necessary to overcome the threat of filibuster. And the threat alone of filibuster is virtually enough to block legislation. Another, of course, is the setting of spending caps on broad categories of governmental activities, forcing a kind of zero-sum game on related agencies such that an

increase in one has to be compensated for by a decrease in one or more of the others, or worse, by a provision for revenue enhancements to cover the increase. This not only forces the discourse toward the margins and away from the substance of government activities, as observed earlier, but also amounts to a decision at the beginning of a congressional session to tie the hands of substantive legislative committees and congressional entrepreneurs, to inhibit any tendency toward substantial innovation.

Still other examples of decision prevention are being sought vigorously by factions in Congress that are majority-size but not yet large enough to pass a constitutional amendment or to overcome a Senate filibuster. The most important of these is the various efforts to impose a three-fifths vote requirement on all tax increases and on all substantive actions that would contribute to an increase in the deficit. The most often proposed measure is the balanced-budget amendment, which would not only constitutionalize discourse that is currently at the margins but would also put virtually all taxation and substantive policy innovation beyond the reach of majoritarian republicanism.

Finally, there is one congressional action that warrants close scrutiny not only because of its intrinsic importance but also because of the likelihood that it will be imitated. This is the Defense Base Closure and Realignment Commission established by Congress in the final days of the Cold War. Special provision was made for the independence of this Commission by giving it the authority to make an annual listing of recommendations for military bases to be closed, with the stipulation that the House and Senate could only vote the entire list of recommendations up or down, with no additions or deletions. Congress gave itself no "line-item veto."

Other such commissions in the pipeline are (1) a commission to correct the Consumer Price Index, which allegedly is overstating the rate of inflation; (2) a commission to give America the campaign finance reform to which neither party can commit; and (3) the institution of special or independent counsel, which is another antirepublican tie-us-to-the-mast example, even though it involves the third branch. Through several metamorphoses since the Watergate crisis, Congress has in effect concluded that it cannot, as an institution, sit in judgment on its own, or executive, or judicial officials, despite the Constitution's provisions that the House of Representatives "shall have the sole Power of Impeachment," that the Senate "shall have the sole power to try all Impeachments," and that "Each House may . . . punish its members for disorderly Behaviour and, with the Concurrence of two thirds, expel a Member." We now have a government of sissies. Where is republicanism now that we need it?

Appraising the Absolute Separation of Powers

Something is rotten in the state of America. It is a functioning system but not a functional one. At a minimum, it is a minimalist solution in a country with maximum demands and expectations. The legitimacy of an enormous democratic politics in a large republican government cannot survive a national governmental process whose operational code is action prevention.

This is no appeal for another forty fat years of governmental growth as a mere by-product of keeping the New Deal coalition together. It is an appeal for common sense over and against knee-jerk denial of capacity to govern.

Signs are all about us that we are trying very hard to deny the republican dream, and these signs are not all as recent as some of the examples given above:

1. Delegation of legislative power away from Congress to the president, 1933–73
2. Delegation of fiscal/monetary power from Congress and the president to an independent and self-financing Federal Reserve System
3. Delegation, nay, a process of emptying, of national power to the extremely narrow and traditionally archconservative states, which have done little to deserve the reputation for virtue they now enjoy, and where class, race, and gender relations were just beginning to emerge from the slime of the nineteenth-century communitarian ideal, thanks only to external—national—pressure
4. Rejection of policy making in favor of marginal analysis
5. Replacement of law with economics as the language of the state
6. Displacement of policy making with bookkeeping
7. Denial of the separateness and integrity of the political, moral, and economic realms

As the old saying goes, "God looks after fools, drunkards, and the United States of America." We have indeed been lucky. Through all of the global stresses of the second half of the twentieth century, America has been a fair-weather system of government. We were able to spend untold trillions of dollars to win the Fifty Years War, 1939–89 (yet are now telling ourselves that we cannot ask our grandchildren to help pay for it). We were able to control world trade to our advantage for most of that same period. We defied the oxymoron "institutionalized innovation," and our government-subsidized research and development inventiveness has kept us just ahead of the curves of runaway inflation and disastrous depression. We survived the one big decision that turned sour, Vietnam (and now we wonder whether we should ever make a big policy decision again).

But can we continue to win every war and muddle through every crisis? What are we going to do when the weather turns foul or when the fat years turn lean? Can we survive, by squeezing without choosing, the unintended consequences of a megapolicy decision not to make policy decisions?

The capacity to govern is not something a nation-state is born with, however free we were born. The capacity to govern is not something that can be provided by even the most enlightened constitutional architecture—although that is an indispensable starting point. The capacity to govern is a skill like any other, and requires a lot of practice. And the legitimacy of a democratic republic requires a lot of experience in surviving the consequences of failed public policy decisions. Governmental capacity and legitimacy in the United States are going to wither and die in the procrustean bed of an Absolute Separation of Powers.

NOTES

1. *Federalist* No. 47 (Madison), at 301, ed. Clinton Rossiter (New York: New American Library, 1961).

2. *Federalist* No. 48 (Madison), at 308.

3. *Federalist* No. 51 (Madison), at 322.

4. See Hamilton's *Report on the Public Credit* (1790); his *Report on Manufactures* (1791); and his valedictory, *Report on the Public Credit* (1795).

5. Woodrow Wilson, *Congressional Government* (New York: Houghton Mifflin, 1913).

6. Richard Neustadt, *Presidential Power and the Politics of Leadership* (New York: Wiley, 1960).

7. *Economist*, Dec. 1995.

CHAPTER 33

Glamis, Yes; Cawdor, Yes— but King of Scotland?

Michael W. McConnell

This is not the first time a group has devoted its discussions to the various "tragedies" that could result from the United States Constitution. That is what the delegates to the Virginia ratifying convention were doing in the early summer of 1788. For the most part, their predictions of constitutional tragedy were not much different from those produced by the panel assembled in this volume: the new federal government could be unfair, unrepresentative, oppressive, and neglectful of the common good. James Madison had this response:

> I have observed, that gentlemen suppose, that the general legislature will do every mischief they possibly can, and that they will omit to do every thing good which they are authorized to do. If this were a reasonable supposition, their objections would be good. I consider it reasonable to conclude, that they will as readily do their duty, as deviate from it: Nor do I go on the grounds mentioned by gentlemen on the other side—that we are to place unlimited confidence in them, and expect nothing but the most exalted integrity and sublime virtue. But I go on this great republican principle, that the people will have virtue and intelligence to select men of virtue and wisdom. Is there no virtue among us? If there be not, we are in a wretched situation. No theoretical checks—no form of government can render us secure.[1]

Madison's answer to the tragedians of his day is worthy of repetition to the tragedians of this volume: do not expect too much from a constitution. If the people of this country do not have virtue and intelligence, no "theoretical checks" will rescue us from that wretched situation. The Constitution does little more than establish a structure of government and protect against a few familiar political pathologies. The rest is left to the people.

Not quite. Madison was not *that* sanguine about the virtue and intelligence of the people. The power of the people was constrained by certain "auxiliary precautions."[2] The central feature of the constitutional structure designed by Madison and his co-Founders was to use the clash of interests and opinions as a proxy for the common good. At first this seems odd. Widespread agreement among different interests, social groups, regions, sects, and so forth is no guarantee of the common good; indeed, it may frustrate the ability of statesmen to accomplish the common good. But it *is* likely to avert tragedy: the "rage" for "improper or wicked project[s]" is "less apt to pervade the whole body of the Union than a particular member of it."[3] No one segment of society can be trusted—not even the social and intellectual elite, not even ourselves. Only by structuring government in such a way that there must be broad consensus among different groups, can we be reasonably confident that the government will not often do improper or wicked things.

Ours is thus a tragedy-averse Constitution—if by "tragedy" we mean doing terrible things.[4] As Madison argued, the virtue and intelligence of the people, structured through institutions that require deliberation and consensus, is a reasonable guarantee against such tragedies.

But our tragedy-resistant Constitution has an Achilles' heel: the judiciary. The least subject of all governmental authorities to the control of checks and balances, deliberately insulated from the will of the people (whether virtuous or otherwise), the judiciary is a top-down hierarchy of power, drawn from an extraordinarily narrow social, economic, and professional subclass (successful lawyers). Lodging power in such a group may be appealing to legal academics, since it is our social class. But if Madison's theory of government is correct, the judiciary is exceptionally dangerous precisely because it is so narrow. One would predict that the judiciary would be the branch of government most prone to hubris, error, folly, and tragedy.

History bears this out. In 1941, then–Attorney General Robert Jackson (later to be one of our greatest Supreme Court justices) wrote that "time has proved that [the Supreme Court's judgment] was wrong on the most outstanding issues upon which it has chosen to challenge the popular branches."[5] He continued:

> Its judgment in the *Dred Scott* case was overruled by war. Its judgment that the currency that preserved the Union could not be made legal tender was overruled by Grant's selection of an additional Justice. Its judgment invalidating the income tax was overruled by the Sixteenth Amendment. Its judgments repressing labor and social legislation are now abandoned. Many of the judgments against New Deal legislation are rectified by confession of

error. *In no major conflict with the representative branches on any question of social or economic policy has time vindicated the Court.*[6]

Indeed, the Court has repeatedly stumbled on what may be the most important moral question that ever reaches a court: whether a category of human persons is unworthy of the protection that is accorded their fellow human beings. Each generation produces a *Dred Scott*, a *Plessy*, a *Korematsu*, or a *Roe*. What will be next?

That judges have the "ways of the scholar," as Alexander Bickel claimed, is no guarantee of virtue. The most important commentary on *Plessy* is Herbert Hovenkamp's "Social Science and Segregation before *Brown*,"[7] which shows that the justices in *Plessy* acted in accordance with the "best" and most "scientific" thinking of their day about race. (It was the much-maligned, profit-motivated railroads who resisted Jim Crow most effectively, for the longest time.)[8] There is no reason to think that the "best" social science and philosophy of our day is immune from a similar moral blindness. One contributor to this volume assured us that "if something is truly evil, the judges will recognize it."[9] That strikes me as precisely the mistake with which the Virginia "gentlemen on the other side" charged the supporters of the Constitution: unwarranted "confidence" in ruling elites. History does not give warrant to such faith in judges, who are as likely as any other narrow social class to overlook evil when it accords with their class interests and prejudices.

The editors of this volume asked us to identify the feature of the Constitution which is most likely to produce "tragedy," but which, as a conscientious interpreter of the document, we are compelled to endorse and support. My nomination: the feature that allows five members of the United States Supreme Court to declare acts of the representative institutions of our government unconstitutional.

This feature is "tragic," in the terms set by the editors of this volume, because it is not a mere mistake. I do not doubt that *Marbury v. Madison*[10] was rightly decided; historical sources leave no doubt that the Framers of the Constitution and the Bill of Rights expected the judiciary to enforce constitutional limits. Without judicial review, it is doubtful that the Constitution would play as central a role as it has in our national life. This would have been a great loss. And I join in celebrating *Brown v. Board of Education*,[11] a great victory for the principles of the Constitution[12] and one of the few instances in which it was a good thing for the judiciary to second-guess the "virtue and intelligence" of the American people.

These great decisions call to mind the opening scenes of Shakespeare's *Macbeth*, in which the witches greet Macbeth as Glamis (his current title), Cawdor (a title that he has just won for valor in battle, though he does not yet know it), and king of Scotland (a title that is not rightfully his, and that can be seized only by illegitimate means). *Marbury*, like Glamis, is the title vested in the judiciary from the beginning. *Brown* represents the judiciary's greatest victory, at a moment of peril to constitutional government. The courts had earned the honor they received from that episode in our history, as Macbeth had earned the title of Cawdor. But Glamis and Cawdor did not entitle Macbeth to seize the sovereign power as king of Scotland. And the principles of *Marbury* and *Brown* do not justify the judiciary in taking upon itself important public questions, about which virtuous and intelligent people are divided, and to which the Constitution, as defined by text, history, practice, and precedent, provides no answer. Not only is this illegitimate, but it can lead, and has led on more than one occasion, to injustice, blood, and death.

NOTES

1. Robert A. Rutland and Charles F. Hobson, eds., *The Papers of James Madison*, vol. 11, at 163 (Chicago: University of Chicago, 1977) (June 20, 1788).

2. *Federalist* No. 51 (Madison), at 322, ed. Clinton Rossiter (New York: New American Library, 1961).

3. *Federalist* No. 10 (Madison), at 84.

4. This same structure aggravates the tendency to a different kind of tragedy, that which comes about through inaction. By requiring a broad consensus before the government can adopt new policies, the Constitution creates gridlock and inaction. These are the logical and predictable outgrowth of a constitutional structure that seeks to avoid the tragedies of improper or wicked acts.

5. Robert H. Jackson, *The Struggle for Judicial Supremacy* x (New York: Vintage Books, 1941).

6. *Id.* at ix–x (emphasis mine).

7. 1985 *Duke L.J.* 624.

8. See Jennifer Roback, "The Political Economy of Segregation: The Case of Segregated Streetcars," 46 *J. Econ. Hist.* 893 (1986).

9. Dan Ortiz posed the question raised in text.

10. 5 U.S. (1 Cranch) 137 (1803).

11. 347 U.S. 483 (1954).

12. See Michael W. McConnell, "Originalism and the Desegregation Decisions," 81 *Va. L. Rev.* 947 (1995).

CHAPTER 34

Brown v. Board of Education

Earl M. Maltz

Any list of constitutional tragedies must include *Brown v. Board of Education*,[1] in which the Court concluded that the maintenance of racially segregated schools was unconstitutional. The tragedy of *Brown* does not lie in the Court's substantive vision. Racial segregation is morally indefensible; moreover, it is terrible public policy, tending to deprive society at large of the potential contributions of talented members of minority races. Instead, the tragedy of *Brown* is that the result in the case cannot be derived from the original understanding of the Fourteenth Amendment.

In measuring the decision in *Brown* against the original understanding, the starting point is, of course, the language of the amendment itself. On its face, Section 1 might appear to be a general, open-ended statement of principles of justice and equality, leaving the judiciary free to fill in the details as it sees fit. However, in the Reconstruction period, privileges and immunities, due process, and equal protection of the laws were all principles with well-established legal pedigrees, whose meanings were uncertain only at the margins—a point of which Republicans were well aware.[2] Moreover, none of these principles had been interpreted by *any* court to bar the maintenance of segregated schools.

The Equal Protection Clause—the centerpiece of the majority's argument in *Brown*—was understood to have a particularly narrow compass. Basically, it was thought to ensure only procedural protection of rights that were otherwise guaranteed by natural or positive law. This concept was so elementary that it was supported even by some who were generally opposed to guaranteeing civil rights to the freed slaves.[3]

Against this background, the Privileges and Immunities Clause emerges as the most plausible support for the *Brown* decision. Courts and commentators have differed sharply over the proper interpretation of this clause. For example, while the *Slaughterhouse Cases*[4] concluded that the concept of privileges and immunities had only a very limited significance, Professor John Harrison takes a quite different view, arguing that "[t]he main point of the [privileges and immunities] clause is to require that every state give the same privileges and immunities of state citizenship . . . to all its citizens."[5] If it accurately reflected the original understanding, Harrison's analysis would justify *Brown*: since all states provide free public education, access to such education would have to be provided on a race-blind basis.[6]

As Harrison clearly demonstrates, the framers of the Fourteenth Amendment were in fact attempting to guarantee intrastate equality in some rights. Nonetheless, his conclusions are flawed, for two reasons. First, one must carefully distinguish between the *nature* of the rights protected and the *measure* of the rights protected. The debates over the Civil Rights Act of 1866 provide a classic example of this dichotomy. As the language of the statute demonstrates, the framers adopted state law as the measure of the rights protected in section 1 of the statute. The list of the rights protected, however, was not derived from state law, but rather from natural or quasi-natural concepts such as "the natural rights of man,"[7] or "the attributes of freedman according to the universal understanding of the American people."[8]

Second, Harrison's argument incorrectly assumes that the framers of the Fourteenth Amendment conflated the rights associated with national citizenship with those derived from state citizenship. Both the language and history of the amendment belie this conclusion. The Citizenship Clause of Section 1 specifically confers *both* state and national citizenship on persons born or naturalized in the United States; by contrast, the Privileges and Immunities Clause by its terms protects only "citizens and immunities of citizens *of the United States.*" Moreover, congressional Republicans drew a clear distinction between the two types of citizenship and sought to provide protection only for those rights that they saw as specifically associated with national citizenship. Thus, for example, Republican representative William Lawrence of Ohio declared that "all privileges and immunities are of two kinds, to wit, those which [are] inherent in every citizen of the United States, and such others as may be conferred by local law and pertain only to the citizens of the state."[9] Similarly, Republican representative Samuel Shellabarger of Ohio distinguished between "those local, and not fundamental, privileges . . . which a State may give to its own permanent inhabitants and deny to sojourners [and] 'fundamental' [rights which] cannot be taken away from any citizen of the United States by the laws of any State."[10]

In each case, Republicans identified the rights to be protected as those appurtenant to national citizenship.

Even when considered in the abstract, the right to a free public education fits comfortably into the mold of a right "conferred by local law and pertain[ing] only to the citizen of the State." Unlike (for example) the right to contract and to be free from bodily restraint, it cannot be viewed as a natural right which preexisted the establishment of governments. Unlike the right to hold real property, it is not the byproduct of allegiance to a federal government with sovereign authority over that property. Instead, public education is a creation of state government, supported by local taxation for the benefit of its own citizenry. As such, access to public education is the quintessential example of a right dependent on state rather than national citizenship, and is thus outside the purview of the Privileges and Immunities Clause.

This conclusion is bolstered by the status of public education under the Privileges and Immunities Clause of Article IV, otherwise known as the Comity Clause. Republican representative John A. Bingham—the author of Section 1 of the Fourteenth Amendment—explicitly identified the Comity Clause as the source of the privileges and immunities language in the Fourteenth Amendment and, differentiating between state and national citizenship, identified the rights protected as the privileges and immunities of citizens of the United States.[11] The identity between the Comity Clause of Article IV and the privileges and immunities language of Section 1 of the Fourteenth Amendment was recognized by many other mainstream Republicans as well.[12]

Against this background, the proper analysis of the Privileges and Immunities Clause of Section 1 emerges rather clearly. The rights protected by the clause are rights of national citizenship, which in turn are identical with those that states must grant to sojourners from other states under the Comity Clause. While the nature of these rights might be unclear at the margins, the right to attend public schools is rather clearly not included. Few (if any) constitutional scholars would claim that a child from state A, visiting for one week in state B, would have a right under the Comity Clause to attend the public schools of state B during his visit. Thus, since the rights guaranteed by the two Privileges and Immunities Clauses were understood to be coextensive, citizens of state B similarly cannot claim the right to attend desegregated schools under the Privileges and Immunities Clause of Section 1.

Any originalist defense of *Brown* must also contend with the historical context in which the Fourteenth Amendment was adopted. School segregation was common in the northern states during the period in which the Fourteenth Amendment was drafted and ratified. Segregation was particularly prevalent in the states of the lower north—the pivotal battleground states in the national elections. Thus, any direct, broad-based effort to attack segregated schools would have carried with it substantial political risks.

The moderate Republicans who controlled the drafting of the Fourteenth Amendment were disinclined to take such risks. Although Section 1 is couched in terms of legal art, the Fourteenth Amendment as a whole was in large measure a campaign document, designed to outline the Republican program of Reconstruction for the upcoming elections of 1866.[13] As such, all of its provisions—including Section 1—were carefully drafted to appeal to swing voters in the post–Civil War electorate. As part of their strategy, mainstream Republicans repeatedly assured these voters that Section 1 would have only a minimal impact on northern state laws—a claim they could not have made if Section 1 had been generally understood to outlaw segregated schools.

The congressional treatment of the District of Columbia school system underscores the unwillingness of Republicans in the Thirty-Ninth Congress to attack segregation in public schools. Issues of federalism did not constrain congressional action dealing with the District of Columbia; thus, on issues such as streetcar segregation, voting rights, and jury service, mainstream Republicans in Congress acted to protect the rights of free African Americans in the district well in advance of the passage of nationally applicable measures. By contrast, contemporaneously with the Fourteenth Amendment, the same Republicans continued to support the segregated school system in the District of Columbia.[14] To contend that Republicans would at the same time knowingly act against school segregation by a nationally applicable constitutional amendment is to attribute to them an almost Orwellian mentality.

Professor Michael McConnell seeks to rebut this evidence by relying on the congressional discussions that ultimately led to the adoption of the Civil Rights Act of 1875.[15] However, Professor McConnell's argument suffers from two difficulties. The first problem is doctrinal; while *Brown* dealt with the impact of the Fourteenth Amendment *per se* on school segregation, the issue in the debate on the Civil Rights Act was whether Congress had the power to require public schools to be desegregated. The second problem is temporal; the Civil Rights Act was not considered and adopted until several years after the Fourteenth Amendment was ratified, and political conditions had changed substantially in the interim.

In doctrinal terms, the constitutional issue that was debated in the 1870s was whether Congress had the power to order school desegregation under Section 5 of the Fourteenth Amendment. This question is analytically distinct from that of whether Section 1 by its terms requires desegregation (although the two issues are obviously related). Moreover, there is substantial reason to believe that at least some Republicans understood this distinction and knew that they were dealing only with the Section 5 issue.

As Professor McConnell notes, Republican representative William Lawrence of Ohio enunciated the basic constitutional theory underlying the provisions of the Civil Rights Bill that dealt with schools. Lawrence argued that "[w]hen the States by law create and protect, and by taxation on all support, benevolent institutions designed to care for those who need those benefits, the [Equal Protection Clause] require[s] that equal provision should be made for all."[16] This theory—also cited by Republican senators Oliver H.P.T. Morton and John Sherman as the justification for including public education in the Civil Rights Bill[17]—draws its support from antebellum legal authorities defining the scope of the right to protection of the laws. These authorities did not rely on either a particular distaste for racial classifications or an assessment of the importance of particular government benefits. Rather, they were based on the view that, where a class of people was taxed to support a given benefit, and then denied access to that benefit, that class was in essence subject to an uncompensated taking, and as such denied the right to protection *from* government.[18]

This doctrine played an important role in the 1860 Senate debate over the funding of education in the District of Columbia. As initially proposed, the bill before the Senate provided simply that the city authorities could impose a general property tax to benefit the public schools in the district, and that the federal government would provide matching funds of up to twenty-five thousand dollars per year. Senate Republicans pressed for an amendment which would have required the city government to use at least part of the funds to educate African Americans as well as whites. One of the mainstays of the Republican argument was the contention that "taxing [African Americans] for the exclusive benefit of the white children . . . would be a kind of legal robbery"[19]—a clear reference to the principles of the state taxation cases. At the same time, however, the limitations of the doctrine became clear when Republican Daniel Clark, the sponsor of the amendment to require that African Americans be admitted to the schools, stated that he would accept exclusion of free African Americans so long as they were exempted from the property tax and their pro rata share of the federal contribution was withheld.[20]

John Sherman, one of the most prominent Republicans in the Senate, took a similarly limited view of the scope of the right protected. In 1872, Sherman explicitly stated that he viewed the maintenance of segregated schools as constitutional, so long as the African-American schools received their pro rata share of school funding.[21] Yet the next day, Sherman voted *against* the Blair amendment, which would have specifically reserved to local governments the right to maintain segregated schools.[22] How can one explain this seeming anomaly?

The simplest answer lies in the Republican conception of the scope of the Section 5 enforcement authority. Many regular Republicans embraced the view of congressional power expressed by Chief Justice John Marshall in *McCulloch v. Maryland*:[23] "Let the end be legitimate, let it be within the scope of the Constitution, and all means which are appropriate, which are not prohibited, but consist with the letter and spirit of the Constitution, are constitutional." Under this view, Congress would clearly have authority to prohibit some actions that would not be prohibited by the Constitution itself. This point was made by Republicans a number of times in the debate over the Civil Rights Act of 1875. Thus, for example, Representative Robert Hale of New York explicitly relied on *McCulloch* in arguing that passage of the Civil Rights Act would not be inconsistent with the Supreme Court's decision in the *Slaughterhouse Cases*.[24] Lawrence also relied on *McCulloch* in his defense of the Civil Rights Bill,[25] declaring that "Congress . . . is the exclusive judge of the means to employ [in guaranteeing the rights secured by the Fourteenth Amendment]"[26] and that "[a] remedial power in the Constitution is to be construed liberally."[27] Against this background, the apparent inconsistencies in Sherman's position can be reconciled. School segregation might not be unconstitutional per se; however, under the *McCulloch* view of congressional power, the Civil Rights Bill might still be constitutional as a device to guarantee that African Americans would in fact receive equal financial support in return for their tax dollars, or (as Sherman apparently believed) as a means to advance the Reconstruction process generally.[28] In neither case would a vote for the school desegregation provisions of the Civil Rights Bill support the conclusion that *Brown* was rightly decided under originalist theory.

Of course, as Professor McConnell clearly demonstrates, a number of Republicans disagreed with Sherman and argued that Section 1 by its terms outlawed school segregation. Even these statements, however, are suspect from an originalist perspective.

Republican pronouncements on constitutional issues in the 1870s are a demonstrably unreliable guide to the original understanding in the period from 1866 to 1868, when the Fourteenth Amendment was drafted and ratified.

As Reconstruction progressed, regular Republicans showed a clear willingness to move beyond the strictures of the Fourteenth Amendment in adopting civil rights measures of nationwide applicability. In pure policy terms, the evolution of the Republican position on the issue of African-American suffrage provides one striking example. During the drafting of the Fourteenth Amendment itself, party regulars explicitly rejected a provision that would have required the states to allow African Americans to vote; moreover, they specifically noted their rejection of the African-American suffrage provision in the committee report accompanying the proposed amendment.[29] Only three years later, by contrast, Republicans united to pass the Fifteenth Amendment, which required states to adopt race-blind qualifications for voting.

For purposes of evaluating Professor McConnell's argument, the evolution of the Republican position on jury service is even more compelling. A section prohibiting racial discrimination in jury selection was included in the Civil Rights Act of 1875, with Republicans citing the Equal Protection Clause as the source of authority for this provision.[30] Moreover, Republican support for the jury selection provision was no less overwhelming than the support for the school provisions: for example, in 1872, an effort to delete the protection for jury service from the Sumner bill was defeated 33–16; among Republicans, only James L. Alcorn of Mississippi, Arthur I. Boreman of West Virginia, Matthew H. Carpenter of Wisconsin, and John A. Logan of Illinois supported the motion.[31]

Given this evidence, the same argument that supports Professor McConnell's position on the issue of racially segregated schools would also suggest that, as originally understood by its framers, the Fourteenth Amendment prohibited states from excluding African Americans from juries. However, a wide variety of commentators—including Professor McConnell himself—have concluded that, in the late 1860s, it was generally conceded by all parties that the Fourteenth Amendment had no impact on political rights, including the right to serve on juries.[32] Thus, the jury service provision stands as a clear example of a case in which regular Republicans of the 1870s were willing to seize on the Fourteenth Amendment as a source of authority for congressional action which went beyond the original understanding of the amendment. There is no particular reason to believe that the school desegregation provision would have stood on any more secure footing. In short, McConnell's originalist defense of *Brown* is ultimately unconvincing.

Against this background, *Brown* emerges as a striking example of a larger tragedy that permeates constitutional law generally. Any honest reading of the historical evidence reveals that, as drafted, the Constitution does not prohibit all or even most of the major injustices that might be perpetrated by the political system. Some might argue that the proper response to this problem is to abandon originalism as a constitutional theory; however, the complete record of the Court's treatment of racial issues—a record that includes not only *Brown* but decisions such as *Prigg v. Pennsylvania*,[33] *Dred Scott v. Sandford*,[34] *The Civil Rights Cases*,[35] *City of Richmond v. J. A. Croson Co.*,[36] and *Shaw v. Reno*[37]—provides little reason to believe that an unconstrained activist Court would truly be a force for social justice. The tragedy is that we have no recourse but to place our trust in the other branches of government and hope for the best.[38]

NOTES

1. 347 U.S. 294 (1954).

2. Earl M. Maltz, "Fourteenth Amendment Concepts in the Antebellum Era," 32 *Am. J. Leg. Hist.* 305 (1988); Cong. Globe, 39th Cong., 1st Sess. 1089 (1866).

3. E.g., Cong. Globe, 39th Cong., 1st Sess. 2891 (1866) (remarks of Sen. Cowan).

4. 83 U.S. (16 Wall.) 36 (1872).

5. John Harrison, "Reconstructing the Privileges and Immunities Clause," 101 *Yale L.J.* 1385, 1388 (1992).

6. Harrison himself seems to tie the right to public education to the fact that whites as well as blacks are taxed to support the system. 101 *Yale L.J.* at 1462–63 and note 294.

7. Cong. Globe, 39th Cong., 1st Sess. 1117 (1866) (remarks of Rep. Wilson)

8. *Id.* at 504 (remarks of Sen. Howard). To the same effect, see *id.* at 474–75 (remarks of Sen. Trumbull).

9. *Id.* at 1836.

10. *Id.* at App. 293.

11. *Id.* at 158, 1034.

12. *Id.* at 1054 (remarks of Rep. Higby); *id.* at 1095 (remarks of Rep. Hotchkiss). While Bingham himself viewed the rights protected by the first eight amendments as protected by the Comity Clause as well, Senator Jacob Howard of Michigan argued that the Privileges and Immunities Clause of Section One protected them *in addition* to those rights protected by the Comity Clause. Cong. Globe, 42d Cong., 1st sess. app. 84 (1871); Cong. Globe, 39th Cong., 1st Sess. 2765 (1866). Even if one were to adopt Howard's view, it would not materially change the analysis.

13. Michael Les Benedict, *A Compromise of Principle: Congressional Republicans and Reconstruction, 1863–1869* (New York: Norton, 1974); Eric McKitrick, *Andrew Johnson and Reconstruction* (Chicago: University of Chicago Press, 1960).

14. E.g., Cong. Globe, 39th Cong., 1st Sess. 708–9 (1866).

15. Michael W. McConnell, "Originalism and the Desegregation Decisions," 81 *Va. L. Rev.* 947 (1995).

16. 2 Cong. Rec. 412 (1874).

17. Cong. Globe, 42d Cong., 2d Sess. 3190–93 (1872).

18. The development of this theory is described in detail in Earl M. Maltz, "Fourteenth Amendment Concepts in the Antebellum Era," 32 *Am. J. Leg. Hist.* 305 (1988).

19. Cong. Globe, 36th Cong., 1st Sess. 1681 (1860).

20. *Id.* at 1680.

21. Cong. Globe, 42d Cong., 2d Sess. 3193 (1874).

22. *Id.* at 3263.

23. 17 U.S. (4 Wheat.) 316, 419 (1819). For an early example of Republican reliance on *McCulloch*, see the defense of the Civil Rights Bill of 1866 by Rep. James Wilson, Cong. Globe, 39th Cong., 2d Sess. 1118 (1866).

24. 3 Cong. Rec. 980 (1875), discussing *Slaughterhouse Cases*, 83 U.S. (16 Wall.) 36 (1873).

25. 2 Cong. Rec. 414 (1874).

26. *Id.*

27. *Id.* at 412, citing *Chisolm v. Georgia*, 2 U.S. (2 Dal.) 419, 476 (1793).

28. Cong. Globe, 42d Cong., 2d Sess. 3192–93 (1872).

29. Report of the Joint Committee on Reconstruction, 39th Cong., 1st Sess. 12 (1866).

30. The evolution of the jury selection provision is described in detail in Earl M. Maltz, "The Civil Rights Act and *The Civil Rights Cases*: Congress, Court and Constitution," 44 *Fla. L. Rev.* 605 (1992).

31. Cong. Globe, 42d Cong., 2d Sess. 3263 (1872).

32. McConnell, "Originalism and the Desegregation Decisions" 1024. See also Maltz, "Civil Rights Act and *The Civil Rights Cases*."

33. 41 U.S. (16 Pet.) 539 (1842).

34. 60 U.S. (19 How.) 393 (1857).

35. 109 U.S. 3 (1883).

36. 488 U.S. 469 (1989).

37. 509 U.S. 630 (1995).

38. Much of this essay is taken from Earl M. Maltz, "A Dissenting Opinion to Brown," 20 So. Ill. L.J. 93 (1995), and Earl M. Maltz, "Originalism and the Desegregation Decisions," 13 Const. Comm. 223 (1996).

CHAPTER 35

Tragedy and Constitutional Interpretation

The California Civil Rights Initiative

Robert Post

We are all familiar with circumstances, like those portrayed by Herman Melville in *Billy Budd*, where the law dictates tragic results. In these circumstances tragedy appears to flow from law's positivism, from the disjunction between legal rules and moral sensibility. The question I wish to address in this paper is whether we can avoid such tragic outcomes by eliminating this disjunction. Specifically, I ask whether we can escape constitutional tragedy by incorporating ordinary moral principles into our practice of constitutional interpretation.

To pursue this inquiry we first need a working definition of tragedy. Classical Greek tragedy, at least as expounded by Aristotle, chronicles the collision between character and fate. Tragedy is in this sense inescapable and therefore not well suited to our present purpose. A more useful concept of tragedy can be derived from the work of R. B. Sewall, who writes that "[b]asic to the tragic form is its recognition of the inevitability of paradox, of unresolved tensions and ambiguities, of opposites in precarious balance."[1] Guido Calabresi and Philip Bobbitt generalize from this concept of tragedy to the notion of tragic decisions, which are "particularly painful" because they involve the necessary compromise of highly important values that are in tension.[2]

A more precise framing of our question, therefore, is whether incorporating general moral principles into our practice of constitutional interpretation will enable us to avoid constitutional tragedy, meaning constitutional decisions that necessarily rupture highly significant values. I note at the outset that this notion of constitutional tragedy is necessarily perspectival, since it depends upon an observer's perception of the values at stake in a decision.

Tragic constitutional decisions are ordinarily figured as involving a conflict between constitutional and extraconstitutional norms. The classic exploration of such tragic decisions may be found in Robert Cover's *Justice Accused*, which delineates the horrific conflict faced by nineteenth-century judges who simultaneously believed that slavery was a great moral wrong and that slavery was constitutional.[3] To decide against slavery would do violence to the law; to decide for slavery would perpetrate a monstrosity. The antislavery judges described by Cover were thus forced to a tragic choice between their duty to the Constitution and their moral responsibility. The obligation of decision required them to violate one value or the other.

The tragedy of these judges springs from the disjunction between general moral principles and the Constitution. The best recent discussion of this disjunction may be found in Henry Monaghan's article "Our Perfect Constitution."[4] Monaghan attacks those who would interpret the Constitution so as to make it "perfect" by construing it to be congruent with "current conceptions of political morality."[5] Citing figures like Frank Michelman, Kenneth Karst, Paul Brest, Laurence Tribe, Owen Fiss, and Ronald Dworkin, Monaghan convincingly argues that this kind of interpretation predominates among modern constitutional theorists.

Monaghan himself wishes to oppose this form of constitutional interpretation, and he offers an alternative account that is roughly textualist or originalist. By thus defending an admittedly positivist and "imperfect" Constitution, Monaghan reintroduces the disjunction between law and political morality. He thereby embraces the possibility of the kind of constitutional tragedy explored by Cover. We may ask, however, whether we can insulate ourselves from such tragedy by rejecting Monaghan's positivism and subscribing to a practice of constitutional interpretation that strives to eliminate the disjunction between political morality and the Constitution.

The question is important to me because I myself do not share Monaghan's commitment to originalism and textualism. Although I cannot here defend the proposition, I think it is clear enough that constitutional interpretation has always been and must ultimately remain "responsive" to the nation's "ethos," by which I mean the values implicit in "our national identity and history."[6] Having adopted this theory of constitutional interpretation, however, have I also protected courts from the possibility of the kind of constitutional tragedy that so tormented Cover's antislavery judges?

Unfortunately the question must be answered in the negative. Consider, for example, the position of a judge who does not share the values of the national ethos. Imagine a judge who is a Christian fundamentalist and who sincerely believes that abortion is murder. If that judge's best interpretation of the values implicit in the nation's identity and history is that they would support the protection of the right to choose as a fundamental right, the judge would be faced with a tragic dilemma, forced to decide between her moral principles and her obligation to the Constitution. She would be in the same horrific position as the antislavery judges described by Cover.

The larger point is, of course, that no plausible theory of constitutional interpretation can attempt to render the Constitution congruent to a judge's subjective conceptions of political morality. The Constitution is a social and public document; it is a repository of collective values. To the extent that any particular judge does not share those values, there remains with respect to that judge the possibility of constitutional tragedy, even though she reads the Constitution as perfectible in Monaghan's sense.

We must press the point, however, and inquire into the position of a judge who participates in the national ethos and who shares the principles of political morality that should appropriately be read into the Constitution. Has such a judge managed to escape the fate of constitutional tragedy? Unfortunately the answer must once again be negative.

A contrary conclusion would require us to envision political morality as a seamless web of internally consistent and coherent obligations. While this hopeful image no doubt underlies the work of some political and moral philosophers, it does not correspond well with the overpowering sense of jagged uncertainty and conflict that most of us experience in ordinary life. That experience is perhaps best captured in the work of those communitarians who respond to the charge that an ethics derived from community norms will lack the resources necessary for critical distance. These communitarians note that in a modern, heterogeneous society like our own, principles of political morality are diverse, complex, and filled with unresolved internal tensions that leave ample room for critical disagreements.[7] Indeed, as Alasdair MacIntyre has written, "A living tradition . . . is an historically extended, socially embodied argument, and an argument precisely in part about the goods which constitute that tradition."[8] Those who take one side of the argument may well err tragically from the perspective of those committed to an opposing position.

It appears, then, that our political morality is not itself perfectible; it unfortunately offers abundant resources to sustain the possibility of tragedy. A practice of constitutional interpretation that closed the gap between the Constitution and political morality would thus not eliminate tragedy. It would instead incorporate the potential for tragedy immanent in our political morality into the Constitution itself. As a consequence, what we had heretofore conceptualized as a conflict between the Constitution and political morality we would now understand as a conflict between competing constitutional norms.[9]

Such a potentially tragic conflict of constitutional norms is presently gestating in my home state of California. Unhappily, California's populism has tended to produce more than its fair share of constitutional anomalies. The most recent example is the enactment in November, 1996, of the California Civil Rights Initiative (CCRI). The initiative is an amendment to the California Constitution that provides that "The state shall not discriminate against, or grant preferential treatment to, any individual or group on the basis of race, sex, color, ethnicity, or national origin in the operation of public employment, public education or public contracting." The precise meaning of CCRI is not clear, but its general thrust is to ban affirmative action except where required by federal or constitutional law. The constitutionality of CCRI has been challenged, and its implementation was enjoined by a federal district court, which was in turn reversed by the United States Court of Appeals for the Ninth Circuit. It is likely that the United States Supreme Court will ultimately pass on its constitutionality.

When it does so, its decision may enact a high constitutional tragedy. This is because there will be two important constitutional values in play, and they will be in serious tension with each other. One of these values is that of democratic self-determination. Affirmative action is a highly controversial method of dealing with social disaffection. It entails state classification of persons on the basis of race, which is always dangerous and always carries significant risks of balkanization, racialization, and essentialism. The Court's current precedents require affirmative action to be subject to strict scrutiny,[10] but even the most liberal justices, like Thurgood Marshall and William J. Brennan, have conceded that these inherent dangers require that affirmative action be subjected to an elevated scrutiny roughly equivalent to that currently applied to explicit gender classifications.[11] To deprive the citizens of a state of the power to regulate such a dangerous and controversial method of addressing social dislocations is to compromise seriously the fundamental constitutional value of democratic self-governance.[12]

There is, however, another constitutional value at stake. California is the nation's most ethnically diverse state; and, at least in my view, CCRI represents a policy disaster of major proportions. We need affirmative action as a means of facilitating upward mobility and social integration. For all its difficulties, affirmative action is the best tool we have to avoid increasingly stark conditions of alienation, division, and oppression. Does this goal engage constitutional values? I believe so. A constitutional order would seem to require a certain minimum of social justice, so as to extend to all a continuing stake in the health and maintenance of the state. Radical alienation, especially when concentrated in identifiable and otherwise oppressed groups, is inimical to the possibility of constitutional democracy. For this reason I personally believe that a decision upholding CCRI will compromise an important constitutional value.

From my perspective, therefore, highly significant constitutional values will be ruptured no matter which way the Supreme Court ultimately decides the case. There will either be deeply felt and justifiable democratic frustration with judicial tyranny, or there will be deeply felt and justifiable despair at our callous disregard of the living consequences of our racist past.

It is important to notice that the tragedy of this dilemma does not turn on any particular method of constitutional interpretation. Even if my reading of the Constitution as requiring a certain minimum of social justice is rejected, the possibility of tragedy persists. That possibility will merely be refigured as a conflict between the constitutional norm of democratic self-governance and the extralegal norm of social justice. The potential for constitutional tragedy is in this sense independent of our substantive practice of constitutional interpretation.

What drives that potential is instead the obligation of decision, the necessity of opting for one value or another. It is striking, therefore, to note that the district court's preliminary injunction barring enforcement of CCRI purports to find unconstitutional only "the manner" in which the initiative prohibits affirmative action.[13] Building upon the Supreme Court's decision in *Washington v. Seattle School District No. 1*,[14] the district court held that CCRI was unconstitutional because it restructured the political process in a way that particularly burdened "the interests of minorities or women";[15] all other groups could receive government preferences merely by lobbying particular governmental agencies, whereas after CCRI minorities and women could receive preferences only by changing the California Constitution.

The district court's opinion was a fair reading of *Seattle School District No. 1*,[16] in which the Supreme Court had struck down an initiative in the state of Washington that in effect barred local school districts from voluntary busing to achieve integration. Although the Court stated that "the simple repeal or modification of desegregation or antidiscrimination laws, without more, never has been viewed as embodying a presumptively invalid racial classification," it nevertheless found the Washington initiative unconstitutional because it lodged "decision making authority over" a question of great interest to minorities "at a new and remote level of government," while leaving decision-making authority over other issues at the level of the local school board.[17]

The California Civil Rights Initiative, analogously, shifts the authority for affirmative action programs to the plateau of constitutional decision making, while leaving authority for other preferences at the level of local governmental agencies. By building on the *Seattle* precedent, therefore, the district court avoided having to decide the constitutionality of affirmative action per se. It thus appeared to conserve both of the values that I have identified as at risk in the case. Democratic self-governance was preserved, for the State of California was told that it could in fact prohibit affirmative action, if only it did so in the proper manner (at the level of particular government agencies). And social justice was preserved, because CCRI was prevented from going into effect.

So far from constitutional tragedy, therefore, the CCRI litigation at the trial court level produced, instead, a form of constitutional comedy, in the sense that "the theme of the comic is the integration of society."[18] The district court's opinion promises a world in which there are no tragic, irresolvable tensions, in which political morality is seamless and internally coherent. And, as we can see from the *Seattle* precedent, this is a highly typical form of legal decision making. That is why the critic Northrop Frye has noted "the resemblance of the rhetoric of comedy to the rhetoric of jurisprudence."[19] Hercules, that is to say, is no Oedipus, regardless of how many riddles he solves. Constitutional law characteristically presents the image of an orderly, stable, and safe social world.

One ought to be careful, however, to distinguish image from reality. The stability of *Seattle*, for example, seems to me largely illusory, because the decision freezes into place a particular allocation of decision-making authority without even purporting constitutionally to analyze the necessity or justifications for that allocation. Thus, while *Seattle* would prohibit the state of Washington from changing its political process constitutionally to constrain local school boards from busing to integrate, it would simultaneously permit another state to regulate its school boards in exactly this way, so long as the latter state need not change its political process in order to do so.[20] The precedent is thus neither safe nor stable; it is constructed on sand.[21]

The ultimate question, therefore, turns on the constitutionality of the power to prohibit affirmative action per se. The elaborate narrative of political process recounted by both *Seattle* and the district court merely defer this question. From the perspective of constitutional tragedy, these decisions demonstrate how the law functions, in the words of Murray Krieger in his essay on "Tragedy and the Tragic Vision," like:

> one of our John Deweys: those of our insistent naturalists who, for all the hardheadedness of their religious disbelief, are yet naively optimistic believers in a structured social morality and in social progress. These are, from the Kierkegaardian standpoint, the men of little heart; those who, evading the atheist's existential obligation to confront nothingness and its frighteningly empty consequences, construct elaborate rational structures based on nothing else: who whistle in the dark as if all were light.[22]

Constitutional law typically whistles in the dark, constructing "elaborate rational structures" to ward off the Kierkegaardian night. It strives to defer and deflect the recognition of incompatible obligations. We might even say that this is the genius of our system of constitutional adjudication. But we should never fool ourselves into thinking that we have actually banished the abyss that we paper over in our efforts to construct sensible political decisions. Despite our Deweyesque commitment to social engineering, despite our endlessly innovative legal techniques, sooner or later yawning inconsistencies will flare frighteningly to the surface.

We can postpone, but we cannot evade, the necessity of constitutional tragedy.

NOTES

1. Richard B. Sewall, "The Tragic Form," in Lawrence Michel and Richard Sewall, eds., *Tragedy: Modern Essays in Criticism* 120 (Englewood Cliffs, N.J.: Prentice-Hall, 1963).

2. Guido Calabresi and Philip Bobbitt, *Tragic Choices* 17 (New York: Norton, 1978).

3. Robert M. Cover, *Justice Accused: Antislavery and the Judicial Process* (New Haven: Yale University Press, 1975).

4. 56 *N.Y.U. L. Rev.* 353 (1981).

5. *Id.* at 358.

6. Robert C. Post, *Constitutional Domains: Democracy, Community, Management* 25–50 (Cambridge: Harvard University Press, 1995).

7. For a good statement, see Michael Walzer, *Interpretation and Social Criticism* (Cambridge: Harvard University Press, 1987).

8. Alasdair MacIntyre, *After Virtue* 207 (Notre Dame, Ind.: University of Notre Dame Press, 1981).

9. So, for example, even if Cover's antislavery judges were to adopt a more modern and liberal theory of constitutional interpretation, they might perhaps rediscover their tragic dilemma as an internal conflict between two constitutional norms: that of personal autonomy and that of precedent (the obligation to effectuate the Constitution as law).

10. *Adarand Constructors, Inc. v. FCC,* 115 S.Ct. 2097 (1995).

11. See *Metro Broadcasting, Inc. v. FCC,* 488 U.S. 547 (1990); *Regents of University of California v. Bakke,* 438 U.S. 265, 324–79 (1978) (opinion of Justices Brennan, White, Marshall, and Blackmun).

12. See, e.g., Cass Sunstein, "Public Deliberation, Affirmative Action, and the Supreme Court," 84 *Calif. L. Rev.* 1179 (1996).

13. *Coalition for Economic Equity v. Wilson,* 946 F.Supp. 1480, 1510 (1996). [As this volume went to press, the Ninth Circuit Court of Appeals reversed the district court and sustained the initiative, 122 F.3d 718 (1997). The Supreme Court then denied further review, 118 S.Ct. 17 (1997).]

14. 458 U.S. 457 (1982).

15. *Coalition for Economic Equity,* at 1510. The district court also ruled that CCRI was preempted by Title VII of the Civil Rights Act of 1964. Both rulings were ultimately rejected by the Ninth Circuit, but only the first would have been a serious issue had the Supreme Court granted certiorari, I believe.

16. See, e.g., Vikram D. Amar and Evan H. Caminker, "Equal Protection, Unequal Political Burdens, and the CCRI," 23 *Hastings Const. L.Q.* 1019 (1996).

17. *Seattle School District No. 1,* 458 U.S. at 483–84.

18. Northrop Frye, *Anatomy of Criticism: Four Essays* 43 (Princeton: Princeton University Press, 1957).

19. *Id.* at 166.

20. While such inconsistent outcomes are typical of process-oriented constitutional restraints, such as those that focus on legislative intent, *Seattle* cannot plausibly be interpreted as imposing a process-oriented constraint, since it is triggered by a set of particular outcomes, namely those that burden the interests of minorities.

21. So, for example, if the California Supreme Court were to interpret the Equal Protection Clause of the California Constitution to bar affirmative action, in the way that Justice Scalia now believes that the Equal Protection Clause of the Fourteenth Amendment bars affirmative action, the effect would be precisely the same as CCRI, and yet *Seattle* would not bar the interpretation. *Crawford v. Board of Ed-*

ucation, 458 U.S. 527 (1982). On the California Constitution, see California Constitution, Article I, Section 7(a). On Scalia, see *Richmond v. J. A. Croson Co.*, 488 U.S. 469, 520 (1989) (Scalia, J., concurring in judgment). This distinction between reinterpreting a "pre-existing" constitutional provision and enacting a new one seems far too obscure to justify a decision of such importance.

22. Murray Krieger, "Tragedy and the Tragic Vision," in Michel and Sewall, *Tragedy* 141.

CHAPTER 36

The Meaning of Blacks' Fidelity to the Constitution

Dorothy E. Roberts

What is the worst outcome the conscientious constitutionalist might be compelled to endorse? Does the possibility of such a tragedy shake our faith in the Constitution? The bite in this line of inquiry depends on the presumption of constitutional fidelity. Within our legal culture, fidelity to the Constitution is usually treated as an unquestioned virtue.[1] For Black Americans, the first question is all too easy; they have stared the answer in the face for three centuries. The most painful tragedy the conscientious constitutionalist might have to concede is her own exclusion from the Constitution's domain. In the case of Black Americans, then, it is much more appropriate to begin with the question, why *should* they be faithful to the Constitution in the first place? How could Black people possibly pledge allegiance to a Constitution that defined them as less than human, was structured to enslave them, and has been interpreted time and time again to keep them subjugated to Whites? In light of all the indignities showered upon Blacks under color of the Constitution, I would think the presumption would be that Blacks should repudiate the document and all the injustice for which it has stood.

Where this project leads us—unsettling the notion of constitutional faith as an indisputable good—is precisely where Black Americans begin. Having been treated as outsiders all along, Blacks confront the Constitution with an unavoidable option of accepting or rejecting it. Surprisingly, many prominent Black thinkers—even the most radical ones—not only have failed to reject the Constitution but have made it a highlight of their advocacy. Black activists from Martin Luther King, Jr., to the Black Panthers have framed their demands in terms of constitutional rights. While King peacefully insisted that segregation violated the Constitution, Huey Newton claimed his constitutional right to bear arms. In this essay I explore the meaning of Blacks' astonishing fidelity to the Constitution.

The Purpose of Constitutional Fidelity

In each historical period, Black Americans have been faithful to a Constitution that looked very different from the version espoused by contemporary courts. It is a Constitution that abolished slavery prior to the Civil War, that provided freed slaves with forty acres and a mule during Reconstruction, that invalidated separate but equal facilities prior to *Brown v. Board of Education*, and that continues to mandate a radical dismantling of discriminatory structures despite the Supreme Court's adherence to the doctrine of color-blindness. Surely Black people are America's chief constitutional idealists, conforming the Constitution's terms to their own sense of justice.[2] No self-respecting person could commit to a covenant that denies her humanity. But why have most Blacks not rejected the Constitution altogether? I think that the answer is that fidelity to the Constitution offers practical advantages to Black people's struggle for full citizenship.

FREDERICK DOUGLASS'S IDEALISM

The transformation of Frederick Douglass's position on constitutional fidelity sheds light on this subject. Frederick Douglass initially adhered to the Garrisonian rejection of the Constitution as a slaveholding document. In 1849, he wrote that "the original intent and meaning of the Constitution (the one given to it by the men who framed it, those who adopted it, and the one given to it by the Supreme Court of the United States) makes it a pro-slavery instrument [which] I cannot bring myself to vote under, or swear to support."[3] In 1850, Douglass argued the Garrisonian position in a debate in Syracuse, New York, proclaiming that the Framers "attempted to unite Liberty in holy wedlock with the dead body of Slavery, and the whole was tainted. Let this unholy, unrighteous union be dissolved."[4]

But Douglass reversed his stance on the Constitution. In his autobiography, Douglass explained the change in his views:

> By such a course of thought and reading I was conducted to the conclusion that the Constitution of the United States—inaugurated "to form a more perfect union, establish justice, insure domestic tranquility, provide for the common defense, promote the general welfare, and secure the blessings of liberty"—could not well have been designed at the same time to maintain and

perpetuate a system of rapine and murder like slavery, especially as not one word can be found in the Constitution to authorize such a belief.[5]

Douglass stuck to his position that America had only two options: either it could abide by a Constitution that recognized Blacks as equal citizens, and therefore prohibited slavery, or the Union would have to be dissolved. It seems Douglass decided it made far more sense to interpret the Constitution to incorporate Blacks than to tear the country asunder. His conversion was not a conservative concession to slaveholders but a radical reinterpretation of the text that recognized Black humanity.

Douglass's constitutionalism was a way of exposing the nation's sins and demanding the nation's repentance. Black activists have simultaneously denounced constitutional evil while relying on constitutional ideals. Indeed, the very point of insisting on the Constitution's ideals is to shine light on the evil practices inflicted in the name of the Constitution. Blacks have criticized racial injustice not by hiding their eyes to constitutional evil but by showing how that evil diverges from the just results of a properly interpreted Constitution. Douglass taunted the Framers when he said "they wrote of Liberty in the Declaration of Independence with one hand, and with the other clutched their brother by the throat!"[6] W.E.B. Du Bois mocked Americans' patriotism when he described White spectators' delight over the burning body of a Black prisoner lynched in Coatesville, Pennsylvania, in 1911: "'Oh, say, can you see by the dawn's early light' that soap box of blackened bones and dust."[7]

The height of Blacks' cynical legalism was the Black Panthers' practice of surrounding police while they arrested a Black man, demanding, law books in hand, that the "pigs" abide by the letter of the law.[8] The Black Panthers, as well as Malcolm X, relied on the Second Amendment to support Black people's right to arm themselves against racist violence.[9] This is the paradox of Blacks' fidelity to the Constitution: Blacks have no reason to have faith in the Constitution that was designed to exclude them, yet in their struggle for citizenship they have remained faithful to the Constitution by relentlessly demanding that its interpretation live up to its highest principles or follow its strictest requirements.

INSTRUMENTAL FIDELITY

The goal of equal citizenship is the heart of Black Americans' fidelity to the Constitution. Black people's first commitment is to establishing their inclusion in the American polity, and fidelity to the Constitution is a way of achieving that objective. Under this instrumental approach, equal citizenship does not arise from the Constitution; it precedes it. The Constitution is not the standard of justice we should faithfully uphold; equal citizenship is. We know how to be just not by immersing ourselves in the Constitution's language but by imagining what it would mean for Black people to be treated like human beings. The purpose of constitutional fidelity is to insist that constitutional interpretations abide by this higher standard of justice. In short, fidelity is a means, not an end, and it is a means to an end that is more fundamental than the Constitution.[10]

Blacks are faithful to the Constitution, then, not because the Constitution deserves their allegiance, for it deserves their cynicism, if not their contempt. They are faithful to the Constitution because Black people deserve to be included in the Constitution's protections and promises. Blacks' fidelity to the Constitution is not a duty, it is a demand—a demand to be counted as full members of the political community. The Black nationalist Malcolm X refused to petition Whites for the recognition of Blacks' civil rights, relying instead on the more fundamental notion of human rights. As Malcolm X explained it, "[h]uman rights are something you are born with. Human rights are your God-given rights. Human rights are the rights that are recognized by all nations of this earth."[11] At the same time, Malcolm X was the consummate pragmatist, advocating that Blacks attempt to win their freedom "by any means necessary." When asked about his attitude toward civil rights organizations, he responded: "I'm for whatever gets results."[12]

The source of Blacks' fidelity to the Constitution is not to be found in the Constitution itself. It comes from the faith that the Constitution will one day be interpreted to include Blacks as full citizens. This faith derives from the belief in oppressed people's determination to be free. It is the faith embodied in the civil rights movement's conviction that "we shall overcome." Malcolm X ridiculed the nonviolent singing of that song as a political tactic,[13] but expressed faith in Black Americans' inevitable victory against oppression: "Time is on the side of the oppressed today, it's against the oppressor. Truth is on the side of the oppressed today, it's against the oppressor. You don't need anything else."[14] Centuries earlier, slave songs vowed that victory yet unrealized on earth would surely be achieved in heaven.

Critiques of Constitutional Fidelity

This instrumental fidelity to the Constitution is the reason for Black critical race studies scholars' disagreement with White critical legal studies scholars over the significance of rights. Scholars such as Kimberlé Crenshaw, Anthony Cook, and Patricia Williams have argued that the crits' rejection of rights discounts the importance of rights to Blacks' struggle for equal citizenship.[15] Critical legal studies theorists rejected rights discourse in part because of its stereotyping of human experience. But Patricia Williams argued that this is a lesser historical evil than having been ignored altogether: "The black experience of anonymity, the estrangement of being without a name, has been one of living in the oblivion of society's inverse, beyond the dimension of any consideration at all."[16] By asserting rights, dispossessed people rebel against this social degradation and demand recognition as full members of society. Williams explains: "For the historically disempowered, the conferring of rights is symbolic of all the denied aspects of their humanity. Rights imply a respect that places one in the referential range of self and others, that elevates one's status from human body to social being."[17] It is not Blacks' assertion of their constitutional rights but America's lack of commitment to these rights that has preserved the oppressive social order.

This instrumental fidelity to the Constitution is also subject to criticism from the opposite direction. Scholars dedicated to constitutional interpretation might contend that an instrumental fidelity is not really fidelity at all; it merely exploits constitutional rhetoric for an ulterior purpose, like a suitor's false profession of love. A second criticism is that equal citizenship is too limited a focus for an approach to the entire Constitution. Although it may help us interpret the Equal Protection Clause, for example, it is useless in construing the meaning of, say, the Second Amendment. Finally, Blacks taking an instrumental approach might be accused of an irrational obsession with race. Race is important, but American politics turns on other important issues as well.

All of these objections crumble in light of the centrality of Black citizenship to the Constitution's meaning.

Whites' persistent mission of denying Blacks the rights of citizenship has stunted official interpretations of the Constitution's terms, even those not directly related to racial equality. Numerous constitutional provisions have been interpreted or deployed to deny Black citizenship. Of course, the Constitution's original accommodation of slavery most blatantly accomplished this end. The Constitution's guarantees of liberty existed alongside its protection of slavery for nearly a century. But the addition of the Reconstruction Amendments that formally acknowledged Black citizenship did not stop an official regime of segregation, disenfranchisement, and terror that practically reduced Blacks to their former status as slaves.[18] The Supreme Court interpreted the Commerce Clause, as well as the Equal Protection Clause, to allow states to segregate public accommodations. More recently, the Court adopted a discriminatory-intent rule because of its fear of the remedies a discriminatory-impact rule would entail, or, as Justice Brennan put it, its "fear of too much justice."[19] Justice Harlan had such confidence in the Constitution's power to preserve White supremacy that he predicted in his dissent in *Plessy v. Ferguson* that the White race would remain dominant for all time if it "holds fast to the principles of constitutional liberty."[20]

Privileged racial status gives Whites a powerful incentive to construe other constitutional provisions in a way that leaves the existing social order intact. Many White Americans view a broad range of reforms as contrary to their self-interest because they perceive Black people's social position in opposition to their own. Under American racist ideology, constitutional interpretations that would benefit Blacks are antithetical to the interests of Whites, because Blacks' social advancement diminishes White superiority. Derrick Bell has argued that Whites in America—even those who lack wealth and power—believe that they gain from continued economic disparities that leave Blacks at the bottom.[21] Thus, racism helps to explain the prevailing understanding of the Constitution that disregards the huge injustice of poverty.

Black activists have claimed that their instrumental approach is more, not less, faithful to the Constitution. Martin Luther King, Jr., saw the Emancipation Proclamation not as an important moment in constitutional history but as the regeneration of constitutional history, "the resumption of that noble journey toward the goals reflected in . . . the Constitution."[22] As he sat in a Birmingham jail, Dr. King predicted:

> One day the South will know that when these disinherited children of God sat down at lunch counters, they were in reality standing up for what is best in the American dream and for the most sacred values in our Judaeo-Christian heritage, thereby bringing our nation back to those great wells of democracy which were dug deep by the founding fathers in their formulation of the Constitution and the Declaration of Independence.[23]

We cannot know what the Constitution means until the precondition of Black citizenship is attained. Without this reason for constitutional fidelity, every attempt at constitutional interpretation makes a mockery of the ideals of equality, liberty, and democracy. If the Constitution cannot incorporate

Blacks as full citizens, there would be no point in even embarking on the enterprise of constitutional interpretation. Relinquishing the belief that the ideal Constitution requires equal citizenship is inconceivable to Blacks. The ideal Constitution *must* reach the deep and profound injustice of denying Blacks equality or it is useless.

Black constitutional scholar Derrick Bell has recently questioned the efficacy of Blacks' constitutional fidelity. Professor Bell's writings, some of the most piercing contemporary critiques of constitutional evil, have become increasingly pessimistic about the chances for racial justice in America.[24] Pointing to Whites' persistent refusal to abdicate their racial domination, Bell draws the conclusion that Blacks' commitment to racial equality can only lead to despair. He therefore proclaims the following bleak manifesto: "We must acknowledge it and move on to adopt policies based on what I call: 'Racial Realism.' This mindset or philosophy requires us to acknowledge the permanence of our subordinate status."[25] Bell argues that this realistic stance is the antidote to the psychological weight of despair, freeing Blacks to try new racial strategies that are more feasible than fidelity to the Constitution.

Other Black scholars have rejected Bell's prescription of racial realism on the ground that it misdiagnoses Black people's problem.[26] John Powell, for example, argues that Bell erroneously attributes the injury suffered by the Black community to its false consciousness about rights rather than the Supreme Court's perpetuation of racial dominance.[27] Black people may suffer from despair, says Powell, but it is "a material problem rooted in the structure of racism," rather than "a psychological problem in the minds of black people."[28]

Professor Bell's sober assessment of racism's intransigence counsels against a naive faith in the moral power of the Constitution alone to bring about racial equality. Yet it need not defeat Blacks' instrumental fidelity to the Constitution as part of a social movement for equal citizenship. Blacks' constitutional fidelity is not the faith that the Constitution will end racism. The constitutional allegiance of Black leaders such as Douglass, Du Bois, and King was grounded in their participation in the social struggle for citizenship rights. They could hold fast to a vision of an ideal Constitution despite their awareness of constitutional evil because of their commitment to a liberation movement. As I concluded elsewhere, "Blacks must continue to struggle for citizenship—not in America as we know it, but in a nation radically transformed by Blacks' very efforts to achieve social justice."[29] It is that struggle that deserves our utmost fidelity.[30]

NOTES

1. J. M. Balkin, "Agreements with Hell and Other Objects of Our Faith," 65 *Fordham L. Rev.* 1703 (1997).

2. Balkin, "Agreements with Hell" (describing "ideal constitutionalism," which "solves the problem of fidelity to an unjust Constitution by conforming the object of interpretation to our sense of what is just").

3. Frederick Douglass, "The Constitution and Slavery," in Philip S. Foner, ed., *The Life and Writings of Frederick Douglass: Early Years, 1817–1849*, vol. 1, at 352–53 (New York: International Publishers, 1950).

4. John W. Blassingame, ed., *The Frederick Douglass Papers, 1847–54*, vol. 2, at 223 (New Haven: Yale University Press, 1992).

5. Frederick Douglass, *The Life and Times of Frederick Douglass* 267 (Citadel Press, 1983) (1841).

6. *Frederick Douglass Papers, 1847–54*, vol. 2, at 223.

7. W.E.B. Du Bois, "Triumph," in Eric J. Sundquist, ed., *The Oxford W.E.B. Du Bois Reader* 376, 377 (New York: Oxford University Press, 1996).

8. David Ray Papke, "The Black Panther Party's Narratives of Resistance," 18 *Vt. L. Rev.* 645 (1994).

9. *Id.*; Malcolm X, "The Ballot or the Bullet," in George Breitman, ed., *Malcolm X Speaks* 23, 43 (New York: Grove Press, 1965).

10. Cf. Richard Delgado, "Rodrigo's Ninth Chronicle: Race, Legal Instrumentalism, and the Rule of Law," 143 *U. Pa. L. Rev.* 379, 388 (1994) (advocating "legal instrumentalism" that treats law as "a tool that is useful for certain purposes and at certain times").

11. Malcolm X, "The Ballot or the Bullet," in *Malcolm X Speaks* 23, 35.

12. Malcolm X, Interview, Station WBAI-FM, New York, Jan. 28, 1965, in *Malcolm X Speaks* 222. Black activists have disagreed as to the best strategies for attaining full Black citizenship, advocating both integrationist and nationalist visions and diverse tactics, including litigation, nonviolent protest, and armed struggle.

13. Malcolm X, "Message to the Grass Roots," in *Malcolm X Speaks* 3, 9 ("Whoever heard of a revolution where they lock arms . . . singing 'We Shall Overcome'? You don't do that in a revolution. You don't do any singing, you're too busy swinging").

14. Malcolm X, "The Harlem 'Hate Gang' Scare," in *Malcolm X Speaks* 68, 64.

15. Patricia Williams, *The Alchemy of Race and Rights* (Cambridge: Harvard Univesity Press, 1991); Anthony Cook, "Beyond Critical Legal Studies: The Reconstructive Theology of Dr. Martin Luther King, Jr.," 103 *Harv. L. Rev.* 985 (1990); Kimberlé Crenshaw, "Race, Reform, and Retrenchment: Transformation and Legitimation in Antidiscrimination Law," 101 *Harv. L. Rev.* 1331 (1988).

16. Williams, *Alchemy* 153–54.

17. *Id.* at 153.

18. Eric Foner, *Nothing but Freedom* (Baton Rouge: Louisiana University Press, 1983); C. Vann Woodward, *The Strange Career of Jim Crow* (New York: Oxford University Press, 3d ed., 1974).

19. Randall L. Kennedy, "*McClesky v. Kemp*: Race, Capital Punishment, and the Supreme Court," 101 *Harv. L. Rev.* 1388, 1413–14 (1988).

20. *Plessy v. Ferguson*, 163 U.S. 537, 559 (1896) (Harlan, J., dissenting).

21. Derrick Bell, *Faces at the Bottom of the Well: The Permanence of Racism* (New York: Basic Books, 1992); Derrick Bell, "After We're Gone: Prudent Speculations on America in a Post-Racial Epoch," 34 *St. Louis U. L.J.* 393, 402 (1990).

22. Martin Luther King, Jr., "The Negro Revolution," in *Why We Can't Wait* 15, 25 (New York: Harper & Row, 1964).

23. Martin Luther King, Jr., "Letter from Birmingham Jail," in *Why We Can't Wait* 76, 94.

24. See, for example, Derrick Bell, *And We Are Not Saved* (New York: Basic Books, 1987); Bell, *Faces at the Bottom of the Well*; Bell, "Racial Realism," 24 *Conn. L. Rev.* 363 (1992).

25. Bell, "Racial Realism" 373–74.

26. See generally "Commentary on Racial Realism," 24 *Conn. L. Rev.* 497, 497–565 (1992).

27. John A. Powell, "Racial Realism or Racial Despair," 24 *Conn. L. Rev.* 533 (1992).

28. *Id.* at 543.

29. Dorothy E. Roberts, "Welfare and the Problem of Black Citizenship," 105 *Yale L.J.* 1563, 1602 (1996).

30. Another version of this essay is included in the *Fordham Law Review*'s Symposium on Fidelity in Constitutional Theory. 65 *Fordham L. Rev.* 1761–72 (1997).

CHAPTER 37

Tragedies under the
Common Law Constitution

David A. Strauss

Some people defend their positions on contested constitutional questions—for example, questions about the religion clauses or the separation of powers—by saying that their approach to constitutional interpretation is to follow the intentions of the Framers. One way to test their commitment to that approach is to ask: Do the Framers' "intentions" just happen to correspond to the things you would favor anyway? Of course, it is possible that the Framers got everything right. But that seems pretty unlikely, and if the Framers' "intentions" are closely aligned with the interpreter's views, then one might reasonably suspect that the interpreter is reaching conclusions on the basis of political (or moral, or ideological) commitments which he or she then attributes to the Framers, not on the basis of dispassionate historical research into the Framers' actual intentions.

Asking someone to identify a "constitutional tragedy" is—if I understand the notion correctly—a more general version of the same challenge. Is there any important point on which your approach to interpreting the Constitution leads to a conclusion different from that which you would have reached if you just openly followed your own moral or political principles? The implicit premise is that constitutional interpretation, if it is really faithful to the Constitution, should not invariably lead to results that coincide with the political views of the interpreter. It might be argued that the premise is perverse, that it is bizarre to celebrate a particular approach to the Constitution on the ground that such an approach would lead one to do (what one considers to be) unfair or unwise things. For reasons that cannot be developed here, I do not think the premise is perverse. But, in any event, the idea that one can show one's fidelity to the law in this way is widespread, so the challenge is worth considering.

Constitutional law is, it seems to me, primarily a common law system.[1] The text plays a significant role, but most of the important principles are settled not by the text but in the same way most of the principles of the law of torts or contracts have been settled: by cases that have been decided and then followed over the years, or by practices and institutions that have been accepted for so long that they have become entrenched. Whether something is just or unjust, fair or unfair, good or bad policy, plays a role in interpreting the Constitution, just as it plays a role in the common law. But it plays that role only within limits—limits set to some degree by the text, but to a much greater degree by decisions and more general understandings that may not be rooted in the text but have become rooted in the legal culture.

There are many examples of unquestionable constitutional principles that owe their rock-solid status not to the text or the original understanding of it but to precedent, both in the sense of judicial precedent and in the sense of practices or understandings that have grown up over the years. Judicial review itself is an example. So is the principle of *McCulloch v. Maryland*,[2] that Congress has broad authority to decide what measures are "necessary and proper" to implement its legislative powers. So are the illegality of secession, an issue settled by the Civil War, not by any textual provision; the principle that states may not have established churches, which if anything is inconsistent with the plain language of the Establishment Clause of the First Amendment; the application of most of the provisions of the Bill of Rights to the states; the prohibition against gender discrimination; the constitutionality of administrative agencies; and many other important principles. In some instances, one can make reasonably plausible arguments for these principles based on the text or the original understandings. But anyone who is candid has to admit that the essentially unchallengeable status of these principles far outruns any textual or original-intent argument that can be made. The principles are part of our constitutional order for the same reason that negligence is a central principle of accident law or consideration a central principle of the law of contracts: the principles have been around for a long time, they have been repeatedly reaffirmed, and they seem to make sense as a matter of policy and morality and to work well.

Against this background, my examples of constitutional tragedies are the unconstitutionality of affirmative action and the constitutionality of capital punishment. I oppose capital punishment, and I think that as a matter of first principles the correct approach to affirmative action would be to leave it to the political process. But if I were a Supreme Court justice, my obligation to follow the Constitution would, I believe, require me sometimes to invalidate affirmative action measures and sometimes to uphold a death penalty. Not to do those things would be the equivalent of a form of civil disobedience.

The reason the Constitution imposes these obligations is not the text. Twenty-five or so years ago, I would have felt free, as a Supreme Court justice, to declare the death penalty unconstitutional in all cases, and to subject affirmative action measures to only the most lenient scrutiny under the Equal Protection Clause. But since that time, constitutional law in these areas has changed, and the positions I would like to hold can no longer be held. After several decisions that began to question the constitutionality of certain aspects of capital punishment, the Supreme Court in 1972 declared capital punishment, as then practiced, unconstitutional (although it stopped short of declaring it cruel and unusual in all circumstances). Within a few years—the story is familiar—the Court backtracked, in the face of a sharply hostile legislative reaction.[3] Since 1976, the principle that capital punishment is constitutional in a significant range of cases has become very well established. Today, of course, no member of the Court casts a vote to the contrary.

Similarly, before the Supreme Court's 1978 decision in *Regents of the University of California v. Bakke*,[4] no precedents stood in the way of a justice who wished to take the position that affirmative action does not present a serious constitutional issue. That is the position I would take today, if the law stood as it did in 1977. Affirmative action in favor of (for example) African Americans is utterly different from discrimination against African Americans; despite much of the rhetoric in the affirmative action debate, I am not sure anyone truly disagrees with that proposition.[5] While there are bad affirmative action measures, there are bad measures of other kinds as well—tax cuts, subsidies, regulatory schemes, etcetera—and it seems to me that the political process is as good a way to deal with affirmative action as it is to deal with those other kinds of measures.

But in the more than two decades that the Supreme Court has been deciding affirmative action cases, that position—that affirmative action measures should be routinely upheld whenever governments choose to engage in it—has never prevailed. In fact, not a single justice has ever explicitly adopted it. Accordingly it seems to me that a justice who is conscientiously following the Constitution can no longer take that position today.

To make the point more generally, when a principle is well established by a line of cases, a judge cannot simply disregard the cases by saying, "They're only cases; they are inconsistent with the real Constitution." To a large extent, the cases *are* the real Constitution. Constitutional law is filled with principles that are far better established than anything in the text or the original understandings would warrant. No purpose is served by saying that we follow those principles as a matter of "stare decisis," not because they are part of "the Constitution." They are as solidly a part of the Constitution as anything in the text. In addition to the examples I gave before—ranging from judicial review to the legitimacy of the administrative state—one could add the prohibition against racial segregation, the core principles of freedom of expression, the expansive power of the federal government, the power of the president in foreign affairs, and many other well-established principles of constitutional law. It would be misleading wordplay to say that these are less part of the Constitution today than the principle that no one under thirty-five years can be president. Unfortunately, from my point of view, the principles that affirmative action must meet a special burden, and that capital punishment need not always be viewed as cruel or unusual, while less well established than the principles I have mentioned, have also, today, become part of the Constitution.

This of course does not mean that no Supreme Court justice could ever vote to overrule a case. Some established principles may be so clearly wrong that they should be overruled at the earliest opportunity. But in general, if a judge thinks a well-established principle of constitutional law is wrong, the right approach is to work against it in the way one would work against a principle in any common law area: to limit its application, to seek to erode the principle, to open up exceptions, to begin to establish an alternative principle. Then, when the "wrong" principle has been undermined by the subsequent cases, the judge (or justice) can properly vote to overrule it.

This is in fact the course that preceded the most famous overrulings of this century. "Separate but equal" was a shell by the time of *Brown v. Board of Education*[6]: it had been decades since a system of segregation had been found to satisfy "separate but equal," and previous cases had all but established that no system of segregation ever could.[7] That is why *Brown* was unquestionably correct, notwithstanding the notorious doubts about its consistency with the original understandings. (In fact *Brown* would have been right even if the separate but equal principle had not been eroded, but it is unnecessary to make that argument in order to justify *Brown*.) Similarly, the constitutional principle of freedom of contract, identified with *Lochner v. New York*,[8] was subject to many exceptions and limitations by the time it was interred.[9]

Of course, the argument that the previous principle was wrong as a matter of policy or simple morality played an important role in *Brown* and in the rejection of *Lochner*, as that argument does in the common law. But that is not the only argument that matters in a common law system, including a common law system of constitutional law. The other virtues of a common law approach—such as humility and a respect for the views of others—also play a role. When a principle has been sustained over a substantial period of time and accepted by a wide range of one's fellow citizens (and predecessor judges), that is a powerful reason to make one's peace with it. That is what produces "tragedies," cases in which a conscientious interpreter of the Constitution must do something at variance with his or her views of the right resolution of the issue. Textualism and originalism are sometimes defended, and a common law approach to interpretation is sometimes attacked, on the ground that the common law approach allows judges to follow their own views.[10] In fact, precedents are probably a more reliable source of limits on judges than either the words of the document read in isolation (which can be subject to a wide range of interpretations) or even the history of the text. Be that as it may, however, if the possibility of "tragedy" is a badge of honor for an interpretive approach, then a common law approach, despite its flexibility and relative lack of connection to the text and the original intentions, qualifies for the badge.

NOTES

1. This idea is developed at greater length in David A. Strauss, "Common Law Constitutional Interpretation," 63 *U. Chi. L. Rev.* 877 (1996).

2. U.S. 316 (1819).

3. The pivotal cases were *Furman v. Georgia*, 408 U.S. 238 (1972), and *Gregg v. Georgia*, 428 U.S. 153 (1976). Such decisions as *Witherspoon v. Illinois*, 391 U.S. 510 (1968), and *United States v. Jackson*, 390 U.S. 570 (1968), can be seen as having begun a common law–like progression that led to *Furman* (but was reversed in *Gregg*).

4. 438 U.S. 265 (1978).

5. The arguments for this proposition are familiar; they were presented in, for example, Justice Stevens's dissent in *Adarand Constructors, Inc. v. Pena*, 115 S. Ct. 2097, 2021–30 (1995).

6. 347 U.S. 483 (1954).

7. See, e.g., Louis Michael Seidman, "*Brown* and *Miranda*," 80 *Calif. L. Rev.* 673, 708 (1992) ("Given what came before, the real question is why *Brown* needed to be decided at all").

8. 198 U.S. 45 (1905).

9. See the discussion in Geoffrey Stone, et al., *Constitutional Law* 829–31 (Boston: Little, Brown, 3d ed., 1996).

10. See, for example, Antonin Scalia, "Common-Law Courts in A Civil-Law System: The Role of United States Federal Courts in Interpreting the Constitution and Laws," in *A Matter of Interpretation* (Princeton: Princeton University Press, 1997).

CHAPTER 38

McCulloch v. Maryland

John Yoo

The last time that the editors of this volume sought out participants, they said they called upon a number of thoughtful and provocative constitutional scholars. I am convinced that I fall into the latter category, for I certainly have yet to show that I belong in the former. In an effort to live up to the provocative billing, and the editors' call for seriousness without seriosity, I propose as a tragic constitutional decision the case of *McCulloch v. Maryland*.[1] But before the traditional pillars of constitutional-law teaching fall around me, I want to attempt to justify my choice based on how we should define a constitutional tragedy.

Once upon a fall semester, as an eager undergraduate, I was in search of a humanities course to satisfy my college's idea of a liberal arts education. I chose a course that I believe was called something like "The Heroic and Tragic Ideal in Ancient Greek Literature," but which was known, due to the large number of football players in attendance, as "Heroes for Zeroes."

We zeroes not only learned about heroes but also about tragedy in the classic sense of the term. As I remember the lectures, tragedy was more than something catastrophically bad. The eruption of a volcano, for example, is not tragic. Rather, tragedy required a hero or heroine, whose tragic flaw (or flaws, in the case of truly great tragedy) compelled him or her to suffer some great downfall. While we in the audience often can see the tragedy looming in the near future, we still sympathize with the hero or heroine because we understand why that character's tragic flaw has left him or her with no alternative but to follow the course to destruction. Sometimes, however, what is tragic for the hero or heroine may produce a good for the broader society.

Thus, Antigone's devotion to her religious beliefs drives her to her end, because by observing the religious rites that require her to bury her traitorous brothers, she violates Theban law. But in executing Antigone, the rule of law and the public safety of Thebes are preserved. Achilles is no less a tragic hero; his hubris and desire to be known as the best of the Achaeans lead to his proud, but ultimately destructive, actions. While his overweening pursuit of glory brings him fame in the war against the Trojans, it also leads to the death of his best friend, Patrocles, and to his own death.

The reason I digress into these matters is to point out why the editors' call for papers on constitutional tragedies need not duplicate the harmony that was produced by their earlier call for papers on constitutional stupidities.[2] That earlier thought experiment was easier than this one, perhaps because most of us can agree on what is "stupid." I doubt that most of the participants in this latter thought experiment can agree on what makes good tragedy, and even if we could, what features of the Constitution or of a Supreme Court decision would qualify.

Under my definition of a tragedy, for example, I am forced to discard several cases that many might consider tragic. *Plessy v. Ferguson*,[3] while a case that had terrible consequences for the nation, was not tragic, because in my mind there was no character flaw in the justices or in the Constitution that forced the Supreme Court to find that "separate but equal" facilities satisfied the Fourteenth Amendment's Equal Protection Clause. No one in the "audience" can display any sympathy or understanding for the manner in which the justices decided the case; Justice Brown and the majority were simply wrong, and dissenting Justice Harlan was simply right.

While perhaps closer to it, *Dred Scott v. Sandford*[4] does not quite fit my definition of a tragedy either. No doubt *Dred Scott* was the most disastrous judicial decision in the history of the Supreme Court and of the United States, but again it seems to me that there was no compulsion or tragic flaw that forced the Court to prohibit the governmental regulation of slavery. There were a number of ways that the Court could have decided the case without sparking such controversy; and, as has been noted, justices on the Court originally had prepared opinions that would have rejected Dred Scott's claims on far narrower grounds.[5] Rather than deciding *Dred Scott* narrowly, the Court chose to expand the scope of the case, because of Chief Justice Taney's hopes to protect the constitutionality of slavery once and for all—a goal that is not worthy of sympathy.

I also cite *Plessy* and *Dred Scott* to show that we should not mistake a case's tragic subject matter for a constitutional tragedy. It was not *Plessy* or *Dred Scott* themselves that were tragic; the tragedy lay in the failure of the nation to answer what Gunnar Myrdal called the "American Dilemma" of race.[6] In my mind, to fit the definition of a constitutional tragedy, the tragedy must have befallen the Constitution, rather than to an issue whose resolution ultimately required judicial intervention. Given Toqueville's observation that Americans have a tendency to turn significant political questions into legal questions, we would expect all national tragedies to become constitutional ones swiftly. But these would not be constitutional tragedies; they would only be national problems that, in the end, sought an answer in the Constitution.

With these ideas in mind, I propose *McCulloch v. Maryland* as a constitutional tragedy. I assert with a straight face that this was a definition in search of a case and not a case in search of a definition. First, *McCulloch* provides the audience with a tragic hero, the great Chief Justice John Marshall. Chief Justice Marshall was not great simply because he was the leader of the Court during its infancy nor, in my mind, because he was chief justice during a nationalizing period in the Court's history. We do not think of Chief Justice Jay or Chief Justice Stone as being "great." Rather, Chief Justice Marshall was great because of his defense of the idea of a written constitution that imposed fixed limits upon the powers of the national government.[7] It was this concept of a written constitution that established the foundation for Marshall's defense of judicial review in *Marbury v. Madison*.[8] As Marshall wrote: "Certainly all those who have framed written constitutions contemplate them as forming the fundamental and paramount law of the nation, and consequently, the theory of every such government must be, that an act of the legislature, repugnant to the constitution, is void."[9] To be sure, some have argued that Marshall was nothing more than a partisan hack who sought to establish the Federalist Party's last bastion behind the barricades of the judiciary. In *Marbury*, however, Marshall spurned the opportunity to strike a political blow against President Jefferson and instead adopted an approach to constitutional interpretation that hewed closely to the text and structure of the Constitution and that gave the judiciary the duty of enforcing the Constitution's written limits on government power.

Chief Justice Marshall's tragic flaw, however, was his ambition to create a strong national government. His clear desire in *McCulloch* to uphold the constitutionality of the national bank overcame his twin goals in *Marbury*: to establish a principled approach to constitutional interpretation and to defend the concept of a written constitution of limited powers. In *McCulloch*, Chief Justice Marshall and the Court upheld the constitutionality of the Second Bank of the United States as an appropriate exercise of Congress's powers under the Necessary and Proper Clause. In the course of that decision, Marshall gave voice to an expansive reading of that clause that bestowed upon Congress broad powers that the Framers never contemplated. Wrote Marshall:

> We admit, as all must admit, that the powers of the government are limited, and that its limits are not to be transcended. But we think the sound construction of the constitution must allow to the national legislature that discretion, with respect to the means by which the powers it confers are to be carried into execution, which will enable that body to perform the high duties assigned to it, in the manner most beneficial to the people. Let the end be legitimate, let it be within the scope of the constitution, and all means which are appropriate, which are plainly adapted to that end, which are not prohibited, but consist with the letter and spirit of this constitution, are constitutional.[10]

One of the most quoted passages in Supreme Court history, this language has led to the constitutional culture we have today, in which Congress may exercise virtually any power so long as it does not violate a specific prohibition in the constitutional text. This was not the view of the Constitution held by many of the framing generation, including Jefferson, Madison, and others.[11] As Madison would write in reaction to *McCulloch*, "those who recollect, and still more, those who shared in what passed in the State conventions, through which the people ratified the Constitution, with respect to the extent of the powers vested in Congress, cannot easily be persuaded that the avowal of such [an interpretation] would not have prevented its ratification."[12] In deciding *McCulloch* as expansively as he did, Marshall reinjected the Supreme Court into the partisan politics of the day,[13] and he undermined the very concept that he had introduced so strikingly in *Marbury*, of a Constitution of limited powers.

Marshall's analysis failed to address the real question of whether the national government even had the implied authority to establish a bank. Indeed, the Constitutional Convention specifically had rejected proposals to give the national government the authority to establish a national university or to grant commercial monopolies, powers very similar to the one upheld by the Court. To be sure, Marshall observed that while the Constitution did not explicitly mention a power to establish a bank, it did grant "the great powers" to wage war, to regulate interstate commerce, to tax, and to borrow money. Marshall, however, never demonstrated whether establishing a bank was truly necessary or proper to effectuate those powers, or, in Marshall's terms, whether the bank was an appropriate means to implement those other constitutional powers and ends.

Marshall's tragic flaw, his predilection for a strong national government, produced a tragedy of constitutional dimensions by undermining the concept and purpose of a written Constitution. At an early stage in the Supreme Court's history, Marshall introduced into the constitutional corpus the idea that the Constitution did not necessarily have a fixed meaning, and that the federal government's powers were not limited. It is *McCulloch,* tellingly, that contains the aphorism, "it is a *constitution* we are expounding." To be sure, Justice Frankfurter thought this phrase "the single most important utterance in the literature of constitutional law—most important because most comprehensive and most comprehending."[14] Nonetheless, this phrase captures Marshall's rejection of the approach to constitutional interpretation he espoused in *Marbury* and his embrace of the idea that the Constitution's meaning could change with changing circumstances, in order to satisfy the social norms and needs of the times. In Marshall's mind, any measure that Congress chooses is constitutional so long as the end is legitimate, and as those ends could change in the future, so could the means.

Of course, the Constitution does not, as Marshall noted, "partake of the prolixity of a legal code," but neither is it a blank check to be filled in with whatever things each generation values. Marshall's language encourages future interpreters to interpret all provisions of the Constitution broadly, as if they embody only policies rather than fixed meanings. *McCulloch* provides authority for the temptation to see in the Constitution what we wish to see. I think that Professor Kurland had it exactly right when he observed that whenever a court quotes the means/ends language in *McCulloch,* "you can be sure that the court will be throwing the constitutional text, its history, and its structure to the winds in reaching its conclusion."[15]

McCulloch also undermined the concept of a Constitution that grants only limited powers to the national government. Marshall's rather unconvincing treatment of the Tenth Amendment transformed the key analytical question in federalism cases. Instead of identifying what powers and rights are retained by the states or by the people, courts henceforth would ask what implied powers are appropriate for the federal government to exercise. Marshall's opinion gave Congress the authority, which it subsequently used, to go beyond the mere act of establishing a national bank. *McCulloch's* reasoning provided the theoretical foundations for the creation of independent regulatory bodies, for the federal administrative state, and for the national security apparatus we have today. For an example of the expansive powers that Marshall's analysis permits, one need only examine the justifications for the measures taken by the North during the Civil War. Legal theorists of the day justified the measures, some of which were of dubious constitutionality, on the grounds that they were necessary and proper for the legitimate constitutional end of "provid[ing] for the common Defence and general Welfare of the United States."[16] It is hard to see what powers would not qualify as necessary and proper given this approach.

McCulloch also contains the seeds of a dangerous doctrine of deference that runs counter to the achievements of *Marbury*. For Marshall not only declared that all means were permissible to reach legitimate ends but also concluded that the courts should not inquire into whether the means were really needed at all. Wrote Marshall: "where the law is not prohibited, and is really calculated to effect any of the objects entrusted to the government, to undertake here to inquire into the degree of its necessity, would be to pass the line which circumscribes the judicial department, and to tread on legislative ground."[17] This language contrasts strikingly with Marshall's language in *Marbury* about the limited powers granted by a written constitution and the judiciary's duty to see that those limits are observed.

McCulloch is finally tragic because, while we can disagree with Marshall's methods, we can still sympathize with him. Marshall certainly had the best of intentions, and it is difficult to argue with his results. Without *McCulloch*, can we be sure that our democracy would have survived the Great Depression, or that the country would have the ability to address the nationwide problems it does today? Without *McCulloch*, can we be sure that the United States would have risen to the status of a great power? Can we be sure that the North would have survived and won the Civil War? *McCulloch* established the foundations for the strong national government that has brought the nation through these crises, but it was at the price of the Framers' original vision of a Constitution of limited powers.[18]

NOTES

1. 17 U.S. (4 Wheat.) 316 (1819).

2. Symposium, "Constitutional Stupidities," 12 *Const. Comm.* 139–225 (1995).

3. 163 U.S. 537 (1896).

4. 60 U.S. (19 How.) 393 (1856).

5. See, e.g., Daniel A. Farber, William N. Eskridge, Jr., and Philip P. Frickey, *Constitutional Law: Themes for the Constitution's Third Century* 11 (St. Paul: West Publishing, 1993).

6. Gunnar Myrdal, *An American Dilemma: The Negro Problem and Modern Democracy* (New York: Harper and Brothers, 1944).

7. Naturally, there is some controversy concerning Chief Justice Marshall and his significance. Early histories had argued that he was a Federalist politician, bent on establishing a strong central government at the expense of the states. Some recent works have treated him more kindly, and some have even argued that he was a great lawyer as well as a great chief justice.

8. 5 U.S. (1 Cranch) 137 (1803).

9. 5 U.S. (1 Cranch) at 177.

10. *McCulloch v. Maryland*, 17 U.S. (4 Wheat.) 316, 421 (1819).

11. See Gary Lawson and Patricia B. Granger, "The 'Proper' Scope of Federal Power: A Jurisdictional Interpretation of the Sweeping Clause," 43 *Duke L.J.* 267 (1993).

12. Max Farrand, *The Records of the Federal Convention of 1787*, vol. 3, at 435 (New Haven: Yale University Press, 1937). Madison's comment is worth quoting in full:

It could not but happen, and was foreseen at the birth of the Constitution, that difficulties and differences of opinion might occasionally arise in expounding terms and phrases necessarily used in such a charter; more especially those which divide legislation between general and local governments; and that it might require a regular course of practice to liquidate and settle the meaning of some of them. But it was anticipated, I believe, by few, if any, of the friends of the Constitution, that a rule of construction would be introduced as broad and pliant as what has occurred. And those who recollect, and still more, those who shared in what passed in the State conventions, through which the people ratified the Constitution, with respect to the extent of the powers vested in Congress, cannot easily be persuaded that the avowal of such a rule would not have prevented its ratification.

13. Marshall's opinion came under vigorous attack by several writers of the period who accused the chief justice of misconstruing the Constitution and of playing partisan politics. Marshall took the extraordinary step of responding in print (albeit under a pseudonym) to his critics. See Gerald Gunther, *John Marshall's Defense of McCulloch v. Maryland* (Stanford: Stanford University Press, 1969).

14. Felix Frankfurter, "John Marshall and the Judicial Function," 69 *Harv. L. Rev.* 217, 219 (1955).

15. Philip Kurland, "*Curia Regis*: Some Comments on the Divine Right of Kings and Courts to Say What the Law Is," 23 *Ariz. L. Rev.* 582, 591 (1981).

16. U.S. Const. Art. I, Sec. 8, Cl. 1. See John Yoo, editor's note, to William Whiting, *War Powers under the Constitution of the United States* (10th ed., 1864, republished by the Legal Classics Library).

17. *McCulloch*, 17 U.S. (4 Wheat.) at 423.

18. I would like to thank Jesse Choper and Paul Mishkin for attempting to dissuade me from choosing this topic, and Bill Eskridge for asking me to participate in this volume.

CHAPTER 39

Antigone and Creon

William N. Eskridge, Jr., and Sanford Levinson

If the selections on constitutional stupidities illuminate the relatively un-adorned document itself, the selections on constitutional tragedies illumi-nate its academic interpreters, and indeed the state of constitutional theory. It strikes us as too harsh to say, as Pamela Karlan and Daniel Ortiz do, that law professors' theories of constitutional interpretation are best character-ized neither as tragedy nor comedy but as farce.[1] Yet it is fair to say that the academy too little appreciates the role of tragedy in constitutional theory, and a goal of this volume is to reengage law professors with tragedy.

The selections in this part of the book reveal, for example, multiple prob-lems with the most famous academic interpreter, Ronald Dworkin's "Her-cules."[2] Hercules got his start as an interpreter of statutes, which he con-strues "so as to make its history, all things considered, the best it can be. . . . His own convictions about justice or wise policy are constrained in his over-all interpretive judgment, not only by the text of the statute but also by a va-riety of considerations of fairness and integrity."[3] Hercules applies a similar methodology to constitutional interpretation, where he seeks to make the Constitution the "best it can be," in light of our constitutional traditions. Note that Dworkin invites tragedy by constraining Hercules' interpretation of legal texts. The problem is that Hercules' actual feats of interpretation seem tragedy-avoiding in practice.

One of us long ago criticized Dworkin's constitutional theory for its strong tendency to produce only "happy endings," that is, its avoidance of tragedy.[4] Dworkin's recent foray into constitutional litigation reinforces the impression that Hercules is (almost?) always "comedic" or "heroic," never "tragic," in his approach to the Constitution. Dworkin was the lead author of the "Philosophers' Brief" filed in the cases where the Supreme Court con-sidered a due process "right to die" in the 1996 Term.[5] The brief argues for a right to die as a matter of constitutional principle, which seems to coincide with the authors' own moral position on the matter. Should that be cause for concern? James Fleming says not: Dworkin's "constitution-perfecting" theory should be proudly embraced, because it makes the Constitution a better document.[6]

Dworkin's and Fleming's reading of the Constitution has just been unanimously—albeit provisionally—rejected by the Supreme Court as we go to press in the summer of 1997.[7] Their general interpretive position has virtually no constituency among judges and, more surprisingly, a diminishing constituency among law professors. Although Laurence Tribe and Frank Michelman argued only twenty years ago that the Constitution guarantees citizens a minimal standard of living,[8] Christopher Eisgruber and Lawrence Sager—card-carrying political liberals—reflect the conventional wisdom when they dismiss that possibility under a normativist reading of the Constitution today.[9] Even Dworkin's most recent book shies away from it.[10] In part, the new conventional wisdom reflects the collapse of political liberalism and the dearth of defenders of the welfare state. In part, it reflects a new insistence by constitutional scholars that there *must* be tragedies—great tragedies—in constitutional interpretation. These include prominent normativists as well as the expected positivists.

Constitutional tragedy is the Achilles' heel of normativist theories such as Dworkin's and Fleming's. It is far from clear, however, that tragedy ensures the triumph of positivism. Put it this way: Has Hercules been supplanted by Antigone? No. Readers may recall that Sophocles' Antigone defied the positive law decreed by the tyrant Creon, in order to fulfill her moral obligation to bury her outlawed brothers.[11] Not having the strength of Hercules or the rhetorical skill of Dworkin, Antigone fell prey to the clash of natural law and positive law, her moral imperative and the severe response of Creon's law. The play *Antigone* can be read as a harbinger of positivism, the separation of law and morals, but note how little support there is among constitutional scholars for so severe a positivism. The positive law in question strikes us as unjust and arbitrary.[12] Either an interpreter will strain to rescue Antigone from the jaws of the law by ameliorative construction, or the legitimacy of the entire state will be in question. Indeed, at the end of the play, Creon is as ruined as Antigone: if the latter has lost her life, the former has lost his son and wife and is in danger of losing the state as well. If there is not some promise of happy constitutional endings at least some of the time, citizens will lose interest in constitutionalism.[13]

Just as few normativists view the Constitution as congruent with modern versions of natural law, few positivists view the Constitution as a document that is unrelentingly tragic. For both kinds of thinkers, the questions then become: What is the role of tragedy in constitutional thinking? What insights into constitutional interpretation does the idea of tragedy press onto us? The foregoing selections in this volume present a multitude of fascinating possibilities.

Invoking the modern tragedy *A Man for All Seasons*, Larry Alexander argues that tragedy is necessary to the rule of law.[14] If the rigorous application of the law does not sometimes yield tragic results, the population and its officials will begin to doubt that law truly is external to the decision maker and reliably protects us all. Alexander's example illustrates the ambiguity of such a claim, though. Sir Thomas More, the tragic protagonist in *A Man for All Seasons*, refuses to use his position as Lord Chancellor to destroy a political enemy, because bending the law to catch the devil undermines law's protection when the devil comes for *us*. This is the positivist's ideal, the judge who refuses to bend the law, even to catch the devil. A problem with this ideal is that the devil and his allies will eagerly bend the law, even if the saintly will not. The Lord Chancellor is thus destroyed, and the rule of law fails to save him. More had not read his critical legal studies, for otherwise he would have realized that the rule of law is plastic in the hands of devilish lawyers. The scrupulous person in a land of scoundrels gets the sucker's payoff.

Gary Jacobsohn deepens Alexander's insight. While a completely tragic vision, such as More's and Alexander's, exaggerates law's determinacy and may undermine its legitimacy, a completely comedic (happy-endings) vision, such as Dworkin's and Fleming's, lacks the humility which is necessary to accomplish small things in a world of limits.[15] As an example, Jacobsohn briefly takes up the issue pursued in Gerard Bradley's essay, the death penalty.[16] Bradley's approach is that of classic tragedy: a morally abominable institution is perpetuated because it does not traverse the conventional limits of the Constitution, properly construed. A comedic approach would find some constitutional device to strike down the practice. Jacobsohn critiques both approaches: the tragic seems defeatist and therefore illegitimate, the comedic baldly manipulative and therefore illegitimate. A "tragicomic" approach would pick its battles, focusing on the racially biased application of the death penalty as a basis for principled constitutional invalidation in at least some instances.

Matters of life and death—capital punishment, assisted suicide, abortion—are an important crucible for thinking about constitutional tragedies.[17] In large part, this is because the issues are ones about which moral theorizing is well developed and participants have intensely held views; hence, the clash between morality and law is particularly well focused and intense. Not only is there temptation to bend the Constitution to reflect one's strongly held moral views, but there is temptation to bend the Constitution in more than one way. A characteristic of life-and-death cases, emphasized by Rebecca Brown and Marie Failinger, is that they force upon judges truly tragic choices, with worthy moral values on either side of the constitutional conflict.[18] Such clashes, with morally attractive norms on both sides of the controversy, seem to be proliferating. The cases often involve conflicts between nondiscrimination and autonomy norms.[19] Examples include a traditionalist group's exclusion of lesbian and gay marchers from its public parade, a college that prohibits different-race dating and marriage for reasons of religious principle, segregation of women in the armed forces because of concerns about fraternization and sexual harassment, a public university's refusal to subsidize journals having religious themes, and compulsory AIDS education in public schools, notwithstanding parental objections.[20]

Different kinds of tragedy are generated by the issue of race, which inspired several essays in this volume. Earl Maltz maintains that *Brown v. Board of Education* is a tragic case; the "right" answer, from an originalist perspective, was to leave state-sponsored segregation in place.[21] Because apartheid is so morally indefensible, the Court could not resist the impulse to read morality into an unyielding Constitution, a judicial lapse which Maltz regrets. Race cases, like death cases, continue to present tragic choices to judges. Racial criteria in busing plans, employment and promotion policies, and university admissions are both defensible and problematic to any fair-minded observer. How is a mere judge to interpret the Constitution to resolve conundrums that divide philosophers and the populace? As Robert Post suggests, judges often insist on procedural requirements—dialogue, mutual accommodation—to avoid or ameliorate tragic choices, but nevertheless many of the choices do not go away.[22] The legacy of slavery and apartheid in America is a tragedy that does not end.

Thus, as Dorothy Roberts and Jack Balkin argue, *Brown* reveals a constitutional tragedy even if one rejects Earl Maltz's analysis.[23] The tragedy involves not the hard choices put to judges and lawyers but a persistent racial caste system that was part of the original Constitution, maintained after the Civil War through constitutionally sanctioned apartheid, and privatized after *Brown* in ways that the judge-created state action doctrine has constitutionally immunized. The plantation and separate restrooms have been replaced by the ghetto and white flight. That judges have backed away from challenging this caste system is less significant than that We the People have created and nurtured it. The depth of the caste system poses Roberts's question: Why should Blacks have constitutional faith? And Balkin's question: Will this ongoing tragedy destroy the country?

A virtue of Roberts's and Balkin's essays on race is their historical understanding of constitutional tragedy. Just as Antigone's tragedy was rooted in the cursed House of Laius (the father of Oedipus), America's greatest tragedy is rooted in the history of race. *Brown* is merely an act in that drama, as is the California affirmative action initiative discussed by Robert Post and the affirmative action cases discussed by David Strauss.[24] But it is possible, albeit sometimes difficult, to believe that the Constitution, correctly interpreted, does require grappling with the implications of our racial history.

As Balkin suggests, what may be most insidious is the quasi-positivist conclusion that the Constitution requires indifference to some great injustice, such as the consequences of relentless poverty, coupled with a psychological predisposition to minimize the importance of this injustice, lest one be forced to confront the legitimacy question that is so rarely addressed in American legal education. One might wonder, for example, how many liberals who have come to concede the constitutional legitimacy of the death penalty also have modified, as Bradley most definitely has not, their views as to its injustice. Even if they remain "abolitionists," they might now say, for example, that "reasonable persons" can differ about the propriety of state-imposed death, etcetera. Similarly, it is hard to square a posture of constitutional disregard for indigence with the belief that this is the very definition of an unjust, perhaps even iniquitous, society. Better to say that there are not really so many people affected as we once thought, that more effort on the part of the poor could lead to happier outcomes, that the law of unintended consequences will necessarily defeat even the best-motivated efforts to alleviate poverty, etcetera.

It is probably fitting that the longest single essay in the volume, Theodore Lowi's on separation of powers,[25] so well joins the various themes of both parts of this volume. Lowi argues that the Constitution started with a stupidity, namely, its separation of the powers of government into three branches. The founding generation soon and wisely compromised that separation and pragmatically commingled functions, to the great advantage of the country. Since World War II, however, structural changes in the polity have stimulated a reinvigoration of separated branches of government. Divided government in the last generation has created an enervating "absolute" separation of powers. Thus, an original constitutional stupidity that was, as a practical matter, limited in its consequences by historical practice has reemerged with a tragic vengeance. Whatever the cogency of Lowi's argument—and we think it considerable—its historical sweep makes it a uniquely insightful approach to constitutional tragedy. Its argumentative structure—starting with a constitutional stupidity and ending with a constitutional tragedy—and seriousness capture what we hope is the overall meaning of the project that began in New Orleans some three years ago.

Consider, in conclusion, some connections between our project and broader intellectual issues of constitutionalism. Because we have no hard-and-fast answers ourselves, we pose these connections as a series of questions.

What theory of constitutional interpretation generates an author's conclusions that provision A is intrinsically and unavoidably "stupid," while provision B is not intrinsically stupid but has "tragically" been construed in an unfortunate way? One lesson we took away from this enterprise was that there is more consensus about constitutional interpretation than one would surmise by reading the academic literature. Even as academics who have read our Derrida, we were struck by the ability of thinkers from many different perspectives to agree that certain rules are hard-wired into the Constitution at least at this point in our political history, while the contest over others is conducted within relatively well-defined limits. Tentatively, we suggest that doomsayers from both the right and left are wrong: the existence of interpretive discretion in some constitutional cases suggests neither the indeterminacy of all constitutional discourse nor the undemocratic nature of any of it.

How much stupidity and tragedy can a constitutive document contain before it becomes useless or irrelevant as a foundational basis for constitutional discourse? Among the founding generation, Thomas Jefferson maintained that "no society can make a perpetual constitution, or even a perpetual law." If it does, then it is only by "an act of force, and not of right."[26] Jefferson would surely be surprised that our Constitution, so chock full of stupidities, has proved serviceable for more than two hundred years. Even if Jefferson were wrong that each generation needs to make a new constitution, however, he might be right that even a good constitution ought not last forever. Should the United States wait for a constitutional disaster to remake its constitution? Or can any potential disaster be handled through a dynamic interpretation of the existing document?

What difference, ultimately, does the document make—especially a document with such open-ended provisions as the Necessary and Proper, the Free Speech, and the Due Process Clauses? A nation can have a constitutional discourse unconnected with a constitution. The departed Soviet Union had a smart-looking, rights-oriented constitution but a stupid constitutional discourse. The United Kingdom has no written constitution at all but enjoys a vibrant and long-standing constitutional discourse. We think the United States has a smart-enough Constitution and a generally astute constitutional discourse, but we are not certain they are strongly connected. The Constitution has not created a culture that both respects the rule of law and imbues it with enough flexibility to handle new social and political developments. Although we think that our nation's tradition of deferring to constitutional procedures and traditions has helped us balance our temporary enthusiasms with our long-term interests and with arguments of justice, we doubt that those procedures and traditions are generated just by the Constitution.

Can constitutional disasters be avoided, as stupidities can be, or are they fated, as tragedies usually are? What responsibilities do We the People bear for the great constitutional mistakes of our history? Written into our original Constitution and inscribed in our culture, slavery was a constitutional disaster that was tragic. The legacies of slavery, apartheid and the racial ghetto, remain our greatest constitutional tragedy, we think. We also worry, however, that we have compounded this ongoing tragedy with stupidity, with constitutional decisions that impede even the modest efforts that have been made to redress a few race-related problems in education and the workplace.

Others would nominate different conundrums, but the point is this: constitutional stupidities and tragedies are intertwined with both the political and the moral fate of our country. Politically, constitutional mistakes are connected with the flourishing or decline of our nation and cannot be disconnected. Morally, we shall be judged by our mistakes. Their nature will define our legacy. Will our mistakes be ones of excessive charity or of meanness? Hubris or timidity? Principle or politics? Will we be remembered as Antigone, the sister who sacrificed her life for family and caretaking, or as Creon, the tyrant who enforced arbitrary rule?

Ultimately, for us, Antigone and Creon define the difference between the worst mistakes and the best ones. If, as Earl Maltz argues, decisions like *Brown v. Board of Education* and *Roe v. Wade* are constitutional mistakes, they are the mistakes of Antigone, excesses of sympathy, perhaps flawed efforts to assure people be treated with equal dignity. If, as we believe, decisions like *McCleskey v. Kemp* (imposing the death penalty notwithstanding evidence of systematic race bias) and *Bowers v. Hardwick* (upholding a law criminalizing consensual "homosexual" sodomy) are constitutional mistakes, they are the mistakes of Creon, failures of empathy, perhaps flawed efforts to deny equal citizenship. The fate of the nation is not only involved, but in important ways molded, by how it handles these issues.

NOTES

1 Pamela S. Karlan and Daniel R. Ortiz, "Constitutional Farce," chapter 31 of this volume.

2. Hercules made his debut as an interpreter in Ronald Dworkin, *Taking Rights Seriously,* chapter 4 (Cambridge: Harvard University Press, 1977), and returned in *Law's Empire* (Cambridge, Mass.: Belknap Press, 1986), where he performed various feats of interpretation.

3. Dworkin, *Law's Empire* 379–80.

4. Sanford Levinson, *Constitutional Faith* (Princeton: Princeton University Press, 1988).

5. See Ronald Dworkin et al., "Assisted Suicide: The Philosophers' Brief," reprinted in *N.Y. Rev. of Books,* Mar. 27, 1997, at 41.

6. James E. Fleming, "Constitutional Tragedy in Dying: Or Whose Tragedy Is It Anyway?," chapter 29 of this volume. Reread Fleming's essay for an eloquent statement of that position, but then reread Marie Failinger, "Jocasta Undone: Constitutional Courts in the Midst of Life and Death," chapter 28 of this volume, for an insistence that the matter is neither morally nor legally so easy as Dworkin and Fleming make it out to be.

7. See *Washington v. Glucksberg,* 117 S. Ct. 2258 (June 26, 1997), *reversing* 79 F.3d 790 (9th Cir. 1996) (en banc).

8. See Frank I. Michelman, "States' Rights and States' Roles: Permutations of 'Sovereignty' in *National League of Cities v. Usery,*" 86 *Yale L.J.* 1165 (1977); Laurence Tribe, "Unraveling *National League of Cities*: The New Federalism and Affirmative Rights to Essential Government Services," 90 *Harv. L. Rev.* 1065 (1977).

9. Christopher L. Eisgruber and Lawrence G. Sager, "Good Constitutions and Bad Choices," chapter 27 of this volume.

10. Ronald Dworkin, *Freedom's Law: The Moral Reading of the American Constitution,* chapter 1 (Cambridge: Harvard University Press, 1996).

11. Sophocles, *The Three Theban Plays: Antigone, Oedipus the King, Oedipus at Colonus,* trans. Robert Fagles (New York: Penguin, 1982); see *id.* at 33–53 (notes by Bernard Knox).

12. Larry Alexander, "Constitutional Tragedies and Giving Refuge to the Devil," chapter 23 of this volume.

13. Dorothy Roberts, "The Meaning of Blacks' Fidelity to the Constitution," chapter 36 of this volume.

14. Alexander, "Giving Refuge to the Devil."

15. Gary Jacobsohn, "Dramatic Jurisprudence," chapter 30 of this volume.

16. Gerard V. Bradley, "The Tragic Case of Capital Punishment," chapter 25.

17. See Bradley, "Capital Punishment"; Failinger, "Jocasta Undone"; Fleming, "Constitutional Tragedy in Dying," chapter 29.

18. Rebecca Brown, "Constitutional Tragedies: The Dark Side of Judgment," chapter 26 of this volume; Failinger, "Jocasta Undone," drawing from Guido Calabresi and Philip Bobbitt, *Tragic Choices* (New York: Norton, 1978).

19. See William N. Eskridge, Jr., "A Jurisprudence of 'Coming Out': Religion, Homosexuality, and Liberty/Equality Clashes in American Public Law," 106 *Yale L.J.* 2411 (1997).

20. These cases are discussed in William N. Eskridge, Jr., and Nan D. Hunter, *Sexuality, Gender, and the Law* (Mineola, N.Y.: Foundation, 1997).

21. Earl Maltz, "*Brown v. Board of Education*," chapter 34 of this volume. A contrary position has been argued in Michael McConnell, "Originalism and the Desegregation Decisions," 81 *Va. L. Rev.* 947 (1995), to which Maltz is specifically responding.

22. Robert Post, "Tragedy and Constitutional Interpretation: The California Civil Rights Initiative," chapter 35 of this volume.

23. See J. M. Balkin, "The Meaning of Constitutional Tragedy," chapter 24 of this volume; Roberts, "Blacks' Fidelity to the Constitution."

24. David A. Strauss, "Tragedy under the Common Law Constitution," chapter 37 of this volume.

25. Theodore Lowi, "Constitutional Merry-Go-Round: The First Tragedy, the Second Farce," chapter 32 of this volume.

26. Letter from Thomas Jefferson to James Madison, September 6, 1789, reprinted in James Morton Smith, ed., *The Republic of Letters: The Correspondence between Thomas Jefferson and James Madison 1776–1826*, at 631, 634 (New York: Norton, 1995).

The Constitution
of the United States

We the People of the United States, in Order to form a more perfect Union, establish Justice, insure domestic Tranquility, provide for the common defence, promote the general Welfare, and secure the Blessings of Liberty to ourselves and our Posterity, do ordain and establish this Constitution for the United States of America.

Article I

Section 1. All legislative Powers herein granted shall be vested in a Congress of the United States, which shall consist of a Senate and House of Representatives.

Section 2. [1] The House of Representatives shall be composed of Members chosen every second Year by the People of the several States, and the Electors in each State shall have the Qualifications requisite for Electors of the most numerous Branch of the State Legislature.

[2] No Person shall be a Representative who shall not have attained to the Age of twenty five Years, and been seven Years a Citizen of the United States, and who shall not, when elected, be an Inhabitant of that State in which he shall be chosen.

[3] Representatives and direct Taxes shall be apportioned among the several States which may be included within this Union, according to their respective Numbers, which shall be determined by adding to the whole Number of free Persons, including those bound to Service for a Term of Years, and excluding Indians not taxed, three fifths of all other Persons. The actual Enumeration shall be made within three Years after the first Meeting of the Congress of the United States, and within every subsequent Term of ten Years, in such Manner as they shall by Law direct. The Number of Representatives shall not exceed one for every thirty Thousand, but each State shall have at Least one Representative; and until such enumeration shall be

made, the State of New Hampshire shall be entitled to chuse three, Massachusetts eight, Rhode Island and Providence Plantations one, Connecticut five, New York six, New Jersey four, Pennsylvania eight, Delaware one, Maryland six, Virginia ten, North Carolina five, South Carolina five, and Georgia three.

[4] When vacancies happen in the Representation from any State, the Executive Authority thereof shall issue Writs of Election to fill such Vacancies.

[5] The House of Representatives shall chuse their Speaker and other Officers; and shall have the sole Power of Impeachment.

Section 3. [1] The Senate of the United States shall be composed of two Senators from each State, chosen by the Legislature thereof,[1] for six Years; and each Senator shall have one Vote.

[2] Immediately after they shall be assembled in Consequence of the first Election, they shall be divided as equally as may be into three Classes. The Seats of the Senators of the first Class shall be vacated at the Expiration of the second Year, of the second Class at the Expiration of the fourth Year, and of the third Class at the Expiration of the sixth Year, so that one third may be chosen every second Year; and if Vacancies happen by Resignation, or otherwise, during the Recess of the Legislature of any State, the Executive thereof may make temporary Appointments until the next Meeting of the Legislature, which shall then fill such Vacancies.

[3] No Person shall be a Senator who shall not have attained to the Age of thirty Years, and been nine Years a Citizen of the United States, and who shall not, when elected, be an Inhabitant of that State for which he shall be chosen.

[4] The Vice President of the United States shall be President of the Senate, but shall have no Vote, unless they be equally divided.

[5] The Senate shall chuse their other Officers, and also a President pro tempore, in the absence of the Vice President, or when he shall exercise the Office of President of the United States.

[6] The Senate shall have the sole Power to try all Impeachments. When sitting for that Purpose, they shall be on Oath or Affirmation. When the President of the United States is tried, the Chief Justice shall preside: And no Person shall be convicted without the Concurrence of two thirds of the Members present.

[7] Judgment in Cases of Impeachment shall not extend further than to removal from Office, and disqualification to hold and enjoy any Office of

honor, Trust or Profit under the United States: but the Party convicted shall nevertheless be liable and subject to Indictment, Trial, Judgment and Punishment, according to Law.

Section 4. [1] The Times, Places and Manner of holding Elections for Senators and Representatives, shall be prescribed in each State by the Legislature thereof; but the Congress may at any time by Law make or alter such Regulations, except as to the Places of chusing Senators.

[2] The Congress shall assemble at least once in every Year, and such Meeting shall be on the first Monday in December, unless they shall by Law appoint a different Day.[2]

Section 5. [1] Each House shall be the Judge of the Elections, Returns and Qualifications of its own Members, and a Majority of each shall constitute a Quorum to do Business; but a smaller Number may adjourn from day to day, and may be authorized to compel the Attendance of absent Members, in such Manner, and under such Penalties as each House may provide.

[2] Each House may determine the Rules of its Proceedings, punish its Members for disorderly Behavior, and, with the Concurrence of two thirds, expel a Member.

[3] Each House shall keep a Journal of its Proceedings, and from time to time publish the same, excepting such Parts as may in their Judgment require Secrecy; and the Yeas and Nays of the Members of either House on any question shall, at the Desire of one fifth of those Present, be entered on the Journal.

[4] Neither House, during the Session of Congress, shall, without the Consent of the other, adjourn for more than three days, nor to any other Place than that in which the two Houses shall be sitting.

Section 6. [1] The Senators and Representatives shall receive a Compensation for their Services, to be ascertained by Law, and paid out of the Treasury of the United States. They shall in all Cases, except Treason, Felony and Breach of the Peace, be privileged from Arrest during their Attendance at the Session of their respective Houses, and in going to and returning from the same; and for any Speech or Debate in either House, they shall not be questioned in any other Place.

[2] No Senator or Representative shall, during the Time for which he was elected, be appointed to any civil Office under the Authority of the United States, which shall have been created, or the Emoluments whereof shall have

been encreased during such time; and no Person holding any Office under the United States, shall be a member of either House during his Continuance in Office.

Section 7. [1] All Bills for raising Revenue shall originate in the House of Representatives; but the Senate may propose or concur with Amendments as on other Bills.

[2] Every Bill which shall have passed the House of Representatives and the Senate, shall, before it become a Law, be presented to the President of the United States; If he approve he shall sign it, but if not he shall return it, with his Objections to the House in which it shall have originated, who shall enter the Objections at large on their Journal, and proceed to reconsider it. If after such Reconsideration two thirds of that House shall agree to pass the Bill, it shall be sent, together with the Objections, to the other House, by which it shall likewise be reconsidered, and if approved by two thirds of that House, it shall become a Law. But in all such Cases the Votes of both Houses shall be determined by Yeas and Nays, and the Names of the Persons voting for and against the Bill shall be entered on the Journal of each House respectively. If any Bill shall not be returned by the President within ten Days (Sundays excepted) after it shall have been presented to him, the Same shall be a Law, in like Manner as if he had signed it, unless the Congress by their Adjournment prevents its Return, in which Case it shall not be a Law.

[3] Every Order, Resolution, or Vote to which the Concurrence of the Senate and House of Representatives may be necessary (except on a question of Adjournment) shall be presented to the President of the United States; and before the Same shall take Effect, shall be approved by him, or being disapproved by him, shall be repassed by two thirds of the Senate and House of Representatives, according to the Rules and Limitations prescribed in the Case of a Bill.

Section 8. [1] The Congress shall have Power To lay and collect Taxes, Duties, Imposts and Excises, to pay the Debts and provide for the common Defence and general Welfare of the United States; but all Duties, Imposts and Excises shall be uniform throughout the United States;

[2] To borrow money on the credit of the United States;

[3] To regulate Commerce with foreign Nations, and among the several States, and with the Indian Tribes;

[4] To establish an uniform Rule of Naturalization, and uniform Laws on the subject of Bankruptcies throughout the United States;

[5] To coin Money, regulate the Value thereof, and of foreign Coin, and fix the Standard of Weights and Measures;

[6] To provide the Punishment of counterfeiting the Securities and current Coin of the United States;

[7] To establish Post Offices and post Roads;

[8] To promote the Progress of Science and useful Arts, by securing for limited Times to Authors and Inventors the exclusive Right to their respective Writings and Discoveries;

[9] To constitute Tribunals inferior to the supreme Court;

[10] To define and punish Piracies and Felonies committed on the high Seas, and Offenses against the Laws of Nations;

[11] To declare War, grant Letters of Marque and Reprisal, and make Rules concerning Captures on Land and Water;

[12] To raise and support Armies, but no Appropriation of Money to that Use shall be for a longer Term than two Years;

[13] To provide and maintain a Navy;

[14] To make Rules for the Government and Regulation of the land and naval Forces;

[15] To provide for calling forth the Militia to execute the Laws of the Union, suppress Insurrections and repel Invasions;

[16] To provide for organizing, arming, and disciplining, the Militia, and for governing such Part of them as may be employed in the Service of the United States, reserving to the States respectively, the Appointment of the Officers, and the Authority of training the Militia according to the discipline prescribed by Congress;

[17] To exercise exclusive Legislation in all Cases whatsoever, over such District (not exceeding ten Miles square) as may, by Cession of particular States, and the Acceptance of Congress, become the Seat of the Government of the United States, and to exercise like Authority over all Places purchased by the Consent of the Legislature of the State in which the Same shall be, for the Erection of Forts, Magazines, Arsenals, dock-Yards, and other needful Buildings;— And

[18] To make all Laws which shall be necessary and proper for carrying into Execution the foregoing Powers, and all other Powers vested by this Constitution in the Government of the United States, or in any Department or Officer thereof.

Section 9. [1] The Migration or Importation of such Persons as any of the States now existing shall think proper to admit, shall not be prohibited by the Congress prior to the Year one thousand eight hundred and eight, but a Tax or duty may be imposed on such Importation, not exceeding ten dollars for each Person.

[2] The privilege of the Writ of Habeas Corpus shall not be suspended, unless when in Cases of Rebellion or Invasion the public Safety may require it.

[3] No Bill of Attainder or ex post facto Law shall be passed.

[4] No Capitation, or other direct, Tax shall be laid, unless in Proportion to the Census or Enumeration herein before directed to be taken.

[5] No Tax or Duty shall be laid on Articles exported from any State.

[6] No Preference shall be given by any Regulation of Commerce or Revenue to the Ports of one State over those of another: nor shall Vessels bound to, or from, one State, be obliged to enter, clear, or pay Duties in another.

[7] No Money shall be drawn from the Treasury, but in Consequence of Appropriations made by Law; and a regular Statement and Account of the Receipts and Expenditures of all public Money shall be published from time to time.

[8] No Title of Nobility shall be granted by the United States: And no Person holding any Office of Profit or Trust under them, shall, without the Consent of the Congress, accept of any present, Emolument, Office, or Title, of any kind whatever, from any King, Prince, or foreign State.

Section 10. [1] No State shall enter into any Treaty, Alliance, or Confederation; grant Letters of Marque and Reprisal; coin Money; emit Bills of Credit; make any Thing but gold and silver Coin a Tender in Payment of Debts; pass any Bill of Attainder, ex post facto Law, or Law impairing the Obligation of Contracts, or grant any Title of Nobility.

[2] No State shall, without the Consent of the Congress, lay any Imposts or Duties on Imports or Exports, except what may be absolutely necessary for executing its inspection Laws: and the net Produce of all Duties and Imposts, laid by any State on Imports or Exports, shall be for the Use of the Treasury of the United States; and all such Laws shall be subject to the Revision and Controul of the Congress.

[3] No State shall, without the Consent of Congress, lay any Duty of Tonnage, keep Troops, or Ships of War in time of Peace, enter into any Agreement or Compact with another State, or with a foreign Power, or engage in War, unless actually invaded, or in such imminent Danger as will not admit of delay.

Article II

Section 1. [1] The executive Power shall be vested in a President of the United States of America. He shall hold his Office during the Term of four Years, and, together with the Vice President, chosen for the same Term, be elected, as follows:

[2] Each State shall appoint, in such Manner as the Legislature thereof may direct, a number of Electors, equal to the whole Number of Senators and Representatives to which the State may be entitled in the Congress: but no Senator or Representative, or Person holding an Office of Trust or Profit under the United States, shall be appointed an Elector.

[3] The Electors shall meet in their respective States, and vote by Ballot for two Persons, of whom one at least shall not be an Inhabitant of the same State with themselves. And they shall make a List of all the Persons voted for, and of the Number of Votes for each; which List they shall sign and certify, and transmit sealed to the Seat of the Government of the United States, directed to the President of the Senate. The President of the Senate shall, in the Presence of the Senate and House of Representatives, open all the Certificates, and the Votes shall then be counted. The Person having the greatest Number of Votes shall be the President, if such Number be a Majority of the whole Number of Electors appointed; and if there be more than one who have such Majority, and have an equal Number of Votes, then the House of Representatives shall immediately chuse by Ballot one of them for President; and if no Person have a Majority, then from the five highest on the List the said House shall in like Manner chuse the President. But in chusing the President, the Votes shall be taken by States, the Representation from each State having one Vote; a quorum for this Purpose shall consist of a Member or Members from two thirds of the States, and a Majority of all the States shall be necessary to a Choice. In every Case, after the Choice of the President, the Person having the greatest Number of Votes of the Electors shall be the Vice President. But if there should remain two or more who have equal Votes, the Senate shall chuse from them by Ballot the Vice President.[3]

[4] The Congress may determine the Time of chusing the Electors, and the Day on which they shall give their Votes; which Day shall be the same throughout the United States.

[5] No person except a natural born Citizen, or a Citizen of the United States, at the time of the Adoption of this Constitution, shall be eligible to the Office of President; neither shall any Person be eligible to that Office

who shall not have attained to the Age of thirty five Years, and been fourteen Years a Resident within the United States.

[6] In case of the removal of the President from Office, or of his Death, Resignation or Inability to discharge the Powers and Duties of the said Office, the Same shall devolve on the Vice President, and the Congress may by Law provide for the Case of Removal, Death, Resignation or Inability, both of the President and Vice President, declaring what Officer shall then act as President, and such Officer shall act accordingly, until the Disability be removed, or a President shall be elected.

[7] The President shall, at stated Times, receive for his Services, a Compensation, which shall neither be increased nor diminished during the Period for which he shall have been elected, and he shall not receive within that Period any other Emolument from the United States, or any of them.

[8] Before he enter on the Execution of his Office, he shall take the following Oath or Affirmation: "I do solemnly swear (or affirm) that I will faithfully execute the Office of President of the United States, and will to the best of my Ability, preserve, protect and defend the Constitution of the United States."

Section 2. [1] The President shall be Commander in Chief of the Army and Navy of the United States, and of the Militia of the several States, when called into the actual Service of the United States; he may require the Opinion, in writing, of the principal Officer in each of the executive Departments, upon any subject relating to the Duties of their respective Offices, and he shall have Power to grant Reprieves and Pardons for Offenses against the United States, except in Cases of Impeachment.

[2] He shall have Power, by and with the Advice and Consent of the Senate, to make Treaties, provided two thirds of the Senators present concur; and he shall nominate, and by and with the Advice and Consent of the Senate, shall appoint Ambassadors, other public Ministers and Consuls, Judges of the supreme Court, and all other Officers of the United States, whose Appointments are not herein otherwise provided for, and which shall be established by Law: but the Congress may by Law vest the Appointment of such inferior Officers, as they think proper, in the President alone, in the Courts of Law, or in the Heads of Departments.

[3] The President shall have Power to fill up all Vacancies that may happen during the Recess of the Senate, by granting Commissions which shall expire at the End of their next Session.

Section 3. He shall from time to time give to the Congress Information of the State of the Union, and recommend to their Consideration such Measures as he shall judge necessary and expedient; he may, on extraordinary Occasions, convene both Houses, or either of them, and in Case of Disagreement between them, with Respect to the Time of Adjournment, he may adjourn them to such Time as he shall think proper; he shall receive Ambassadors and other public Ministers; he shall take Care that the Laws be faithfully executed, and shall Commission all the Officers of the United States.

Section 4. The President and all civil Officers of the United States, shall be removed from Office on Impeachment for, and Conviction of, Treason, Bribery, or other high Crimes and Misdemeanors.

Article III

Section 1. The judicial Power of the United States, shall be vested in one supreme Court, and in such inferior Courts as the Congress may from time to time ordain and establish. The Judges, both of the supreme and inferior Courts, shall hold their Offices during good Behaviour, and shall, at stated Times, receive for their Services, a Compensation, which shall not be diminished during their Continuance in Office.

Section 2. [1] The Judicial Power shall extend to all Cases, in Law and Equity, arising under this Constitution, the Laws of the United States, and Treaties made, or which shall be made, under their Authority;—to all Cases affecting Ambassadors, other public Ministers and Consuls;—to all Cases of admiralty and maritime Jurisdiction;—to Controversies to which the United States shall be a Party;—to Controversies between two or more States;—between a State and Citizens of another State;—between Citizens of different States;—between Citizens of the same State claiming Lands under Grants of different States, and between a State, or the Citizens thereof, and foreign States, Citizens or Subjects.

[2] In all Cases affecting Ambassadors, other public Ministers and Consuls, and those in which a State shall be a Party, the supreme Court shall have original Jurisdiction. In all the other Cases before mentioned, the supreme Court shall have appellate Jurisdiction, both as to Law and Fact, with such Exceptions, and under such Regulations as the Congress shall make.

[3] The trial of all Crimes, except in Cases of Impeachment, shall be by Jury; and such Trial shall be held in the State where the said Crimes shall have been committed; but when not committed within any State, the Trial shall be at such Place or places as the Congress may by Law have directed.

Section 3. [1] Treason against the United States, shall consist only in levying War against them, or in adhering to their Enemies, giving them Aid and Comfort. No person shall be convicted of Treason unless on the Testimony of two Witnesses to the same overt Act, or on Confession in open Court.

[2] The Congress shall have Power to declare the Punishment of Treason, but no Attainder of Treason shall work Corruption of Blood, or Forfeiture except during the Life of the Person attainted.

Article IV

Section 1. Full Faith and Credit shall be given in each State to the public Acts, and Records, and judicial Proceedings of every other State. And the Congress may by general Laws prescribe the Manner in which such Acts, Records and Proceedings shall be proved, and the Effect thereof.

Section 2. [1] The Citizens of each State shall be entitled to all Privileges and Immunities of Citizens in the several States.

[2] A Person charged in any State with Treason, Felony, or other Crime, who shall flee from Justice, and be found in another State, shall on demand of the executive Authority of the State from which he fled, be delivered up, to be removed to the State having Jurisdiction of the Crime.

[3] No Person held to Service or Labour in one State, under the Laws thereof, escaping into another, shall, in Consequence of any Law or Regulation therein, be discharged from such Service or Labour, but shall be delivered up on Claim of the Party to whom such Service or Labour may be due.

Section 3. [1] New States may be admitted by the Congress into this Union; but no new State shall be formed or erected within the Jurisdiction of any other State; nor any State be formed by the Junction of two or more States, or Parts of States, without the Consent of the Legislatures of the States concerned as well as of the Congress.

[2] The Congress shall have Power to dispose of and make all needful Rules and Regulations respecting the Territory or other Property belonging to the United States; and nothing in this Constitution shall be so con-

strued as to Prejudice any Claims of the United States, or of any particular State.

Section 4. The United States shall guarantee to every State in this Union a Republican Form of Government, and shall protect each of them against Invasion; and on Application of the Legislature, or of the Executive (when the Legislature cannot be convened) against domestic Violence.

Article V

The Congress, whenever two thirds of both Houses shall deem it necessary, shall propose Amendments to this Constitution, or, on the Application of the Legislatures of two thirds of the several States, shall call a Convention for proposing Amendments, which, in either Case, shall be valid to all Intents and Purposes, as part of this Constitution, when ratified by the Legislatures of three fourths of the several States, or by Conventions in three fourths thereof, as the one or the other Mode of Ratification may be proposed by the Congress; Provided that no Amendment which may be made prior to the Year One thousand eight hundred and eight shall in any Manner affect the first and fourth Clauses in the Ninth Section of the first Article; and that no State, without its Consent, shall be deprived of its equal Suffrage in the Senate.

Article VI

[1] All Debts contracted and Engagements entered into, before the Adoption of this Constitution, shall be as valid against the United States under this Constitution, as under the Confederation.

[2] This Constitution, and the Laws of the United States which shall be made in Pursuance thereof; and all Treaties made, or which shall be made, under the Authority of the United States, shall be the supreme Law of the Land; and the Judges in every State shall be bound thereby, any Thing in the Constitution or Laws of any State to the Contrary notwithstanding.

[3] The Senators and Representatives before mentioned, and the Members of the several State Legislatures, and all executive and judicial Officers, both of the United States and of the several States, shall be bound by Oath or Affirmation, to support this Constitution; but no religious Test shall ever be required as a Qualification to any Office or public Trust under the United States.

Article VII

The Ratification of the Conventions of nine States shall be sufficient for the Establishment of this Constitution between the States so ratifying the Same.

Done in Convention by the Unanimous Consent of the States present the Seventeenth Day of September in the Year of our Lord one thousand seven hundred and Eighty seven and of the Independence of the United States of America the Twelfth.

ARTICLES IN ADDITION TO, AND AMENDMENT OF, THE
CONSTITUTION OF THE UNITED STATES OF AMERICA, PROPOSED
BY CONGRESS, AND RATIFIED BY THE LEGISLATURES OF THE
SEVERAL STATES, PURSUANT TO THE FIFTH ARTICLE OF THE
ORIGINAL CONSTITUTION

Amendment I [1791]

Congress shall make no law respecting an establishment of religion, or prohibiting the free exercise thereof; or abridging the freedom of speech, or of the press; or the right of the people peaceably to assemble, and to petition the Government for a redress of grievances.

Amendment II [1791]

A well regulated Militia, being necessary to the security of a free State, the right of the people to keep and bear Arms, shall not be infringed.

Amendment III [1791]

No Soldier shall, in time of peace be quartered in any house, without the consent of the Owner, nor in time of war, but in a manner to be prescribed by law.

Amendment IV [1791]

The right of the people to be secure in their persons, houses, papers, and effects, against unreasonable searches and seizures, shall not be violated, and no Warrants shall issue, but upon probable cause, supported by Oath or affirmation, and particularly describing the place to be searched, and the persons or things to be seized.

Amendment V [1791]

No person shall be held to answer for a capital, or otherwise infamous crime, unless on a presentment or indictment of a Grand Jury, except in cases arising in the land or naval forces, or in the Militia, when in actual service in time of War or public danger; nor shall any person be subject for the same offence to be twice put in jeopardy of life or limb; nor shall be compelled in any criminal case to be a witness against himself, nor be deprived of life, liberty, or property, without due process of law; nor shall private property be taken for public use, without just compensation.

Amendment VI [1791]

In all criminal prosecutions, the accused shall enjoy the right to a speedy and public trial, by an impartial jury of the State and district wherein the crime shall have been committed, which district shall have been previously ascertained by law, and to be informed of the nature and cause of the accusation; to be confronted with the witnesses against him; to have compulsory process for obtaining witnesses in his favor, and to have the Assistance of Counsel for his defence.

Amendment VII [1791]

In Suits at common law, where the value in controversy shall exceed twenty dollars, the right of trial by jury shall be preserved, and no fact tried by a jury, shall be otherwise re-examined in any Court of the United States, than according to the rules of the common law.

Amendment VIII [1791]

Excessive bail shall not be required, nor excessive fines imposed, nor cruel and unusual punishments inflicted.

Amendment IX [1791]

The enumeration in the Constitution, of certain rights, shall not be construed to deny or disparage others retained by the people.

Amendment X [1791]

The powers not delegated to the United States by the Constitution, nor prohibited by it to the States, are reserved to the States respectively, or to the people.

Amendment XI [1798]

The Judicial power of the United States shall not be construed to extend to any suit in law or equity, commenced or prosecuted against one of the United States by Citizens of another State, or by Citizens or Subjects of any Foreign State.

Amendment XII [1804]

The Electors shall meet in their respective states and vote by ballot for President and Vice-President, one of whom, at least, shall not be an inhabitant of the same state with themselves; they shall name in their ballots the person voted for as President, and in distinct ballots the person voted for as Vice-President, and they shall make distinct lists of all persons voted for as President, and of all persons voted for as Vice-President, and of the number of votes for each, which lists they shall sign and certify, and transmit sealed to the seat of the government of the United States, directed to the President of the Senate;—The President of the Senate shall, in the presence of the Senate and House of Representatives, open all the certificates and the votes shall then be counted;—The person having the greatest number of votes for President, shall be the President, if such number be a majority of the whole number of Electors appointed; and if no person have such majority, then from the persons having the highest numbers not exceeding three on the list of those voted for as President, the House of Representatives shall choose immediately, by ballot, the President. But in choosing the President, the votes shall be taken by states, the representation from each state having one vote; a quorum for this purpose shall consist of a member or members from two-thirds of the states, and a majority of all the states shall be necessary to a choice. And if the House of Representatives shall not choose a President whenever the right of choice shall devolve upon them, before the fourth day of March next following, then the Vice-President shall act as President, as in the case of the death or other constitutional disability of the President. The person having the greatest number of votes as Vice-President, shall be the

Vice-President, if such number be a majority of the whole number of Electors appointed, and if no person have a majority, then from the two highest numbers on the list, the Senate shall choose the Vice-President; a quorum for the purpose shall consist of two-thirds of the whole number of Senators, and a majority of the whole number shall be necessary to a choice. But no person constitutionally ineligible to the office of President shall be eligible to that of Vice-President of the United States.

Amendment XIII [1865]

Section 1. Neither slavery nor involuntary servitude, except as a punishment for crime whereof the party shall have been duly convicted, shall exist within the United States, or any place subject to their jurisdiction.

Section 2. Congress shall have power to enforce this article by appropriate legislation.

Amendment XIV [1868]

Section 1. All persons born or naturalized in the United States, and subject to the jurisdiction thereof, are citizens of the United States and of the State wherein they reside. No State shall make or enforce any law which shall abridge the privileges or immunities of citizens of the United States; nor shall any State deprive any person of life, liberty, or property, without due process of law; nor deny to any person within its jurisdiction the equal protection of the laws.

Section 2. Representatives shall be apportioned among the several States according to their respective numbers, counting the whole number of persons in each State, excluding Indians not taxed. But when the right to vote at any election for the choice of electors for President and Vice President of the United States, Representatives in Congress, the Executive and Judicial officers of a State, or the members of the Legislature thereof, is denied to any of the male inhabitants of such State, being twenty-one years of age, and citizens of the United States, or in any way abridged, except for participation in rebellion, or other crime, the basis of representation therein shall be reduced in the proportion which the number of such male citizens shall bear to the whole number of male citizens twenty-one years of age in such State.

Section 3. No person shall be a Senator or Representative in Congress, or elector of President and Vice President, or hold any office, civil or military, under the United States, or under any State, who, having previously taken an oath, as a member of Congress, or as an officer of the United States, or as a member of any State legislature, or as an executive or judicial officer of any State, to support the Constitution of the United States, shall have engaged in insurrection or rebellion against the same, or given aid or comfort to the enemies thereof. But Congress may by a vote of two-thirds of each House, remove such disability.

Section 4. The validity of the public debt of the United States, authorized by law, including debts incurred for payment of pensions and bounties for services in suppressing insurrection or rebellion, shall not be questioned. But neither the United States nor any State shall assume or pay any debt or obligation incurred in aid of insurrection or rebellion against the United States, or any claim for the loss or emancipation of any slave; but all such debts, obligations and claims shall be held illegal and void.

Section 5. The Congress shall have power to enforce, by appropriate legislation, the provisions of this article.

Amendment XV [1870]

Section 1. The right of citizens of the United States to vote shall not be denied or abridged by the United States or by any State on account of race, color, or previous condition of servitude.

Section 2. The Congress shall have power to enforce this article by appropriate legislation.

Amendment XVI [1913]

The Congress shall have power to lay and collect taxes on incomes, from whatever source derived, without apportionment among the several States, and without regard to any census or enumeration.

Amendment XVII [1913]

[1] The Senate of the United States shall be composed of two Senators from each State, elected by the people thereof, for six years; and each Senator shall have one vote. The electors in each State shall have the qualifica-

tions requisite for electors of the most numerous branch of the State legislatures.

[2] When vacancies happen in the representation of any State in the Senate, the executive authority of such State shall issue writs of election to fill such vacancies: *Provided,* That the legislature of any State may empower the executive thereof to make temporary appointments until the people fill the vacancies by election as the legislature may direct.

[3] This amendment shall not be so construed as to affect the election or term of any Senator chosen before it becomes valid as part of the Constitution.

Amendment XVIII [1919][4]

Section 1. After one year from the ratification of this article the manufacture, sale, or transportation of intoxicating liquors within, the importation thereof into, or the exportation thereof from the United States and all territory subject to the jurisdiction thereof for beverage purposes is hereby prohibited.

Section 2. The Congress and the several States shall have concurrent power to enforce this article by appropriate legislation.

Section 3. This article shall be inoperative unless it shall have been ratified as an amendment to the Constitution by the legislatures of the several States, as provided in the Constitution, within seven years from the date of the submission hereof to the States by the Congress.

Amendment XIX [1920]

[1] The right of citizens of the United States to vote shall not be denied or abridged by the United States or by any State on account of sex.

[2] Congress shall have power to enforce this article by appropriate legislation.

Amendment XX [1933]

Section 1. The terms of the President and Vice President shall end at noon on the 20th day of January, and the terms of Senators and Representatives at noon on the 3d day of January, of the years in which such terms would have ended if this article had not been ratified; and the terms of their successors shall then begin.

Section 2. The Congress shall assemble at least once in every year, and such meeting shall begin at noon on the 3d day of January, unless they shall by law appoint a different day.

Section 3. If, at the time fixed for the beginning of the term of the President, the President elect shall have died, the Vice President elect shall become President. If a President shall not have been chosen before the time fixed for the beginning of his term, or if the President elect shall have failed to qualify, then the Vice President elect shall act as President until a President shall have qualified; and the Congress may by law provide for the case wherein neither a President elect nor a Vice President elect shall have qualified, declaring who shall then act as President, or the manner in which one who is to act shall be selected, and such person shall act accordingly until a President or Vice President shall have qualified.

Section 4. The Congress may by law provide for the case of the death of any of the persons from whom the House of Representatives may choose a President whenever the right of choice shall have devolved upon them, and for the case of the death of any of the persons from whom the Senate may choose a Vice President whenever the right of choice shall have devolved upon them.

Section 5. Sections 1 and 2 shall take effect on the 15th day of October following the ratification of this article.

Section 6. This article shall be inoperative unless it shall have been ratified as an amendment to the Constitution by the legislatures of three-fourths of the several States within seven years from the date of its submission.

Amendment XXI [1933]

Section 1. The eighteenth article of amendment to the Constitution of the United States is hereby repealed.

Section 2. The transportation or importation into any State, Territory, or possession of the United States for delivery or use therein of intoxicating liquors, in violation of the laws thereof, is hereby prohibited.

Section 3. This article shall be inoperative unless it shall have been ratified as an amendment to the Constitution by conventions in the several States, as provided in the Constitution, within seven years from the date of the submission hereof to the States by the Congress.

Amendment XXII [1951]

Section 1. No person shall be elected to the office of the President more than twice, and no person who has held the office of President, or acted as President, for more than two years of a term to which some other person was elected President shall be elected to the office of the President more than once. But this Article shall not apply to any person holding the office of President when this Article was proposed by the Congress, and shall not prevent any person who may be holding the office of President, or acting as President, during the term within which this Article becomes operative from holding the office of President or acting as President during the remainder of such term.

Section 2. This article shall be inoperative unless it shall have been ratified as an amendment to the Constitution by the legislatures of three-fourths of the several States within seven years from the date of its submission to the States by the Congress.

Amendment XXIII [1961]

Section 1. The District constituting the seat of Government of the United States shall appoint in such manner as the Congress may direct:

A number of electors of President and Vice President equal to the whole number of Senators and Representatives in Congress to which the District would be entitled if it were a State, but in no event more than the least populous State; they shall be in addition to those appointed by the States, but they shall be considered, for the purposes of the election of President and Vice President, to be electors appointed by a State; and they shall meet in the District and perform such duties as provided by the twelfth article of amendment.

Section 2. The Congress shall have power to enforce this article by appropriate legislation.

Amendment XXIV [1964]

Section 1. The right of citizens of the United States to vote in any primary or other election for President or Vice President, for electors for President or Vice President, or for Senator or Representative in Congress, shall not be denied or abridged by the United States or any State by reason of failure to pay any poll tax or other tax.

Section 2. The Congress shall have power to enforce this article by appropriate legislation.

Amendment XXV [1967]

Section 1. In case of the removal of the President from office or of his death or resignation, the Vice President shall become President.

Section 2. Whenever there is a vacancy in the office of Vice President, the President shall nominate a Vice President who shall take office upon confirmation by a majority vote of both Houses of Congress.

Section 3. Whenever the President transmits to the President pro tempore of the Senate and the Speaker of the House of Representatives his written declaration that he is unable to discharge the powers and duties of his office, and until he transmits to them a written declaration to the contrary, such powers and duties shall be discharged by the Vice President as Acting President.

Section 4. Whenever the Vice President and a majority of either the principal officers of the executive departments or of such other body as Congress may by law provide, transmit to the President pro tempore of the Senate and the Speaker of the House of Representatives their written declaration that the President is unable to discharge the powers and duties of his office, the Vice President shall immediately assume the powers and duties of the office as Acting President.

Thereafter, when the President transmits to the President pro tempore of the Senate and the Speaker of the House of Representatives his written declaration that no inability exists, he shall resume the powers and duties of his office unless the Vice President and a majority of either the principal officers of the executive department or of such other body as Congress may by law provide, transmit within four days to the President pro tempore of the Senate and the Speaker of the House of Representatives their written declaration that the President is unable to discharge the powers and duties of his office. Thereupon Congress shall decide the issue, assembling within forty-eight hours for that purpose if not in session. If the Congress, within twenty-one days after receipt of the latter written declaration, or, if Congress is not in session, within twenty-one days after Congress is required to assemble, determines by two-thirds vote of both Houses that the President is unable to discharge the powers and duties of his office, the Vice President shall continue to discharge the same as Acting President; otherwise, the President shall resume the powers and duties of his office.

Amendment XXVI [1971]

Section 1. The right of citizens of the United States, who are eighteen years of age or older, to vote shall not be denied or abridged by the United States or by any State on account of age.

Section 2. The Congress shall have power to enforce this article by appropriate legislation.

Amendment XXVII [1992?][5]

No law varying the Compensation for the services of the Senators and Representatives shall take effect, unless an election of Representatives shall have intervened.

NOTES

1. Repealed by the Seventeenth Amendment.
2. Repealed by the Twentieth Amendment, Section 2.
3. Altered by the Twelfth Amendment.
4. Repealed by the Twenty-First Amendment.
5. This text, initially drafted in 1789 as one of twelve amendments proposed by the First Congress, did not receive the requisite number of ratifications and was long considered "dead." It was, however, rediscovered in the 1970s and ultimately received, by 1992, sufficient additional ratifications to bring the total, beginning with Maryland's 1789 ratification, to that required by Article V (three-fourths of the states). Whether this 203-year-long period of ratification is in accordance with Article V is debatable, and the reprinting of the text in this Appendix labeled "Constitution" should not be taken as evidence that either of the editors believes that it clearly *is* part of the Constitution. See Sanford Levinson, "Authorizing Constitutional Text: On the Purported Twenty-Seventh Amendment," 11 *Const. Comm.* 101 (1994). Neither of the editors, however, believes that it is either "stupid" or "tragic," whatever might be said of a reading of Article V that allows ratification after 203 years.

About the Contributors

Larry Alexander is the Warren Distinguished Professor of Law at the University of California at San Diego. He is the coauthor, with Paul Horton, of *Whom Does the Constitution Command?* (1988).

Akhil Reed Amar is the Southmayd Professor of Law at Yale University. He is the author of *The Constitution and Criminal Procedure: First Principles* (1996). His many articles on issues of constitutional history, structure, and law are among the most cited in the legal academy.

J. M. Balkin is the LaFayette S. Foster Professor of Law at Yale University. He is the author of numerous articles on constitutional law and other humorous topics.

Philip Bobbitt is the A. W. Walker Centennial Chair of Law at the University of Texas. He is the author of several books, including *Tragic Choices* (1978), coauthored with now-Judge Guido Calabresi.

Gerard V. Bradley is a professor of law at Notre Dame University. He is the author of several articles on constitutional and natural law and of *Church-State Relationships in America* (1987).

Rebecca L. Brown is a professor of law at Vanderbilt University. She is the author of several articles on constitutional tradition and interpretation.

Steven G. Calabresi is a professor of law at Northwestern University. He is the author of several articles on constitutional structure and interpretation.

Lief H. Carter is a professor of political science at the University of Georgia. He is the author of *Contemporary Constitutional Lawmaking: The Supreme Court and the Art of Politics* (1985).

Christopher L. Eisgruber is a professor of law at New York University. He is the author of several articles on constitutional law and jurisprudence.

William N. Eskridge, Jr., is a professor of law at Georgetown University. He is the author of several articles and books on constitutional and statutory interpretation, including *Dynamic Statutory Interpretation* (1994) and *The Case for Same-Sex Marriage* (1996).

Marie A. Failinger is a professor of law at Hamline University School of Law. She is the author of several articles on constitutional law and gender and the law; she is an editor of the *Journal of Law and Religion*.

Daniel A. Farber is the Henry J. Fletcher Professor of Law at the University of Minnesota. He is the author of numerous articles on issues of constitutional and statutory interpretation and is the coauthor, with Philip Frickey, of *Law and Public Choice* (1991). He is the coauthor, with Frickey and William Eskridge, of *Constitutional Law* (1993), a casebook.

James E. Fleming is an associate professor of law at Fordham University. He is an author of several articles on constitutional law and the coauthor, with Walter Murphy and Sotirios Barber, of *American Constitutional Interpretation* (2d ed., 1995), a casebook.

Mark Graber is a professor of political science at the University of Maryland. He is the author of several articles on constitutional history and interpretation and of *Rethinking Abortion: Equal Choice, the Constitution, and Reproductive Politics* (1996).

Stephen M. Griffin is an associate professor of law at Tulane University. He is the author of *American Constitutionalism: From Theory to Politics* (1996).

Gary Jacobsohn is the Woodrow Wilson Professor of Government at Williams College. He is the author of *The Supreme Court and the Decline of Constitutional Aspiration* (1986) and is currently conducting a comparative study of the constitutions of India, Israel, and the United States.

Pamela S. Karlan is a professor of law and the Roy L. and Rosamond Woodruff Morgan Research Professor at the University of Virginia. She is the author of numerous articles on constitutional law and voting rights.

Randall Kennedy is a professor of law at Harvard University. He has authored numerous articles on constitutional issues and race theory. He is the founding editor of the journal *Reconstruction* and is the author of *Race, Crime, and the Law* (1997).

L. H. LaRue is an associate professor of law at Washington and Lee University. He is the author of several articles on constitutional law and interpretation and recently authored *Constitution Law as Fiction: Narrative in the Rhetoric of Authority* (1995).

Sanford Levinson holds the W. St. John Garwood and W. St. John Garwood, Jr. Chair of Law at the University of Texas Law School and is also a member of the university's Department of Government. He is the author of *Constitutional Faith* (1988), the editor of *Responding to Imperfection: The Theory and Practice of Constitutional Amendment* (1995), and the co-editor of *Processes of Constitutional Decisionmaking* (3d ed. 1992) and *Interpreting Law and Literature: A Hermeneutic Reader* (1988).

Theodore J. Lowi is the John L. Senior Professor of Political Institutions at Cornell University. He is the author of numerous articles on political theory and constitutionalism. His books include the profoundly influential *The End of Liberalism* (2d ed., 1979).

Earl M. Maltz is a Distinguished Professor of Law at Rutgers University (Camden). He is the author of numerous articles on constitutional law and of *The Constitution and Congress, 1863–1869* (1990).

Michael W. McConnell is a Presidential Professor at the University of Utah. His articles on constitutional law and issues of religion and the state are among the most cited in the legal academy.

Matthew D. Michael is a scholar of public policy in Washington, D.C. He is the author of papers on the American political system.

Robert F. Nagel is the Ira C. Rothgerber Professor of Constitutional Law at the University of Colorado. He is the author of *Constitutional Cultures: The Mentality and Consequences of Judicial Review* (1989).

Daniel R. Ortiz is the John Allen Love Professor of Law and the Elizabeth D. and Richard A. Merrill Research Professor at the University of Virginia. He is the author of several articles on constitutional law and voting rights.

Michael Stokes Paulsen is an associate professor of law at the University of Minnesota. He is the author of several articles on constitutional text, structure, and interpretive paradoxes.

Robert Post is the Alexander F. and May T. Morrison Professor of Law at the University of California at Berkeley. He is the author of numerous articles on constitutional law and of *Constitutional Domains: Democracy, Community, Management* (1995).

L. A. Powe, Jr., is the Anne Green Regents Chair at the University of Texas Law School. He is the author of several award-winning books on constitutional law, including *The Fourth Estate and the Constitution: Freedom of the Press in America* (1991).

Dorothy E. Roberts is a professor of law at Rutgers University (Newark). She is the author of several articles on constitutional law and race theory and a coeditor, with Donald Lively, of *First Amendment Anthology* (1994).

Jeffrey Rosen is an associate professor of law at the George Washington National Law Center and the legal affairs editor at the *New Republic*, where he has written many articles on issues of public law and jurisprudence.

Lawrence G. Sager is the Robert B. McKay Professor of Law at New York University. He is the author of numerous articles on constitutional law and interpretation.

Frederick Schauer is the Frank Stanton Professor of the First Amendment at the John F. Kennedy School of Government of Harvard University. He is the author of several books, including *Playing by the Rules* (1991).

Louis Michael Seidman is a professor of law at Georgetown University. He is the author of numerous articles on constitutional law and the coauthor, with Mark Tushnet, of *Remnants of Belief: Contemporary Constitutional Issues* (1996). With Tushnet, Geoffrey Stone, and Cass Sunstein, he is the coauthor of *Constitutional Law*, the leading casebook in the field, now in its third edition.

Suzanna Sherry is the Earl R. Larson Professor of Civil Rights and Civil Liberties Law at the University of Minnesota. She is the author of numerous articles on constitutional law and the coauthor, with Daniel Farber, of *A History of the American Constitution* (1990).

David A. Strauss is the Harry N. Wyatt Professor and Russell Baker Scholar at the University of Chicago. He is the author of numerous articles on constitutional law and theory.

Laurence H. Tribe is the Ralph S. Tyler Professor of Constitutional Law at Harvard University. He is the author of numerous articles and several books on constitutional law. His *American Constitutional Law* (2d ed., 1988) is the leading constitutional law treatise.

Mark Tushnet is the Carmack Waterhouse Professor of Constitutional Law at Georgetown University. His many articles on issues of constitutional history and law are among the most cited in the legal academy. He is the coauthor, with Michael Seidman, of *Remnants of Belief: Contemporary Constitutional Issues* (1996). With Seidman, Geoffrey Stone, and Cass Sunstein, he is the coauthor of the leading casebook on *Constitutional Law*, now in its third edition.

John Yoo is an acting professor of law at the University of California at Berkeley. He is the author of several articles on constitutional law and history.

Index